Launching the
New Enlightenment

The Reaffirmation of
the Social Contract

Michael Jaffey

ISBN-10: 1492977934
ISBN-13: 978-1492977933
Library of Congress Control Number: 2013920864
CreateSpace Independent Publishing Platform
North Charleston, South Carolina

For my Dearest Diana

Launching the
New Enlightenment

The author, Michael Jaffey, graduated as an engineer, and then, as a Rhodes Scholar at Oxford, read philosophy, politics, and economics, which changed his world view. After first working as an engineer, he became a systems analyst, and then worked more broadly studying our society's problems. He has long believed that inside our sick society is a good society, struggling to get out, and that we must help it, and without delay.

Table of Contents

• •

List of Figures

List of Tables

Preface

About fifty years ago I sketched out my view of a seriously ailing society, and then, ten years later, I asked 'Does this hypothesis represent an *idée fixe*' , a mere obsession, 'or is it an internally consistent model with strong underpinnings of reality?[1] ' Looking now at my early formulation of the hypothesis I am struck by how little it differs from the present version, and that indeed might suggest an *idée fixe*, even a neurotic delusion, after all, as far as I am aware, no one else shares my particular diagnosis of our society's ills. In this book I argue that, far from suffering from delusion, somehow I managed, whether by good fortune or by meritorious effort, all those years ago, to identify deep seated governance faults whose malign effects are now so much in evidence. Now there is much agonising about the future of Western society, especially its American part (there is also deep concern for the future of Europe, but that is due less to the governance faults than to the ill-conceived adoption of the Euro common currency, and the defective Brussels pseudo-government).

My purpose, in the present work, in identifying our governance flaws, is to propose what must be done to correct them. Fortunately, I argue, the governance faults are readily correctable, and if we make the reforms which are the subject of this book, our Western society can resume its upward path in a New Enlightenment. But we must act quickly as the world faces climate calamity – a calamity in the main due to these same governance faults, which have hindered our efforts to curb our carbon emissions. As far as I am aware, although many writers are now writing on the West's decline, few, if any, are like me, suggesting what we must do to heal our society.

It will be observed that on occasion I quote from earlier, unpublished, papers. One reason for doing this is that I can't think of a better way to make the point, but more important, I want to emphasize how deep-seated and enduring some societal malfunction is. Some might argue that the governance faults of the society of fifty years ago have little relevance for a society that has changed beyond recognition, now so many people interconnected as a result of electronic wizardry and the new social media. On the contrary, I argue, it is all the more pressing to correct the deep seated governance faults if mankind is not to be bounced into what might be a very nasty future – humans must have some control over their destiny. I have further emphasized the unchanging, deep-seatedness of our society's misgovernment by attaching an appendix on the history of the 'hypothesis of underlying society malfunction'.

There are several themes that recur throughout my scribbles over the years: Our troubles in the main arise from our neglect of the Social Contract according to which the only justification for society is that it serve the people, but that through our misgovernment we have failed to ensure that our magnificent, innovative, business corporations serve us, and as a result they have run amok – that the fault is ours, not theirs, we have governed badly. Another theme is that I have been pro-West, the splendid heritage from ancient Greece and Rome, leading eventually to the Renaissance, the Reformation, and then the Enlightenment. Out of all this came the 'western attributes', the rule of law, human rights, and individual liberty. But that in recent times, especially in the United States, the Social Contract has been misinterpreted, and the business corporations and special interests, rather that the people, are in control. And I have so often complained that societies see only what they want to see, and ignore the obvious, hence the need for the small boy to exclaim 'but the King isn't wearing *any* clothes at all!' – so often the mother says 'Johnny behave yourself!' And then pessimistically I exclaim: *'gotterdammerung*: those whom the gods will destroy they first make mad' – we're are a useless lot, they are going to try something else.

In nothing have I been more fixed than in my loathing for what I call the American model of broadcasting, paid for by and serving business corporations and special interests, not by the people to serve them. A disgusting disease of the body-politic I have called it, the very symbol, the essence, of deep societal dysfunction. And I never tire of saying, no the blame is not corporations', corporations *will* be corporations, no, the blame falls squarely on ourselves, how absurd, how pathetic has been our misgovernment.

Over the years, until now, I have never published my work, though I have pestered many individuals with particular papers, and usually without avail. But fortunately several distinguished persons (named in my 'Acknowledgements') responded positively. I cannot exaggerate how important their comments were in reassuring me that I might be saying something worthwhile. It was these that emboldened me to try to communicate with Canada's politicians. In 2007 I sent to every member of the Canadian parliament a proposal for curbing carbon emissions. Then in 2010 I expended much effort trying to communicate with the leader of the opposition on a new party platform, not only on cutting emissions, but also to bring about the institutional reforms that are the subject of this work. It was only when these efforts failed totally that I decided to write this book – the only book I have ever written.

And there is the question of what this work should be named, it is a synthesis of diverse parts. Consistently I have talked of societal rot and recovery therefrom, of our breach of the Social Contract, of the failings of our economists. And I have expended much energy on the Great Battle of the Climate[2]. My writings on the latter were accompanied by a brief companion paper, 'Auxiliary Measures for the Battle of the Climate', the improvements of our societal governance if we were to engage successfully in the Battle. Most of our terrible woes are related: Had our governance, and our so-called 'economics', been grounded on the Social Contract, we would not have emitted huge amounts of carbon, nor would we now be in degradation and decline. I have chosen to name this work 'Launching the New Enlightenment', but with little reorganization it could equally have been called 'The Great Battle of the Climate', or 'The Great War of Civilization, or 'The League of the Social Contract', or 'The New Science of Economics'. Indeed several years ago I started writing a book of the latter name, but abandoned it when I found that another book (the present) that I was writing was saying much the same thing.

In writing this work, continually I must amend it, in rapid succession events overtake what I write: in December 2011, the IMF warns of a repeat of the 1930 Great Depression, and the Euro is in terminal crisis, but now in January 2013, the Euro appears to have recovered somewhat, but at the World Economic Forum in Davos the world's financial leader warn that all is not well with the global economy.

And becoming more burningly obvious, fast changing technology is taking over, and bouncing us all into a future we may not like, a 'runaway world' Martin Rees calls it. And, and in any case, a world we were never given an opportunity to discuss, let alone to decide on, whether the new future that is arriving is one that is desirable, one that improves our quality of life. As my elderly sister-in-law recently exclaimed, 'I'm living in a foreign country, I don't understand what's happening'.

And lately 'social media' has become a part of the vocabulary, and on Facebook, one in seven people on the planet, and perhaps a half of young westerners, are exchanging trivia with a host of casual acquaintances, is this an advance for mankind? A recent study has shown that 40 percent of Twitter tweets are 'meaningless babble'.

The tail is very much wagging the dog, we are being driven by technology used to meet the goals of business corporations, and their stables of young geeks. And the Western advanced economies in the United States and Europe are being hollowed out, the middle classes having difficulty finding jobs, partly because of 'globalization' – the 'outsourcing', or rather, 'offshoring', by multinationals of their work to Asia, and partly by the advance of technology and relentless mechanization, machines replacing people – and sometimes in a way that reduces people's quality of life, the lives of ourselves as consumers of the economy's output, machines doing things badly and annoyingly for us, machines that are a pain in our necks. The Social Contract is being breached, society and the economy have only one justification for existing, and that is the service and the comfort of the people.

We are on a roller coaster ride. We, the people must take control. Without control by the people there can be no talk of a New Enlightenment.

Finally I must excuse myself in advance on several counts: This work ventures very wide, I am by way of being a generalist with little expertise in most of the areas I have tried to tie together. Ideally such a work as this should be conducted by a team who could delve into the statistics of many areas. Even so, I don't believe such improved research would materially change my main conclusions. For many people parts of this work may be seen as far-fetched, wild, weird prognostications, mad proposals. But our society is in a dire state, climate change is accelerating, new thinking is fast required, and what must be done is off the beaten track, people must start coming up with different ideas.

I should also add in this preface that I'm feeling a little ashamed that so often the words 'I' and 'me' appear. It is because this is, in the main, a chronicle of my own musings over many years that I find it difficult to avoid frequently writing in the first person.

Introduction

This work is about mending a deeply sick society. But perhaps we should hesitate a moment. How sick are we really? Is our society really sick, or merely going through a rough patch? Is it merely that humans being imperfect, all human societies have their good points and their bad points, but that certain dyspeptic individuals see only the latter, *O tempora, O mores* – Oh the times, oh the customs – Cicero when the Roman Empire had still 400 years before it expired.

To me it appears that our Western society is staggering, sickening on its own glut and profligate misspending, while as a result of its dysfunctional institutions, it has brought about accelerating dangerous climate change, and through its incompetence now struggles to emerge from deep recession. And in December 2011, from the Durban climate conference: 'Rarely, or never, has such an epic problem as global warming been so dismally handled'[3], is the battle to save the climate lost? And there have been reports of methane gas bubbling from the tundra, a green house gas twenty five times as potent as carbon dioxide – is this work a waste of effort, eat, drink and be merry because *apres moi la calamité*? But let us continue.

Meanwhile, much talked about is Western decadence and decline, and a fast-rising China and an end to Western hegemony. This ceding of power is, of course, not necessarily a Western woe, if the West mends its sickness, remains strong, and regains its qualities as an exemplary civilization that serves its people well.

But I may be merely a dyspeptic person, one of those malcontents that even the best societies throw up, who blame their unhappiness not on their own shortcomings, but on their society. To obviate this possibility, rather than taking it for granted that our society is in deep trouble and on its way down, I instead take a clinical approach, it's the annual check-up, the doctor asks many questions as a result of which he diagnoses a serious malady, but fortunately the sickness is curable, provided the correct measures are taken.

Through this process, I hope to take the reader with me: Yes, our society exhibits these phenomena, and yes, they are nasty, and surely can only be symptoms of severe societal disorder, caused through some serious malfunction of our society's governance organs. But fortunately there is a cure, our governance can be mended, and if we act determinedly, we can restore our society so that it will no longer be sick, it will enjoy a new renaissance.

This is what I hope here to demonstrate: Our grave difficulties, dithering ineffectively with global warming, economic depression, and decadence and decline, can exist only because the Western nations have particular faults of governance. These faults have been evident over many years, but societies do not see what they do not want to see, the status quo is comfortable for the vast majority – or they have long adapted to it, and believe it is, quite simply, the way the world is. The aim of this work is to convince that I have laid out a coherent argument: yes these phenomena are symptoms of severe societal disorder, in particular, illness in certain vital institutions, and yes, if we enact these reforms, then the giant ship of Western society can change course, and launch itself in a new renaissance.

But steady, a note of caution: Perhaps, here at the outset, the reader needs to be convinced just how crass have been our faults of governance, and that our difficulties are not due to ordinary human backsliding and burying of heads in the sand. First take human-induced global warming and our emissions that have caused it. In the words of the eminent scientist, Martin Rees. 'Within fifty years . . . the amount of carbon dioxide in the atmosphere, which over most of earth's history had been slowly falling, began to rise anomalously fast' [4]. But did that matter? But for its atmosphere the earth's surface would be very cold. The atmosphere is what has kept the earth's surface at a temperature that supports life. And not just any atmosphere, but one with a certain composition: Our sister planet Venus has an atmosphere that is 96% carbon dioxide, and as a result of the greenhouse effect its surface temperature is 462 degrees C[5]. A well governed society would not recklessly have extracted vast quantities of carbon from the earth, now billions of tons annually, and then dumped it in the world's atmosphere, which supports all life on the planet. Or having started the process it would long ago have stopped and found another way forward.

Fortunately, one hopes not too late for remedial action, alarm built up in the 1980s, leading to the establishment in 1988 of the Intergovernmental Panel on Climate Change (IPCC), and to a gathering of the world's nations in Rio in 1992. That produced the UN Framework Convention on Climate change that led eventually to the Kyoto Protocol, which was to come into force only after 55 countries, which together produced at least 55% of the world's emissions, had ratified the agreement. These conditions were met in 2005, when the Accord came into effect.

But since that time, most of the world's nations' performance in cutting their emissions can only be called pathetic, and this is most strange, as the required measures are quite obvious – any engineer or physicist can tell you precisely in a few words what must be done, and it needs no new technology – if these scientists can remove themselves from the thrall of society's current paralysis. And the symbol of this idiocy is – what? Giant windmills, desecrating lovely landscapes with miles of monsters. A thousand square miles of wind turbines will produce as much electricity as a single conventional one thousand megawatt generating station – but only when the wind blows. And can the United States governance institutions be sound if an increasing majority of Americans believe that man-made global warming is based on 'junk science', and in any case they should not make any effort to combat it?

I shall give just one more example here to convince the reader of the incompetence of our society's organs of governance, and that is its highly dubious 'economic science' – here are our doctors of the economy whom we count on to tell us when the economy is sick, and how to fix it, above all, how to avoid deep depression and unemployment. But they have failed. We can split the atom and land on the moon but we cannot keep all our people fully employed all the time, and now especially when there is so much to be done. Boom and bust is surely an archaic absurdity. Another of the many failures of so-called economic science is the Eurozone crisis – can the common currency survive? When the currency was launched, twelve years ago, it should have been obvious to economists that the present crisis was likely to occur (Some, I am now discovering, did warn but one heard little of this in the media and public discourse). At the time I wrote that 'Maastricht may serve as a cruel yoke for some nations, turning them into depressed areas' [6]. That wasn't clever, anybody with common sense would have seen the currency's flaws – had they not assumed that the experts must know what they were about. Is what is now called 'economics' a genuine science that understands how the complex social, political physical, informational, monetary, environmental system functions? The evidence is not.

Having just reread Martin Rees' book already referred to, 'Our Final Hour: A scientist's warning' I have avoided a serious blunder. I had thought that if we mend our sick society and reduce our emissions we shall enjoy a happy future. Martin Rees gives humanity only a fifty percent chance of surviving this century, but the threat is not only of environmental disaster, but also of error, and of terror perpetrated by fanatics like al Qaeda, and Anders Breivik in Norway. But perhaps if we mend our faults of governance, we shall have a society more competent in avoiding the terror and error that could wreck mankind.

This work has been several years in the writing, and latterly momentous events are overtaking what I write. Now as I complete this work, a doom-laden statement appears in the press, two leading British scientists[7] having concluded that our institutions have failed us, our carbon dioxide emissions will continue their rapid growth, and disastrous climate change is now inevitable. We must therefore 'prepare for the challenging times ahead'. Consequently they are creating 'a forum for the public to discuss the issues with leading climate scientists'. Does this mean that efforts such as mine are futile? I believe not, indeed all the more reason to mend our faulty institutions, which is the subject of this book.

There are elements of terrible tragedy in the West's present plight. The present situation is so needless. In fact within the West is a marvellous, enlightened civilization struggling to get out. All the ingredients of such a society are there, but their promise is being nullified by some governance flaws which we must now rapidly mend. True, climate damage has been allowed to progress too far, but over that, if we correct the flaws, we can get some control, and emerge in the coming decades if battered, and a little warmer, nonetheless highly civilized, indeed in a new Age of Enlightenment.

This work has four parts[8]. Part One, Symptoms, catalogues what I believe to be our society's indications of disease, what might also be called 'woes' except that many people may not see them as woes, over many years they have adapted to them, 'that's the way the world works, what one must learn to cope with, or even enjoy'. But then when we step aside and look at them in the light of the Social Contract, that society exists to serve us, not for us to serve it, or some part of it, we see them in their true light.

Next, in Part Two comes our 'Diagnosis' in which we explore the nature of the disease responsible for the symptoms, and what changes we must make in our society's governance mechanisms so they disappear and our society can rise to the grim challenges of our times.

Part Three then sets out the strategy of our launch, how we can convert our diagnosis into a programme that pulls back our society from the brink, and puts it on the course to recovery.

Finally in Part Four is our Action Plan for the Great War for Western Civilization, the battle order, what must be done, by whom, when. At this stage, all our thought at all levels is only on execution, waging the great Battle of Civilization.

Part One

Symptoms of Societal Disorder

In this part I have grouped what I believe are symptoms of disorder in our society. There are three sorts. The first sort are incontestably 'woes', nobody in their right minds can see them as anything other than a blemish, a nasty thing bringing discomfort or misery to large numbers of people. There should be little difficulty in seeing them as indicators of grave societal dysfunction – surely a healthy society would not permit such travesties of good sense to exist. These are the subject of Chapter 1.

A second category of symptom are items that most people probably shrug off, that's the way the world is, or is becoming, to talk of them as woes brands you as a complainer, an old fogey – hey man, lighten up, get with it, keep up with the times. The Observer columnist, Katherine Whitehorn, once complained that new gadgets should be sold with an attached seven-year old boy to show you how to use it. These symptoms of disorder are discussed here under the heading 'We, the people, are not in control', if the people were really in control of their society, they would see that the items in question were a very odd way for a well- run country to arrange matters. For example unsolicited phone calls waste your time when you're busy, trying to sell you something – you may even rudely say 'drop dead' if you are not well brought up, and slam down the receiver. The German federal government has legislated against these calls, and two years ago introduced a penalty of 50,000 euros for perpetrators[9]. Clearly here is a nation that places great value on the privacy of individuals – as any well governed nation should. This category of symptom is the subject of Chapter 2.

The third category of symptom is the sort, perhaps, that the average person couldn't care less about – he's got other things on his mind. This category is the subject of Chapter 3, concerned with deep, underlying matters, societal decadence and decline, and the shift of global power away from West to East.

CHAPTER 1

Incontestable Woes, Travesties of Good Sense

Recession and unemployment

Perhaps the woe most pressing on many minds now is grim unrelenting recession which has most Western nations in its grip. This is a phenomenon that only a few individuals will not think a woe, even if they still have a job and secure income – only a certain kind of fundamentalist will believe that the jobless' plight is celestial punishment for lazy freeloaders living on unemployment benefits, and welfare bums.

It was over five years ago that the American economy went into a tailspin, in the wake of the credit crisis and sub-prime mortgages, and other nations, especially Western, followed suit. This downturn, the 'Great Recession', the worst since the Great Depression of the thirties – not much then in the way of unemployment and social welfare benefits, or Keynesian stimuli, to remedy the situation. Very slowly, and in fits and starts, the Western economy has now been recovering, there have been some signs of improvement in the United States, but deep pessimism continues there, according to a recent report, 80% of Americans believe that the economy is in a sad state, 38% gave unemployment as the worst problem, and 28% the budget deficit, which tells us that Americans feel they are between a rock and a hard place. To cut the deficit requires cutting government spending, (or raising taxes, another US bugaboo) but doing so immediately raises the unemployment rate, or through reduced 'entitlements' hurts the public. Somehow those who press for deficit reduction appear to have assumed that this fiscal rectitude will bless the nation and the economy will re-ignite and unemployment will disappear.

In July 2011, grand farce played out in the United States, threatening to throw not only that country, but the world economy into crisis. The American Tea Party Republicans accept as a categorical imperative, 'Thou must balance the budget' and proposed a constitutional amendment.

In Britain the conservative government, loathers of the deficit and of government spending, have enacted austerity, cut government jobs, reduced benefits such as university student support, and despite all this, unemployment and low economic growth continues. Indeed, this deficit phobia increases unemployment, and prevents recovery. And now, the news is of the depth of Britain's double dip recession, and the Chancellor, George Osborne is being pummelled in the press.

But unemployment and low economic growth are not even throughout the West. As of January 2013 the Eurozone nations collectively have 12 % unemployment, even higher than the United States, but it is very uneven. Greece and Spain's unemployment is 26 percent, but Germany's with its brilliant manufacturing industry exporting to the world has only 7 percent, and in what might be called Western Europe's little wonders, the Scandinavian nations, and the Netherlands, one might ask 'what recession?' In Switzerland unemployment is a low 3.3 percent, and the economy continues to grow. Japan is very interesting. Despite its persisting low economic growth rate, and hideous government debt, its unemployment rate remains low at 4.1% and it continues to have a large international balance of payments surplus. Not only this, despite its stratospheric debt, far higher than that of the US and Britain, the yen's value has until recently risen against the dollar and the euro. The most likely reason for Japan's lack of unemployment may simply be that Japan looks after its people well, and so do the people each other. That is made strikingly clear by Martin Jacques, in his recent book 'When China Rules the World', and he quotes a Japanese colleague telling him that while on the outside the Japanese are Western, on the inside they are, well, Japanese. A visit by the Japanese prime minister and cabinet to Fukushima is illuminating. Following the prime minister's speech to tsunami victims, the prime minister was harangued by an angry man, at which the whole cabinet abased itself in abject apology, lowering their foreheads to the floor.

Now there are some signs of recovery in the United States, there is some rehiring by business, though unemployment remains stubbornly high. Keynes- inspired stimulus spending by the Obama administration probably averted deeper unemployment. But the signs are that the recovery such as it is, will repeat the old pattern, driven by the American way of broadcasting, an advertising medium, telling people to buy, buy, our marvellous stuff, it will make you so happy, whoopee! . This is a nation that relies hugely on consumer spending to keep its economy aloft, and when a public accustomed to buying on the never-never, was suddenly frightened it stopped shopping – that was really quite easy, much of what they bought wasn't really necessary anyway. The bubble has burst, all the signs are there of an unhappy, perhaps deeply sick, nation.

Meanwhile the rising Asian giants continue their climb, thereby slightly moderating the extent of world recession. Up with gross unemployment China will not put, when the depressed West reduces its imports of Chinese goods, China's authoritarian rulers switch production to the building of national infrastructure.

But what kind of woe is massive unemployment and economic depression? Just one of the laws of the Medes and the Persians, divinely ordered, seven good years and then seven lean? Just get used to it, that's the way the world is. The reality is that we humans have been clever enough to invent computers and land on the moon and replace actual travel by virtual travel, to do these amazing things, but we still do not have the wit to keep everybody who wants to work employed, and especially so when there is so much to be done – in the United States the infrastructure is crumbling, bridges are falling down, and huge projects are needed to moderate global warming.

Affluence or Mirage?

Even now in the present Great Recession and with high unemployment, Western nations can be said to be very wealthy, yet there remains considerable poverty, and in the United States, with the largest GDP per person of any major nation, this poverty is dire. J. K. Galbraith's 'Affluent Society' of fifty years ago required only a single breadwinner, and now with two breadwinners, and doubled output per worker, affluence must have much more than doubled – or has it? In the United States the difficulties of the middle classes are a major issue, as is the state of the public infrastructure which has not been maintained, and the lack of health coverage for many Americans. Logically there can be only three causes – the failure of governments to transfer adequate income to the unemployed and disadvantaged, very unequal remuneration of the employed, and, perhaps this is the most important, the nature of the bountiful supply of the consumer goods, produced. A major part of people's income has been spent on often inessential goods that fast become obsolete, at the expense of the basic necessities of life.

Gross increase in income inequality is an important factor in many Western nations but most particularly in the United States. There, between 1979 and 2006 the share of total household income received by the richest one percent of households increased from 10% to 23%. Since 2000, 91% of income growth went to the top 10% of households, while most families have had stagnant or falling incomes[9]. Forty percent of all American personal income is received by one third of one percent of the U.S. population, and in December 2011, half of the population, if not classed as poor, were struggling to make ends meet[10]. It defies belief. The anger now at this mal-distribution of income, as the recession persists, has occasioned the Occupy Wall Street demonstrations which have spread to other Western capitals.

These extraordinary figures of poverty in the midst of plenty surely indicate severe dysfunction of the western body-politic, and most especially in the West's economic heartland. And this poverty is made all the more unbearable by a monstrous level of consumer debt[11], and the biggest cause of personal bankruptcies is high medical expenditures.

Taxation Misery

This most certainly is a woe, even the very rich do not like parting with their money. But should we just endure it, nothing is inevitable but death and taxes – or is it possible to change that so only death is inevitable?

Most of the goods and services we need or would like to have we pay for directly through our personal spending, but how are we to pay for the vital public services we need? At present we pay for these through various forms of taxation, of which a large part is the personal income tax. The income tax is not pleasant, so very often politicians promise that they won't raise taxes – or that they will even cut them. A large section of the American public have a particular aversion to the income tax, in that it pays for government, and government isn't good, it is bloated and too big, and for many Americans it is the oppressor, interfering in their lives, directly descended from the British government against which they gloriously rebelled. So government must be shrunk. But is American government really so vast? In fact, the overall size of American government, at all levels, of both government-performed services and transfer payments to the unemployed and disadvantaged, is one of the lowest in the Western world, 39% of GDP compared with 53% in Sweden and France.

But now we are in times when we need more public funds than ever. Vast projects must be launched for the great Battle of the Climate, and funds are needed for our public institutions that have in recent years been starved of money. Museums, art galleries, and centres for the performing arts which were once totally funded by government grants, that is, paid for out of taxes, now must supplement these grants by seeking corporation donations – so called 'corporate social responsibility'. Why is a society that once could give government grants to these institutions now unable to do so? I suggest that at least part of the reason has been the increasingly intense advertising drive which has made private consumption of a stream of new products the be-all and end-all of people's lives. Private consumption has grown at the expense of public consumption. In the United States, where advertising is particularly intense, private consumption is over 70% of GDP.

Global warming paralysis

This is probably the grimmest woe of all, the threat to future life on the planet, though many people don't even see it as a woe, having relegated it to a corner of their consciousness, or even refuse to believe it is happening at all.

In the United States it has lately disappeared from the public agenda, as indicated by a headline in the New York Times asking 'Where did global warming go'[12]? Politically the very word has become a no-no: 'Though the evidence of climate change has, if anything, solidified, Mr Obama now talks of "green jobs" mostly as a strategy for improving the economy, not the planet. He did not mention climate change in his last State of the Union address [13] . . . . The United States is the one significant outlier in responding to climate change', elsewhere it is a priority matter. 'In the United States, the right wing of the Republican Party has managed to turn scepticism about man-made global warming into a requirement for electability'. 'Michelle Bachmann, one of the leaders of the Tea Party movement which has up-ended American politics, in a statement in the U.S. House of Representatives said 'Carbon dioxide is natural, it is not harmful. We're being told we have to reduce this natural substance to create an arbitrary reduction in something naturally occurring on the earth'. (As a Canadian I must correct the New York Times: In Canada too the subject has disappeared from the public discourse. There the headlines are about how to export oil from the notorious oil sands, of which James Hansen, the head of the NASA Goddard Institute for Space Studies, has been widely quoted as saying that if the oil sands are exploited 'it will be game over' for the climate).

What is really woeful here is not Bachmann's ignorance and wrong-headedness on a hugely important matter, but the fact that democracy, despite its overall benign qualities, sometimes makes difficult the formulation and prosecution of vital public policies – problems sometimes less difficult for authoritarian governments. The Chinese leadership pronounces nuclear stations and fast train services will be built forthwith, and they get built pronto.

World-wide the dire news builds up, a recent report that as a result of logging and drought, the Amazon forest, the world's major sink absorbing some of its carbon dioxide emissions, is losing its capacity to do so, and by an amount each year greater than what is annually emitted by the United States. Meanwhile we have reports that the North Pole will soon be ice-free in summer, but only in the context of a race among nations to start drilling there for oil, rather than of accelerating man - induced climate disaster. We may be the generation that could have rallied to save the climate, but failed ignominiously.

But some nations are being far more effective than North Americans. Recently [14] it was reported that the UK's climate watchdog has said two more nuclear reactors may be needed if targeted emission cuts are to be achieved. This body advises the British government on progress in meeting its target of 50 percent emission reduction below their 1990 level by 2050.

Not only is there a widespread state of global warming denial, there is an equally astonishing blindness about what must be done to cut our emissions. This is quite extraordinary as what must be done is obvious, and needs no new technology, any physicist or engineer can quickly see that only one course of action is open to us to avert climate disaster. A paper I wrote in 2005 laid out what measures were required, and my later papers have scarcely changed at all. In a 2008 paper called 'The Inexorable Logic of the Battle of the Climate' I was trying to emphasize that there was no other way: 'While the world – some European nations excepted – buries its head in the sand . . . the experts' prescriptions of what to do are woefully inadequate. And this is most strange, what must be done is obvious, and requires no new technology. We must replace our fossil fuels through total electrification of the economy, using nuclear power – there is no alternative – and also convert to a low energy way of life based on new transportation systems, telecommunications, and urban redesign. (I would now amend this - a large, though rather less large, emission reduction is possible through total electrification of the economy but still using fossil fuels, especially natural gas, for electricity generation). Something must be blocking our society's ability to act intelligently and decisively. So we have *two* great challenges, not just one: Not only must we vastly reduce our greenhouse gas emissions, we must also remove the institutional hindrances now preventing us from acting.

Deficit Phobia

This is not only a woe, it is sometimes a deep delusion – the US Tea Party fears it so much that in July 2011 it was ready to plunge the entire world's financial system into disarray. And the British Chancellor of the Exchequer is equally convinced that Britain's first priority is to cut the deficit[15]. 'George Osborne has faced down fierce pressure to reverse police cuts in the wake of this week's riots . . "Let me make clear not only in the House of Commons but to the whole world: ours is an absolutely unwavering commitment to fiscal responsibility and deficit reduction"' Osborne would appear to be suffering from Immanuel Kant's categorical imperative, thou shalt not under any circumstances run a deficit, repeating the actions responsible for the depth of the thirties Great Depression, the error of viewing a government deficit as the same sort of evil as a household in debt or a business running at a loss. But surely restoring what is called fiscal balance is the last thing that will restart an economy in the depth of a recession. Once growth and employment are restored in the economy, that is the time to balance the budget. Osborne brings to mind Alec Guinness in the film 'Kind Hearts and Coronets', where playing a not very bright battleship captain, his ship on a collision course, gives the order 'Hard to port!' – 'surely sir, you mean starboard' scream his subordinates? No, port! shouts the captain, and then crash! The battleship plummets to the bottom of the ocean.

What to me it is inexplicable is that according to both IMF and Eurostat (the EU agency), the UK – along with Germany – had the lowest public debt of the G7 nations, 74% of GDP for 2010, while the US's was 93% (in August 2011 it reached 100%), Italy's was 118%, and Japan's was 226%. It is a woe indeed, something is extraordinarily unsatisfactory, when governments and the economists who advise them can be driven in such absurdly different directions in coping with the present economic turmoil. It is believed by many in Britain, and by the present government, that the nation's official debt figure grossly understates the government's real indebtedness, because it does not include the future pension payments it will have to make to retired government workers. But, as argued here later, it can convincingly be argued that this is fallacious thinking.

Another absurdity on which no one seems to have commented is why, if the deficit is such a threat to the economy, the sky hasn't fallen in on Japan with its monstrous public debt. An article in the Financial Times[16] is on a growing fear of the 'Japanisation' of Western nations, people are fleeing from equities to bonds despite low yields, the yield on US treasury bills has fallen below 2 percent for the first time in sixty-one years, a level that Japanese government bond debt has not risen above for fifteen years. (It is impossible in writing this book to keep up with the fast developing times: now in mid-2012, not only is the yield on US 10 year bonds only 1.5%, so is it on British 10 year bonds. No doubt George Osborne believes he is responsible for that – which may console him as the nation is baying for his blood, at Britain's severe double dip). And all the while, the yen has until very recently increased in value by over 30 percent against the dollar since the start of the recession, and despite Japan's low economic growth rate, and now the Fukushima tsunami, nuclear station, disaster. This can only mean that despite deficit phobia and the rating agencies' downgrading of Japanese debt, the nation is not in a perilous state. And it should be added that the Japanese unemployment rate is the lowest of the of the G7 economies. And the nation's balance of payments surplus, high like those of Germany and China, suggests much that's healthy in the Japanese economy. It is surely a woe that so much remains murky in the field of economic management.

Traffic Gridlock, Urban Ugliness and Sprawl

Would our society, had it been better governed, have wished upon itself the loss of a part of people's lives in bumper-to-bumper commuting and city centre traffic gridlock, its monster urban periphery shopping malls with their acres of parking lots? And the ugliness and tackiness of it all? The approaches to many North American cities have become an appallingly ugly commercial sprawl. Traffic spotter planes over Toronto show fifteen lanes full of crawling metal creatures, the handiwork of recently collapsed General Motors. What an incredibly obtuse way to convey a million people daily to work. There is absolutely no need for this sort of blight. In Britain, for example, urban sprawl is controlled, and the difference is profound, the visual landscape can be a delight. The same is true of the Portuguese island of Madeira and the American state of Vermont.

CHAPTER 2

We the People
are not in Control

The Broadcasting Perversion

What I here call the 'broadcasting perversion' – over the years I have used other epithets, the 'broadcasting obscenity', the 'broadcasting calamity', each equally suitable – is a phenomenon that for most people, particularly in North America, is not viewed as a woe – it has been a part of their sight and sound ambiance all their lives, which they assume to be part of the natural order of things. But in fact, the American model of broadcasting, increasingly dominant worldwide, is a disgusting disease of the body politic. Ostensibly serving the public and society, it is in fact paid for by business corporations, its so-called programmes no more than consumer bait for peddling their wares, many of dubious utility. Imagine other great services for people similarly organized, on highways, motorists stopping every fifteen minutes in front of giant commercials, symphony concerts in theatres, classes in schools, hospital operations even, interrupted at frequent intervals, promoting some underarm deodorant or brand of toilet paper. But of course the American model of broadcasting is not really a service for people, it an advertising service for business corporations, paid for by them for that purpose – of course it is. The term I have adopted for it is 'advertising-broadcasting' as distinct from 'broadcasting', which I reserve for 'broadcasting' provided for people, analogous to other services for people, education, the health services, and many others.

It is not as if many people don't know that the commercial interruptions are awful, the radio arm of Canada's so-called public broadcaster, the CBC, has no advertising, and actually boasts about it. It's television arm on the contrary has the same amount of advertising, 20% of airtime, as the commercial broadcasters.

Somehow North Americans assume that it is natural for broadcasting to be punctuated by advertising breaks, that's the way broadcasting is. At some level of their consciousness they realize that the commercials are nasty, smelly things, they are like going to the bathroom, everybody has to go there, one just doesn't talk about it. The TV announcer delicately says 'the programme will continue after these messages' or 'after the break' or even more delicately 'after this', or 'stay with us'. And in solemn times, the broadcasting system avoids going to the bathroom at all. For several days after 9/11, the Twin Towers calamity, the US networks nobly carried no commercial breaks at all. And when President Obama addresses the nation over what continues to be, despite the huge array of electronic innovations, the main means of public mass communication, there are no commercial interruptions.

Average viewing time of TV is about four hours daily in major Western countries, so clearly a broadcasting system is a vital modern service for the people as are their other great services, all of which are paid for by the people, not as an adjunct to their business corporation advertising and public relations activities. One could say the United States has no broadcasting service, apart from the donation - supported public broadcasting service, PBS. In both the United States and Canada the small minority of people who wish for better programmes watch PBS, and in Canada, the provincial broadcasters such as TV Ontario. About one quarter of PBS 's revenue is provided by the public – 'viewers like you' – donations from whom are solicited in tedious week-long campaigns, conducted by earnest public-spirited volunteers, which interfere with regular programming. Business corporations also give 'donations', quite transparently as a public relations exercise, to show how public-spirited they are. These are eerily similar to 'corporate social responsibility' donations, discussed later – indeed perhaps they are actually so-designated in corporation accounts. Interestingly these TVO and PBS viewers, who willingly make donations, accept the notion that regular broadcasting must be funded by advertisers. I recall that many years ago Andrew Coyne, now the editor of Canada's Maclean's magazine, wrote that of course regular, commercial TV is bad, when one considers its purpose, but that if one wants better fare one should pay for it. But gladly, I am sure, many people would pay for it, but they can't – for example, in Ottawa, the 2012 Masters' Golf Tournament could only be seen by people willing to endure commercial breaks, whose frequency increased in the last suspenseful few holes of the tournament. This is patently absurd – there are two important parties to a great sports event, the players themselves, seeking glory, and the huge public avidly watching them – but one must remember, in the United States, what business, here the advertiser, wants, business gets – it's called the American Dream. There is pay-to-view television, but it is mainly for movies and 'adult' fare, good old porn.

Just how dreadful is the American travesty of a television service for people, frequently interrupted by ghastly commercials, is made clear by viewing the contrary, the programmes on offer in Canada from TV Ontario and PBS, partly paid for by viewer donations. For drama, comedy, and documentaries these use many imported British programmes, one supposes because the American model of broadcasting does not lend itself to produce the equivalent. Television properly managed is a great boon, for example in England one can have a seat on Centre Court at Wimbledon, seven hours daily, for two weeks, but be in one's living room at home.

Mistakenly, the viewer regards advertising-broadcasting as free, but it is more expensive than genuine people-serving broadcasting would be, its costs hidden in the price of consumer goods, inflated by the huge sums spent in making television commercials and paying sports stars and celebrities to attract viewers. It has no compensating virtues. Neither economists nor communications experts claim that it is a necessary evil, to keep consumers buying, thereby maintaining economic growth and employment. They are probably wrong, and if so, what an absurd way for a society to decide how to deploy its production capacity.

Advertising-broadcasting over the years has been spreading. These were the years in which market fundamentalism and the ideas of Milton Friedman flourished, and helped to trigger off the present Great Recession In 1995 the BBC, all of whose domestic programmes are free of advertising, 're-branded' its international TV service, BBC World News, as a commercial broadcaster. In other countries too, advertising-broadcasting has spread, but far less so in some European countries, especially Switzerland and the Scandinavian countries, while in the United States – and also New Zealand – it constitutes nearly half of all advertising, a veritable blitz of commercial interruptions on radio and television, regarding which few complain, of course, silly, TV has commercials!

'Corporate Social Responsibility'

Here is a phenomenon that like advertising-broadcasting is not seen as a woe by the general public. The misappropriation of the airwaves is now being extended to other public functions. At Canada's National Art Centre we are told that 'this concert was made possible by Mark Motors Audi', and in the centre of the foyer a shining new Audi is displayed, as in a motor show room. And this despite the small proportion of the concert's total cost borne by Mark Motors.

Mark Motors' motivation is very like that of advertisers who buy broadcasting time, it is a public relations exercise, Mark Motors is a worthy citizen who helps pay for our concert tickets, and therefore we will have warm feelings towards Audi cars. Orchestral concerts are superior music, Audi are superior cars.

This phenomenon, 'Corporate Social Responsibility' (CSR), exhibits many forms. In Ottawa's celebrated annual 'Winterlude' on its canal, the 'world's longest skating rink', Roger's Wireless is now a 'partner' with the National Capital Commission in staging the event. 'We wanted' says the Rogers marketing manager 'to have a large-scale, branded interaction that was relevant to Winterlude and the Rideau Canal. Our own branded rink made perfect sense'. Marketeese gobbledygook.

But in a healthy society, the sole function of business corporations is to provide the people with the goods and services they choose and pay for, and their success in doing this is measured by their 'bottom line'. All their disbursements are operating expenses to this end, as are their 'donations', which are public relations expenses passed on to the public by raising the price of their goods and services.

The anomalous new situation can only imply that 'We, the people, (having departed from our senses) have delegated to you, Rogers' Wireless, the job of knowing what causes we deem deserving of our support, then supporting them, with *our* money, by raising the price of the goods you sell to us, and then getting the credit for being the beneficent supporter of good causes. And this closely parallels the broadcasting scam: We pay for our television sets, and for cable service, and then for the commercials you beam at us, along with a wasteland of 'programmes', which we also pay for, thank you, Dear 'Sponsor'. The grand daddy of all con-jobs.

About eight years ago The Economist had a leading article decrying CSR. 'One of the biggest corporate fads of the 1990s was the flowering of "corporate social responsibility". CSR is now an industry in itself, with full-time staff, websites, newsletters, professional associations and massed armies of consultants'. But, The Economist comments: 'It is philanthropy at other people's expense . . . . Supporting good causes out of [the managers'] own generous salaries, bonuses, deferred compensation, options packages, and incentive schemes would be admirable. Doing it out of income that would otherwise be paid to shareholders is a more dubious proposition. Anyway, is it really for managers . . . to decide social-policy priorities among themselves? In a democracy, that is a job for voters and elected politicians'.

The Economist might have added that not only the shareholders are deprived of income, the public too, as they must pay more for their consumer goods. Corporations raise their prices to cover these 'charitable donations' which the public had no part in deciding on. The mechanism is the same as the one described above for broadcasting, the so-called 'free' programs of advertising-funded broadcasting are in fact paid for by a hidden tax buried in the price of consumer goods.

It is interesting that this Economist article sank without a trace. There was little comment in the form of letters to the editor, or any follow up in The Economist. Perhaps behind the scenes there was some uproar and The Economist backed off, the magazine has many business readers and half its readership is in the United States. At the time, I phoned the offices of the Canadian branch of the CSR activity, and enquired regarding their reaction to The Economist article. I was told briskly 'typical right wing attack' So CSR is on the side of the liberal Great and Good, and stands with the Davos demonstrators, yes, make the bastards give some of their ill-gotten gains to charity.

I have tried to find out what the total is of CSR donations in Canada. I supposed that the amount would be huge, for example just for a single recipient, Ottawa's National Arts Centre Orchestra, concert programmes list donating corporations – seven of which 'donate' $100,000 or more each – for a total of several million dollars annually. Surely for all Canadian institutions that are beneficiaries of CSR donations, the total donated must be very large. It is rare that Google fails to reveal available facts, but my search was fruitless – a great deal of information was provided on CSR's noble aims, and on the exemplary behaviour of corporations – reams of gooey waffle no doubt generated by the marketing departments of the corporations concerned, but no indication of how much was given. And not only business corporations, public service entities also – with our tax dollars. I have no doubt that this CSR activity runs rife not only in the bureaucracies of huge corporations but also in those of public bodies aping them. And that somehow the CSR central industry association has been able to block revelation of the overall size of these grand 'charitable' donations? Such ability I know does exist.

For example, Canada's central statistical agency, Statistics Canada, provides minute information on most activities of Canadians, but will not divulge television viewing statistics, which programmes are the most popular – I was advised that this was proprietary information, owned by Nielsen, the rating agency. We the people are not allowed to know what television we watch.

And now corporate social responsibility is being extended to Canada's publicly provided schools, 'This swimming pool courtesy of Coca Cola' – and being lauded for doing this in an editorial in the Globe and Mail, Canada's leading newspaper[17]. But what business has a soft drink company paying for our children's education?

The Facebook phenomenon, and hyperconnectivity

How much of a woe is this – or is it a woe? It is beyond my ken, I have not had an opportunity to immerse myself in Facebook and the social media, but certain facts are quite clear and well known. Take the hugely popular Facebook, nearly half the United States population now are users – and obviously a much larger proportion of the young. And not only in the United States: soon one in seven people on the planet will be on it. And it is free to the user (or any rate, like perverted broadcasting, seems to him free). So who does pay for it, that is, directly? The business corporations, those who purvey consumers goods and services, of course. They pay the Facebook Corporation to permit them to put their advertising to appear on your computer or smart phone screen when you are 'social networking' with your group of friends and acquaintances. You, the user, are the recipient of targeted advertising, tailored to your special tastes and needs. How is this achieved? For you to become a Facebook user, you must first provide a profile of yourself. The Facebook corporation then 'mines' these profiles and informs companies what someone like you is likely to buy so they can target you. Now just consider: When Mark Zuckerberg and colleagues devised Facebook, it was presumably merely for the purpose of communication and amusement among themselves and their friends. But then somebody had the bright idea that this could be a gold mine, and presto, Facebook took off as a phenomenal business success story (perhaps not so phenomenal after all, a report in July 2012 tells us that Facebook has run into privacy problems revealing what's in people's profiles, and its shares have plunged).

But, still can Facebook be called a woe? After all, the user can ignore the ads on his computer or smartphone screen. But consider more broadly: Users may be spending time in aimless communication of trivia and babble at the expense of the real kind of actual communication, face to face with real people, that humans have had for perhaps the 40,000 years since *homo sapiens* first emerged on our planet. And more recently, by letter or email.

And it is not just Facebook. An article in The Economist[18] has the title 'Slaves to the Smartphone: the horrors of hyperconnectivity – and how to restore a degree of freedom' 'Smart devices' we are told 'are sometimes empowering. They put a world of information at our fingertips. They free people to work from home' and so on . . .'But for most people the servant has become the master . . . This is partly because smartphones are addictive . . , BlackBerries and iPhones provide relentless stimuli . . . The faster smartphones become and the more alluring the apps devised for them, the stronger the addiction will grow. Spouses can help by tossing the damned devices out of a window or into a bucket of water'. The article is in The Economist's business section, and discusses the growing problem for businesses, and concludes that 'ultimately it is up to companies to outsmart the smartphones by insisting that everyone turn them off from time to time' But somehow the smartphone purveyors have a hammerlock on the situation, a friend who lectures at a university tells me she is forbidden to order the students to de-activate their gadgets.

So woe or not? Something, surely, is rotten in the state of society – the world is becoming a less comfortable, or perhaps less civilised, place for humans. Of course, all this brilliant new smartphone technology could be of great benefit to mankind, if properly used, with the comfort and benefit of the people the only consideration governing their use.

Renaming grand edifices

This is akin to CSR – public relations stuff. When the railway companies built Canada's great landmark hotels they named them the Chateau Laurier (in 1912), the Royal York (1929), and the Queen Elizabeth (1958), but now when Fairmont acquires them they suddenly become the *Fairmont* Chateau Laurier, the *Fairmont* Royal York. As for the Queen Elizabeth Hotel, where the Queen has stayed four times, would she, visiting again, now stay at the *Fairmont* Queen Elizabeth?

The Pestilential Pop-Ups

This is a terrible annoyance of the same ilk as advertising interruptions in broadcasting. On the internet one is reading a newspaper article or viewing some website, and suddenly the screen is totally blocked by a pop-up of something completely different – some promotion or other. One often has to hunt for where one can 'click' to get rid of the nuisance – in some cases there is no such place, one has to wait for the damn thing to go away of its own accord.

The advertisers / broadcasters are always trying something on. When one is watching television one can always mute the advertisements that interrupt a programme – at least one can shut out the sound of the absurd 'messages' – but there was a period recently in Canada when the moment one pressed the mute button, the advertising message immediately appeared in written form. Fortunately this phase did not last long, no doubt there was a barrage of complaints.

Sports Marketing

'Sports Marketing' is a new industry that took off with the 'commercialisation and Americanization' of the Olympic Games in California in 1984[19]. Now, as soon as a promising young sportsman starts winning, sports marketing firms help him to get on the endorsement gravy train. Sports marketing is another phenomenon, like advertising-broadcasting and CSR, in which business corporations are exceeding their proper functions to serve their marketing and public relations purposes.

Is anything more absurd, pathetic, than the Tiger Bubble, as the New York Times called it. We have been regaled by the grand farce of Tiger Woods' disgrace – a trivial matter? Or is it an omen in our skies, our society is gravely ill? The butcher, the baker, the candlestick maker, indeed, the writer, the lawyer, even the prime minister, all serve the public, and the public pays each for his service. The sportsman, whom the public avidly watches, whom does he serve? The public? Or giant corporations to help them peddle their product? The public paid Tiger $112 million annually to watch him play, but of this, only $12 million was for his actual playing, and that is all we would have to pay if the times were not out of joint. The rest, $100 million, we pay to Nike and the other corporations through the raised price of their products, and they then pass it on to Tiger for the right to use him as a role model to enhance the image of their products.

Philandering, wife cheating, are common in the world, and get attention in the tabloids, but the Tiger Bubble so obviously stank. Tiger's obviously carefully contrived public statement of contrition reeked of hypocrisy and damage control double-talk, no doubt crafted in the marketing departments of the business corporations. *L'affaire Tigre* is just the latest, and most in-our-faces, manifestation of the contravention of the Social Contract in the continuing tilt to untrammelled business power. And it is *we* who are to blame, corporations are merely being corporations. We have not governed well.

Countless Irritations, exasperating useless production

As if all this were not enough, we allow business corporations to impose countless irritations on us. I've never heard a word said in defence of the mindless time-wasting telephone answering systems that now are a blight in people's lives. And they are getting worse, you talk to a jolly machine that asks you questions, and then mis-hears everything you say, you say Ottawa, and the machine hears it as Oshawa. Who designs them to be so awful? And frequent computer software versions one never asked for, which require enormous effort relearning; new electronic gadgets galore, cell phones that do innumerable things you may not be interested in, described in badly written manuals — I know that for many of the young now these things are the be-all and end-all of their lives, but should they be? – I don't know, perhaps mankind, willy nilly, is being bounced into some future world, everybody social-networking, exchanging trivia, tweeting. A new magazine has just arrived in the mail for devotees of these gadgets, whose cover story is 'Does (not 'do') Social Media Work?' – if its editor had spent less time on gadgetry he might know that 'media' is the plural of 'medium'. For us oldies the present is now a foreign country. Perhaps this is just an oldie beef, not a serious woe?

And now this one has goaded me to rage. All our parking meters in Ottawa have just been replaced by modern machines. Meters were handy, next to where you'd just parked your car. You just dropped coins in them and proceeded to your destination. Too easy, some manufacturing company persuaded some municipal functionary that meters were old fashioned, stone age stuff, time for modern technology. Result: A single tall machine that replaces all the meters, you have to walk to it, read obscure instructions about what to do, which buttons to press for your choice of payment method. Say you wish to use coins, what must you do? You guess, the 'Buy time' button. A message appears, 'please wait' (what for, for God's sake – for the machine to gather its wits?). Then, after quite a long time the 'please wait' fades away. What does that mean? You guess it means that you can now drop in your coins? Anyhow you then do that, in one of the machine's orifices. Then you presume that you must now press the button designated 'Print Ticket', You do so, you guessed right, and a ticket laboriously is extruded by the machine, under a flap you must raise. Then you must walk back to your car, open the door, and display the ticket on the dashboard, so that a traffic warden can read it. So much wasted time and effort. The central machine may be fifty yards away from your car, and you have to make the trip twice, before you can proceed to your destination. *Cui bono ?* The machine manufacturer, of course, the public be damned. Several individuals have disagreed with me about the new machines, they are perfectly resigned to them, they're now part of their routine. My point is that, the comfort and the convenience of the public wasn't in the minds of the machines' makers, had it been, they would instead have made an improved version of the individual meters, that calculated for you your expiry time, and also allowed you the option of using your credit card.

Then approximately the same happened in the underground parking garage at Ottawa's National Gallery, which for years I had visited weekly. One simply paid a person in a booth at the garage exit as one left, and got a reduction by showing one's gallery membership card. But that was too easy, and not modern enough. The man at the booth was replaced by a machine placed near the gallery entrance. I haven't yet been able to try to use it, too many members of the public have been clustered round the machine, trying to understand what to do. Fortunately now redundant former booth persons have been retained, so many people were flummoxed, to stand at the garage exit who use a machine there for you. But how do you get your gallery member's reduction? When you enter the Gallery you must first walk to the reception desk, perhaps queuing, where you will get a card that enables you to get a two dollar reduction,. And you must put this card as well as your other card, into the machine as you leave the garage. I was told by the employees stationed at the garage machine to help people use it that there had been a furore, annoyed public and gallery members.

These new ways of paying for parking are not only inconvenient for the public, they may also constitute wasteful production, use of the economy's productive capacity to produce things that the public don't need or want at the expense of useful production raising the quality of life. Companies may think they are reducing costs by mechanisation – one cannot be sure – but even if they are, the fundamental principle is ignored, that ultimately it is the public who should be served, improving the public's quality of life. Besides the former parking attendants, perhaps individuals not cut out for any other sort of employment, are put out of work.

A problem of our society much commented on is that with fast advancing technology, people are being replaced by machines. That is a long term matter that must be ultimately addressed in an intelligent way, possibly by a shorter work week, but the principle in a good society should always be observed, innovations must never add to the woes, or inconvenience, of the public that the economy exists to serve. Please, dear reader, don't get me wrong. Modern technology is wondrous, if properly used it can be a great boon – but only if it is borne in mind that it is the comfort and convenience of the public that must come first.

There are other unnecessary items produced which are less annoying to the public, who can just ignore them. (I'm using the first person here as I haven't conducted a survey of what other people feel).

I like my toothbrush, I've used the same one for years. But every time, twice yearly, when I get my routine tooth cleaning and check, I'm given a new toothbrush and other cleaning aids, which I subsequently throw away. When I get my annual eye examination I'm now given a bottle of glasses cleaning fluid and cloth (which I don't use because just holding my glasses under a tap for a moment is effective). And here is another new absurdity, waist-high devices like parking meters, 'Gemstar instant hand sanitizers' have sprouted up around buildings. These dispense hand-cleaning fluid, and urge you to 'Please sanitize your hands to help maintain a healthy environment' Really! I've seldom seen anybody using them. Another such unnecessary item has lately popped up in doctors' and dentists' waiting rooms, disposable plastic foot covers – one is supposed to remove one's shoes and place the plastic cover over one's socks. Many patients do what they are told, but others ignore the hint to participate, and no one, neither receptionist nor doctor, says a word.

And what about unnecessary elaborate packaging with an impregnably resistant plastic cover, and no instructions on how to remove it? You dance in rage, trying to wrestle the thing open, having first found a heavy duty pair of scissors or pliers. Add to this the waste that must be disposed of, and that of course adds to the price of the product.

It doesn't take much thought to see another side to all these useless devices coming into being. That is where some of the affluence goes that we are supposed to have, which Galbraith wrote of fifty years ago, but which we don't now really have. This unnecessary stuff adds to GDP, and high GDP per capita is supposed to signify affluence, a high living standard. Here it properly is negative and a reduction of living standards.

Nirvana of gadgetry

Face-book, Twitter, Blackberry, iPhone, iPod, Myspace, social networking, mobile mania, now the preoccupation and highest aspiration of our young. A television commercial shows a room with a large television screen, and happy youths, standing, sprawled on sofas, on the floor, engrossed in a nirvana of these gadgets – or is this dystopia, Orwell's proles kept happy with honky-tonk? And everywhere the noise, loud pop and rock, little children cowering in their mothers' laps in high-decibel movie theatres, the poor mites' fingers in their ears. *Gotterdammerung,* the twilight of the gods, the crescendo of madness of a sinking society?

And one's vocabulary must expand. Lately a new word has suddenly come onto our scene, 'apps', which only lately I discovered was short for 'application software', related to the electronic gadgets. One must race to keep up with the modern world – but is it worth it, is a proliferating gadget-happy civilization where we really want to go, or are we being willy-nilly bounced into it? I don't know, but it is a matter needing discussion: (yes, I know, some of these gadgets are, or could be, marvellous contributions to the quality of life, but the matter shouldn't be left entirely to the business corporations and their high pressure sales promotion).

Misuse of the wonders of modern technology

Make no mistake, modern technological ingenuity has been a boon. All sorts of products have made our lives easier. And in recent decades email and the internet have been a most useful innovation. Without Google and Wikipedia, and my word processor, this work would have been much more difficult to write. As important has been the immediate access the internet gives me to the world's newspapers. And I don't doubt that many of the gadgets now existing – I myself have not had the time to immerse myself in them, smart phones, blackberries, and many more – if used intelligently can be enormously helpful. Google is amazing, one can quickly find out anything about anything. In a conversation somebody said to me 'Cry Havoc and let slip the dogs of war', and I typed 'cry havoc' into Google and was instantly told that the words were uttered by Mark Antony in Shakespeare's Julius Caesar, Scene 1, Act 3.

But there is what might be called a negative woe, the absence of the improvements in our life quality as a result of the misuse of the new technologies. It is not only the false nirvana, modern youth spending their time in mindless perpetual intercommunication – every second young person walking down the street with a cell phone or suchlike gadget glued to their ear, surely at the expense of thoughts engaged in more worthwhile matters of our fascinating diverse world. According to surveys[20] 72 percent of Facebook's 800 million users worldwide are under 34 years old, and 50 percent of Twitter tweets are pointless babble, self-promotion, or spam, and 38 percent conversational. But it is not only these gadgets, but also far larger equipment, notably the motor car, over-sized, stuck in urban traffic grid-lock, and difficult to park. And it need not be so, indeed all these items of communication and transportation if not misused can be a great boon. For example some one I know who lives on the outskirts of a city in England has minibuses passing his house every 20 minutes which take him into the city centre which is totally pedestrianised and car-free, a delight to walk around, shop in, or go to restaurants, with pleasing urban architecture. He depends on the car only for venturing further into the countryside, going to the golf course, and for longer trips – though a good intercity train service also helps there.

The reader may have the idea that I have a jaded view of life, look through the opposite of rose tinted glasses. Not so, there is much these days to be thankful for. One important thing is life expectancy, over 80 years in most Western nations. It is striking how short lives once were. One hundred years ago life expectancy at birth in the US and the UK was only 50. In the UK infant mortality fell from 14% to 0.5%. According to one source, 80% of improved life expectancy is due to clean drinking water, and universal sanitation, and 20% due to better nutrition and medical care.

What I'm getting at here is that because of serious shortcomings in our modern societal governance, the wonders of modern technology are often grossly misused, in particular to serve the marketing and profit goals of business corporations run amok – and I insist it is far more our fault, not business corporations', we have not made sure that we, the people, are in control – that the economic system exists to serve us, not we it. Unless we take action very soon humanity will be bounced into a very nasty world. But, if we just pull ourselves together we could make sure that instead we move into a delightful, humanity-serving world.

All–American Woes

This work would be incomplete if it didn't mention this woe of what Samuel Huntington called the 'core state' of Western civilization – he too thought our society was in decline – and what I have called the heartland of the West's sickness. Sixteen percent of American GDP in now spent on health care, which means about 23% of all personal spending. And despite this huge expenditure, about 17% of the population have no coverage, while about as many more have insufficient coverage. At the same time, statistics show that the United States has one of the highest rates of child mortality, and lowest life expectancy of all the world's advanced nations. But no doubt the affluent portion of the US population gets very good health care and medical attention.

How can this be so in what not only is one of the wealthiest nations, but also the most godly – love thy neighbour, faith, hope and charity, and of these the greatest is charity – but it's OK if the poor people's cancer goes untreated.

Also all-American is the gun fixation, the sacred right to bear arms, and the accelerating succession of gun slaughters, at the time of writing, the horror of Newtown, Connecticut.

CHAPTER 3

Decadence and Decline

There is a large and growing literature of Western decadence and decline, but can one be sure that one's society is really on the way down? Is pessimism justified? Oliver Bennett, in his 'Cultural Pessimism', writes that 'cultural pessimism arises with the conviction that the culture of a nation, a civilisation, or of humanity itself, is in an irreversible process of decline'. In Bennett's view 'in the last few decades, narratives emerged throughout the West, that were deeply pessimistic'. He discusses the literature of decline, such familiar names as Spengler, Toynbee, and more recently, Huntington, and Fukuyama. The heartland of decline, Bennett believes, is the Anglo world, in particular the United States, Britain, and New Zealand. There is no doubt that at present there is huge unease in the United States at the state of the nation. Most recently Niall Ferguson presented a television series, 'Is the West history'?, and a magisterial work by Martin Jacques is entitled 'When China Rules the World: The rise of the Middle Kingdom and the End of the Western World'. And now, in the depth of the Euro crisis, there is pessimism about Europe's future.

But even so, the difficulty of determining whether a civilization is in decline is something like the problem of the group of blind men describing an elephant after touching it – each touches a different part. As I stated in the introduction, my approach here is 'clinical', linking together three things, symptoms, diagnosis, and cure. If through this approach one produces a convincing, coherent, 'model' of reality, then one can get past the conflicting blind men's testimonies, and arrive at a sound conclusion. But I am leaping ahead here, the reader should withhold judgment until later, has a convincing case been made?

At this point though, one can talk of one's deep suspicion of grave societal dysfunction. The following journalist's view seems to me expressive of the state of much of our Western society:

> 'If advertising holds up a mirror to society, then the slogan that best reflects our times is surely "Have It Your Way", used by Burger King .... the fragmentation of society into millions of individuals who .... want it their way now .... Life has become a supermarket ... manners, discipline, censorship, shame, standards of dress, respect for tradition ... has been chucked in the trash can .... one result is the growth of "rage" incidents, explosions of anger over minor setbacks, often accompanied by violence .... mass or multiple killings, such as the Oklahoma City bombing ... the Columbine High School massacre'.

And this from the Financial Times[21], scarcely a fierce, anti-establishment propagator of extreme views. But when I encounter such views I have always wondered why the particular role is never mentioned of our perverted broadcasting system, relentlessly dinning in its message, buy, buy, buy, this will make you so, so happy. The FT article was written long before the present economic crisis, and now, in 2012, the same newspaper is running a series of articles on 'The Crisis in Capitalism'.

The Seeming Power Shift to Asia

No matter is now more discussed than the rise of China, and to a somewhat lesser extent of India. These two economies are rising fast, and given that together they have one third of the world's total population, 2.8 times more than that of the entire developed world, they are bound within, say, two decades to match their economies.

But can we call this a woe? Clearly, only to the extent that these countries' rise affects the quality – and safety – of our own civilization. What here we are concerned with is whether we are in a state of decadence and decline, as well as misery in our lives. And if one allows that the route from ancient Greece, through Rome, the Enlightenment, and modern Western democracy is the most beneficial for humanity, our decline is a setback for the whole world.

And we must retain perspective. We should surely separate China and India, they are as different as chalk and cheese. Racially, culturally, linguistically, and in their political systems, they differ hugely, and they are separated physically by the barrier of the Himalayas. And there is little love lost between them, their differences may be bigger than those between any two members of the European Union, say between Sweden and Greece.

Very often the comparison is made between the United States, the present hegemon, and the hegamon-to-be, China. At purchasing power parity (at what a nation's currency can buy internally) China's GDP is now 69% the size of that of the United States. Its present growth rate of about 9% is surely unsustainable, to a considerable degree dependent on the huge 'outsourcing' of globalization due to Western business corporations transferring production to Asia to profit from its cheap skilled labour, with a consequent 'hollowing out' of Western industry. Perhaps in a New Enlightenment, with a new degree of control over corporation behaviour, such outsourcing might be reduced, as part of a Western attempt to recover from its present economic meltdown. Also making possible China's huge capital investment is its astonishing 45% family saving rate, the share of income not spent on personal consumption. Although these unusual conditions cannot last indefinitely, China's growth rate will surely continue to be high. A little arithmetic will show how fast the Chinese economy must grow in order to overtake the American in fifteen years, that is by 2027. Assuming the American economy continues to grow at its present rate, say 2.5%, then if the Chinese economy grows at only 5.1% it will draw even by 2027 in purchasing power parity terms.

More grave than the size of China economy, is China's carbon emissions. These are indeed a woe. Already China produces nearly a quarter of the world's CO_2 emissions, and they are fast increasing. China has a very dirty economy, it is a huge user of coal, the dirtiest of fossil fuels. But is also true that China has the world's largest programme of new nuclear station construction as well as new high speed electric trains. But it will be a woe indeed, a huge obstacle to any new renaissance, if China cannot be fast induced to convert fast to a far cleaner economy. And the same is true of such other fast-growing emerging giants such as India, Brazil, and Indonesia.

We should also note here that some of the appearance of power transfer from east to west is due to the United States' consumption of more than it produces, helped by mortgaging part of its economy – ' *now leased out . . . . like to a tenement or pelting farm²²*' – to China which now holds more than a trillion dollars of US Treasury bills. Mind you China has some vulnerability, if the US defaults on its debt payments.

A Dirge for our Times, aka
Modern Popular Music

Is this a societal woe or is it just a kinky personal woe? For me it is one of the blights of our time, that I sometimes have difficulty escaping, when radios in taxis, restaurants, even doctors' waiting rooms, are tuned to commercial stations which when not belting out selling 'messages', are belting out pop. Other people sitting round me in waiting rooms seem to be tuning it out, reading, or chatting with others, this is the backdrop to modern North American life, its sound ambiance. I have seen people coming into a room where the television happened to be switched off, walk up to the set, switch it on, and then sit down and start chatting with someone.

But, really is modern popular music as awful as I think it is – or sounds, in Mark Twain's words – or is this thing just part of my dyspepsia? To me, it is rarely anything but foul, when one compares it with the popular music of earlier times, Jerome Kern, Smoke gets in your eyes, Latin America tangos, rumbas, and cha, cha, chas, tea for two, and two for tea – and also such tuneful music of our times as Andrew Lloyd Webber – lots of lovely stuff. I often ask myself whether the current thump, thump, thump of rock, the menace of rap, are a dirge, portending a sick and dying age – or is merely different, not worse, the sounds of a new age, and of a people fast becoming different, and that evolution, natural selection and random mutation, linked to electronic gadgetry, and the social media, are accelerating, a new kind of human being is taking over, and I think of H. G. Wells' 'Time Machine' and a ghastly world of the future.

But, I am sure, this is overblown, this ranting of mine is idiosyncratic. Even so, I'll continue, as politely as I can, to ask the taxi driver if he would mind turning his radio down – and he correctly receives this as a request to switch it off – he has his tip in mind.

Part Two

Diagnosis

The phenomena just discussed in Part One were called 'symptoms of societal disorder', but are they really? – societies have always had blemishes, there are always individuals who complain, it wasn't like this when I was young, and people who cry doom, so let us here play devil's advocate:

'Diagnosis' presupposes a problem, but do we *really* have a problem? Global Warming? All right, that *is* awful, and yes, it's time we got going on that. Recession? – we've always had boom and bust, and this will eventually bottom out. And your 'woes', really! What's so terrible about television advertisements? they're often better than the programmes - hey man, get a life! So power is tilting to business? Doesn't bother me, let them make charitable donations and support the Symphony – besides I trust them more than I do government bureaucrats.

And what do you mean, our affluence is a mirage – we have hundreds of things we never had before, travel abroad, computers, two cars, dining out in restaurants, – so what if all the kids spend their time with Twitter and Facebook and have cell phones glued to their ears? China and India rising, I couldn't care less – but just be sure we keep our powder dry. Decadence? Every generation complains 'it wasn't like this when I was young', just get on with, stop whining.

Alright, I allow that there is only one thing we must act on, and act on immediately. We are on the countdown to Doomsday, accelerating global warming, and the risk of runaway warming when the methane in the soil is released, 20 or more times worse than carbon emissions.

Not only this threat, but precisely what must be done to combat it, have long been starkly clear. Why then have our efforts been so pathetic, sleepwalking to our doom? There must be some serious weakness in our society's governance institutions, which has paralysed us, that allows this paralysis to endure. We must fast make the reforms in our governance that will enable us to save the planet from catastrophe. But these faults of governance are the same ones that have driven our society into decadence and decline, and by correcting them we will at the same time be on the way to a new renaissance.

Now to our diagnosis. The chapters of Part Two lay out the defects of our governing institutions, and what must be done to correct them, not argue about all the other woes, or indeed whether our society is decadent and in decline. But soon we shall start to realize that our society is less sick, there will be fewer works published on the decline of the West.

CHAPTER 4

The Hypothesis of Underlying Societal Malfunction

Already in 1969[23] it was possible to postulate the following:

'Through our so-called free enterprise system we have created a magnificently efficient, flexible, inventive means of production. Our mechanism for enjoying the fruits of this wonderful machine – of getting it to produce the things we really want, or would ask for if the mechanism existed for presenting us with the options – has not kept pace. An economic system should exist to satisfy the real wants of the people, but that is being lost sight of.

'An imbalance has developed in our system. In order to overcome the problems of overcapacity and unemployment caused by accelerating productivity, and assure continued profits and growth, the sales promotion function has grown beyond reason. An increasingly frantic assault is being made on the consuming public, to stimulate 'wants'. The effect of this may well be to make people feel poorer than ever (despite the 'highest' living standard the world has ever known), and get them deeper in debt, a situation facilitated by increasingly easy credit. Some people may actually be getting poorer, in living fundamentals such as food, shelter, clothes, medical care, leisure, pleasant surroundings, fast transportation, as a result of spending their money on the artificially stimulated wants (this could have been written yesterday!).

'This situation in which supply now creates its own demand, rather than the position of orthodox economic theory in which demand governs supply, has been called by J. K. Galbraith the "revised sequence".

'It is arguable that this imbalance that has crept into our society contributes to a corruption of values, crime and violence, growing unrest and disaffection, and blunders in military and foreign policy. It may be no coincidence that the word "sell" has acquired a connotation far broader and more pervasive than its original specific meaning . . . an analysis of our complete social-economic-political system may be called for . . . . . . In my view our Western system is still basically the world's hope. To paraphrase Churchill: it is a bad system, but nothing better has yet been devised. With enough determination and intelligence, we can get it back "on track".

'In our society the problem of financing the urgently needed collective expenditures to improve our general environment has not yet been solved . . . . How to finance this type of public enterprise without additional psychologically bad income tax? – the General Motors president is paid not much under a million dollars a year to offset personal tax (in 2011 he was paid seven million, low because of GM's government bailout – Ford's president was paid thirty million dollars).

'One answer appears to be to 'bleed' money out of the productive processes, by a variety of production or sales taxes. One gathers that . . . some moves in this direction are occurring in . . . . eg the Netherlands. There are problems to applying the method: it can be made to seem painless to the man in the street, and there might be a danger of loss of democratic control and abuse'.

That was my diagnosis in 1969, and the following are its main points.

(i) 'Through our so-called free enterprise system we have created a magnificently efficient, flexible, inventive means of production'.

(ii) 'Our mechanism for enjoying the fruits of this wonderful machine – of getting it to produce the things we really want, or would ask for if the mechanism existed for presenting us with the options – has not kept pace'.

(iii) 'An economic system should exist to satisfy the real wants of the people, but that is being lost sight of': (As I have put it in this present work, our society is contravening the great Social Contract of Hobbes, Locke and Rousseau, that the only justification of society is that it serve the people, otherwise why not return to the state of nature, where life is 'nasty, brutish, and short'?).

(iv) 'In order to overcome the problems of overcapacity . . . caused by accelerating productivity, ... the sales promotion function has grown beyond reason. An increasingly frantic assault is being made on the consuming public, to stimulate "wants".

(v) 'The effect of this may well be to make people feel poorer than ever (despite the "highest" living standard the world has ever known), and get them deeper in debt, a situation facilitated by increasingly easy credit. Some people may actually be getting poorer, in living fundamentals such as . . . . medical care . . . . pleasant surroundings, fast transportation, as a result of spending their money on the artificially stimulated wants'.

(vi) 'It is arguable that this imbalance that has crept into our society contributes to a corruption of values, crime and violence, growing unrest and disaffection'.

(vii) 'our Western system is still basically the world's hope. With enough determination and intelligence, we can get it back 'on track'.

(viii) 'In our society the problem of financing the urgently needed collective expenditures to improve our general environment has not yet been solved . . . . . How to finance this type of public enterprise without additional psychologically bad income tax'.

(ix) 'One answer appears to be to "bleed" money out of the productive processes, by a variety of production or sales taxes'.

That remains essentially my diagnosis now, except for one omission, the absurdity of boom and bust – it is a grave weakness of the current discipline called 'economics' that people cannot be kept employed all the time. In recent years I have also elaborated on item (iv), the overdeveloped sales promotion function, focussing on the perversion of the broadcasting system to serve as an advertising medium paid for by business corporations, and more lately other such perversions. I have also developed a way of 'bleeding money out of the productive processes' (item ix), by recognising a new, third, factor of production 'Society', which like the factors, 'Labour' and 'Capital', must receive its return.

But over all these years have I merely been prey to an *idée fixe*? Already in 1973[24], a decade after I had originally sketched it out, I was struck by how little my view had changed, and asked 'Does this hypothesis of mine simply represent an *idée fixe*[25] of long standing' or 'whether an internally consistent model has been forming in my mind with strong underpinnings of reality?' Can it be a fixed idea, an obsession, a delusion? Stafford Beer, at the time an influential expert on operational research and management cybernetics, discussed how belief is fixed in humans. 'Every time a particular pathway is traced through a set of nerve cells (in the brain) . . . it becomes easier to trace that path again in the future. This is rather like the situation on a network of snowbound roads: every vehicle that passes makes it easier for the next to pass, until certain routes through the network of roads must obviously be preferred to others'.

I asked that question and now forty years later I am still asking it, and increasingly I have become convinced that the hypothesis is right, even more so with the present economic meltdown, and the especial difficulties of the US economy in getting restarted. As already observed in Chapter 1, it has been a bubble economy, a frantically buying consumer economy, held aloft by a stream of television commercials telling people to 'buy, buy, this will make you so happy. An economy that is held aloft by a bubble that has burst, with little attempt at purposeful spending to meet real needs such as building needed infrastructure and launching the huge projects needed to save the climate.

But if correct why has it escaped the attention of our society's thinkers'?

If this diagnosis is correct, and for me its rightness seems to be obvious, why has it escaped the attention of our economists and policy makers? I suggest there are three reasons. One is the colossal inertia of the great ship society which has the policy makers in thrall; another is the stubbornness of orthodoxy, what J. K. Galbraith called the conventional wisdom of the economists, who have a huge influence on public policy; and finally, and perhaps the most important, economics is not now a genuine science, it needs to be replaced by a new science of how the economy functions, a genuine science like physics and chemistry, deserving of a Nobel Prize. Already macro-economics and the Keynesian school have been laying groundwork for what can become a genuine science. Some Keynesians, the Nobel Prize winners, for example Paul Krugman and Joseph Stiglitz, and the late Kenneth Galbraith have done valuable work. I'll say a word on each of these forces preventing an understanding of what is obviously wrong with our economic system.

The inertia of the giant supertanker, Society: As to society, it is difficult to deflect the giant vessel from its present course. Each individual person, ourselves, is programmed to play his present part, both at work and play, that he or she has been taught to do since infancy, over his lifetime he has acquired deeply ingrained habits, skills, routines, way of life. He may profess grand thoughts for change, he may write books that are well reviewed, but the giant ship continues heedless on its course: 'words, words, is that all you blighters can do'? trilled Julie Andrews[26], when its comes to action his programming prevails.

The stubborness of the conventional wisdom: Economics like other disciplines has a body of orthodoxy that its exponents learn and practise, which, for the economists, J. K. Galbraith called 'the conventional wisdom . . . People invest heavily in these ideas, and so are heavily resistant to changing them. They are only finally overturned when new events occur which make the conventional wisdom so absurd as to be impalpable'[27]. And now in 2012, there is a great deal in the present wisdom that is 'impalpable' but unfortunately has not yet been recognised as such.

In the physical sciences the corresponding process was described by Thomas Kuhn[28] in his highly influential 'The Structure of Scientific Revolutions' which was published in 1962. 'Normal science' is the occupation of scientific orthodoxy, refining the current paradigm, until one day, when its shortcomings become increasingly evident, a new paradigm is put forward. Copernicus proposed a universe that no longer goes round the earth, Newton the laws of motion, Darwin evolution, and then Einstein relativity. New paradigms have been fiercely opposed – Galileo was tried by the Inquisition for espousing Copernican views, and spent the rest of his life under house arrest.

Economics not a real science. This is surely the single most important reason why our society has not diagnosed the cause of its woes. The present discipline of economics has the disadvantage of not being a real science, the genuine study of the exceedingly complex social, economic, political, informational, environmental, system that is our society. Years ago I studied this system, producing flow diagrams of its physical, monetary, information, resource, environmental flows, and present economics is simply a monetary abstraction that ignores the other flows. By way of example, a major economist of recent times, the Nobel laureate Paul Samuelson, devoted only one quarter of a page of his 750 page text book to advertising, not even distinguishing the broadcasting variety. Yet how can a genuine science of economics ignore this hugely powerful force in the economy?

That economics is not now a genuine science is demonstrated in having two warring orthodoxies. In a genuine science, physics, say, or chemistry, there is a single great body of what is taken as correct, which is updated as a result of research, new discovery, and ratiocination. Economics' two orthodoxies are, on the one hand, the view that the economy should be left to itself, that market forces will bring full employment, and on the other, Keynesian management of the economy. A new genuine science of the economy is needed, and, I believe, one which will build on Keynes' thought, incorporating many aspects of the societal system at present absent in economics. When Keynes' launched his ideas the world, at least outside the United States, lacked our broadcasting perversion and our other contraventions of the Social Contract that influence the functioning of the economy. A new economics paradigm must surely include advertising, and the question of who should control the airwaves. But that is only part of it, present economics has manifold shortcomings.

Now in the world's deep recession there is huge disagreement between the competing economics orthodoxies about what to do. For the 'leave it to business and the market' orthodoxy, priority must be given to cutting the budget deficit and pruning government spending – witness the British Conservative government's savage government cutting measures, and in more extreme form the shouts of the Tea Party for 'government just to get off our backs and leave it to us, the people'. The other orthodoxy, that of the Keynesians, calls for stimulus, leave the deficit for later, just concentrate on restarting the economy and half the deficit will go away by itself. Even from a purely common sense point of view that makes more sense. Certainly that means more public debt interest will have to be paid for a while, but that is a fleabite of a problem compared with that of an unemployed economy.

Reflecting economics' dubious claim to being a genuine science was the brouhaha about a move by the Federal Reserve Board's to boost the US economy. The Wall Street Journal of the 15th November 2010, under the headline 'Fed's QE move faces rough ride' (QE is so-called Quantitative Easing') we are told that 'a group of Republican-leaning economists . . . is launching a campaign calling on the Fed chair to drop his plan to buy $600 billion more in U.S. treasury bonds. The planned asset purchases risk currency debasement and inflation' and will not 'achieve the Fed's objective of promoting employment' . . . 'The economists have been consulting several Republican lawmakers . . . and have begun discussions with potential GOP presidential candidates'. Most strange. When one is arranging a space flight to Mars does one ask what political party the space scientists belong to?

Or when one is about to have an operation, whether the surgeon is a Democrat or a Republican?

Equally interesting was the riposte from a Fed spokeswoman: 'The Chairman has also noted that the Federal Reserve does not believe that it can solve the economy's problems on its own . . . That will take time and the combined efforts of many parties, including the central bank, Congress, the administration, regulators, and the private sector'. Well now, and everybody thought the Fed by fiddling with the money supply could fix the economy. But seriously, is it not a joke science where its experts contest whether the central bank alone, or whether every organ of government, plus the business corporations must work together to restart the economy? Some science, some scientists! And to round out the farce, we are told that 'potential Republican presidential candidate Sarah Palin delivered a stinging speech on the Fed move'.

Martin Wolf of the Financial Times, a leading economics commentator, writes thus[29]: 'The Chancellor presents the proposal for cutting fiscal deficits and reducing the share of public spending of gross domestic product as "unavoidable". This is not so . . . . The Chancellor presents the hypothesis of looming national "bankruptcy". If so, the UK must have been bankrupt for much of the last two centuries . . . The Chancellor and the Treasury are confident and persuasive. . . . having written on the UK economy for 23 years, I know it was ever thus. Yet, in retrospect, the government was wrong perhaps half the time. Economics is an art, not a science. . . . This may be a great policy success or the biggest fiscal blunder since the early 1930s'. Because of its vital part in managing the economic system and launching the New Enlightenment I discuss the question of a new genuine science of economics, that is no longer an art, at some length later.

The essential point of this diagnosis is that our society lacks a mechanism to ensure that it serves only us, the people, not some other element of society – or indeed to ensure that it is not aimless, a huge entity out of control lurching along without purpose. In other words it lacks machinery to ensure that it fulfils the great Social Contract. But before discussing this missing mechanism, let us first discuss the Social Contract, and how it is now being contravened.

CHAPTER 5

The Social Contract

In this chapter we discuss the very nature of what constitutes the good society. Our goal is to launch a new enlightenment and renaissance, and we do not wish to bring into being something that is less than good, that falls short of what a society should be. Let us start then at the most fundamental level. What is the justification of societies, why should there be society at all ? Perhaps there are two sorts of way of answering this, the scientific, Darwinian way, and the values, morality sort of way. Or perhaps a blend of the two. A Darwinian answer might be that early men, hominids, who grouped together cooperatively had a survival advantage over those that remained solitary, and since that time power and force have ultimately determined the shape of societies, whether within each nation, or between nations. An answer based on values would say that the form of a society will ultimately depend on the value and moral judgment of the people.

The philosopher, Bertrand Russell was awarded the 1950 Nobel laureate in Literature, 'in recognition of his varied and significant writings in which he champions humanitarian ideals and freedom of thought'. In his 'The History of Western Philosophy'[30], Russell compares Nietzsche with Buddha: Nietzsche writes of that 'blockhead John Stuart Mill . . . . I abhor the man's vulgarity when he says "do not unto others that which you would not that they do to you"'. Nietzsche admired Napoleon, 'a great man defeated by petty opponents. It is necessary for higher men to make war against the masses, and resist the democratic tendencies of the age, for in all directions mediocre people are joining hands to make themselves masters'. Over most of human history, observes Russell, authoritarian regimes have prevailed, and 'the governments of all large states were aristocratic until the American and French Revolutions'.

How to resolve the matter? 'Some find pleasure in the infliction of torture, others, like Buddha, feel they cannot be fully happy so long as any living thing is suffering'. Russell concludes 'I agree with Buddha . . But I do not know how to prove he is right . . . I think the ultimate argument lies not in an appeal to the facts, but in an appeal to the emotions. Nietzsche despises universal love; I feel that it is the motive power to all that I desire as regards the world. Coming down on the side of Buddha and Russell, the value judgment I have made is that the good society is one that fulfils the Social Contract, that is, a society that is at the service of the *entire* people, not just one, powerful segment of the people.

Two contending ways of fulfilling the Social Contract

There are now, especially with the rise of China, and the West's current disarray in the United States and Europe, two contending forms of political organisation for fulfilling the Social Contract. We in the West presume that our slowly and painfully evolved democratic institutions are the be-all and end-all of good government. They were slowly, and painfully, built up in stages, from ancient Greece, later from the tribunes of the people of ancient Rome, and a thousand years later from Magna Carta, then the rule of law, individual rights, freedom of expression, elected government, and universal suffrage. But this requires some careful thought. On reflection one can see that the Social Contract does not *logically* demand democracy – one might argue that the mass of people, not everybody well informed, or the least bit interested in matters political, each person with his own narrow preoccupations and prejudices, and capable of being swayed by demagogues, one might argue that the mass of people are not equipped to make a wise choice of government.

Over the last two centuries the West has enjoyed hegemony – the world has in a sense been a Western world, the fast rising developing giants are seeking a Western standard of living, using Western technology, acquiring Western style consumer goods. There has been a tendency to assume that as economies advanced, Western notions of democracy and human rights would also become the world norm. But perhaps that is a question that needs reflection, we want to be sure that the New Enlightenment's foundations are not built on sand. This is especially important as a challenging conception of the good society is fast rising in the East, in China in particular, and the West, in the United States and Europe, is in a state of agonized turmoil.

So our question is, is the benign society that fulfills he Social Contract necessarily one that embraces what might be called the 'western attributes', the rule of law, freedom of speech, civil liberties, human rights, democratically elected government? Confucius, who wrote 2500 years ago, also believed in benign government for the benefit of all, but how this was to come about was anything but democratic. Benign government was hierarchical, and whether between the ruler and the ruled, or the father and the son, 'the former party was expected to protect the latter, and in return the latter was expected to be obedient to the former'. And the 'ruler should also ensure that his own behaviour to his subjects was a model of paternal benevolence, since this would lead to emulation by all others in a comparably superior situation[31]'. And rising China is now reemphasizing Confucius, as was made explicitly clear in the opening ceremony of the 2008 Beijing Olympic Games[32], implying that there is a ruling caste of specially educated people, whose function is to govern – scholars steeped in the ancient wisdoms figure much in Confucian teachings.

In his recent work 'When China Rules the World; The Rise of the Middle Kingdom' Martin Jacques throws interesting light on the matter. He shows the superficiality of the Western assumption that grew out of its last two centuries' of hegemony, that when the non-western countries become highly developed, for example Japan and more lately the Asian tigers, South Korea, Taiwan, and Singapore – they of necessity adopt our 'western attributes'. No says Jacques, there is not only one way of being modern. Japan he convincingly argues is only superficially Western. And in its own way Japan is exceedingly benign, it takes care of, and is kind to, its people. This was illustrated following the Fukushima tsunami-nuclear disaster, when the visiting prime minister and cabinet ministers, after being harangued by angry Fukushima victims, abased themselves, their foreheads on the floor.

China and truth

Undoubtedly China is one of the world's great civilizations, and the Chinese are a highly civilised people, and no doubt in many respects they are well governed. But consider just one question, the place of truth. In the Western view of the benign society a fundamental tenet is that truth is a great good in itself, but this has not been the Chinese view. Historically the truth in China can sharply switch – Confucius good, Confucius bad, Confucius good. Perhaps that alone should be enough to disqualify China as participating in a drive to reaffirm the Social Contract and reverse decadence and decline: Truth is of the very essence of the heritage of the enlightenment, the question of truth, the plain unvarnished truth, in no way doctored to suit the political needs of the moment. For Kant truth was a categorical imperative. In a democracy, all its best thinkers, or for that matter everybody, Tea Party and flat earthers included, is free to put forward what they believe to be true, and the people, and society, are free to choose whom or what they believe. But in an autocratic society, what is absolutely true is what the great leader, Big Brother, says is true. And so it is in China. The Confucian view has had its ups and downs over the centuries. More recently, the nationalist Chiang Kai-Shek favoured Confucius, but then Mao Tse-tung denounced Confucius as having kept China backward vis-a-vis Japan and the West. But then a *volte face,* under Mao's successors, truth's name is again Confucius, and now in parts of China there are more statues of Confucius than of Mao. Orwell's '1984' comes to mind, suddenly black is white and white is black. But perhaps some might argue that truth is not supreme in all circumstances, that what is supreme is human well-being and happiness, what the Social Contract calls for. Western philosophy would have difficulty demoting truth so far, perhaps allowing only an occasional little white lie, in some special circumstances, for example so as not to hurt someone's feelings, or more seriously in the situation where a desperate man tears up to you and says 'there are men chasing me who will kill me, tell them I went *that* way', and the man then streaks of in the opposite direction'. If you don't lie to his pursuers you will cause his death.

The lack of belief in the western attributes of the current Chinese leadership is breathtakingly strong, who demonstrate this in word and deed. Its treatment of the blind dissident, Chen Guangcheng in May 2012 arouses deep Western disgust. One can greatly admire China, it has achieved remarkable wonders since Mao's death, a prodigiously fast development catchup with the Western world, on the brink of becoming the world's largest economy, but now at this pivotal stage in human history, we must face stark reality. Consider the words of the Chinese foreign minister, Yang Jiechi, during his recent visit to Zimbabwe, once the 'jewel of Africa', with a highly developed infrastructure and democratic institutions, but now sent plunging by Mugabe and his gang of thugs, in a total negation of the western attributes. China is fast seeking to exploit Africa's raw materials, and on 16th February 1911 Yang Jiechi gave a news conference after emerging from a meeting with the malign Zimbabwe dictator, Robert Mugabe: 'China', he said, 'believes that Africa belongs to African countries and African people. African people are their own masters and all the others are guests. We believe all nations should respect each other's sovereignty and territorial integrity'. Yang called for an end to the sanctions that the European Union and the United States have placed on travel by Mugabe and his cronies. That is the Chinese mantra, for ever in use, non-interference in the internal affairs of other countries. The lack of Chinese grasp of, or interest in, the western attributes is profound. It is not the Zimbabwean people who are masters of their own house, it is Comrade Mugabe and his thugs who are the masters, and are plundering the land. In fact Yang's statement invites scepticism. China, it is reported, is a deeply racist society, within China it is not politically incorrect to refer to darker people in the most offensive terms, and most particularly the darkest people of all, those from Sub-Saharan Africa[33].

China has had a tempestuous history over the millennia, with uprisings and civil wars. It believes in authoritarian government under an elite class exercising benevolent rule in the Confucian fashion, and its greatest dread is its own instability, consider Tianmen Square, and now, fearful of contagion from the Middle East uprisings, is arresting dissidents, and has made disappear its outspoken artist and activist, Ai Weiwei, who helped design China's Olympic Games edifice but is a dissident. The publication 'China Daily' of 11 March 2011 reports that 'The country's top legislator on Thursday warned of a possible "abyss if internal disorder" if China strays from the "correct political orientation". China will never adopt a multiparty revolving-door system or other Western-style models'.

Democracy too can be flawed

But if China's claim to represent a good society is seriously blemished, is that to say that the Western democratic model represents what the good society should be? The answer is that the Western model can in practice sometimes have grave shortcomings. For example the American model falls short in several important respects. The first is its faulty interpretation of the Social Contract that elevates the business corporation to the highest level of sanctity. And another is the severe problems of national governance, in particular the American gridlock now in the news as a result of the division of powers between the three arms of government, Congress – the Senate and the House of Representatives, the President, and the Supreme Court, whose sometimes odd reliance on a the US Constitution crafted under conditions prevailing two and a quarter centuries ago produces strange rulings. A recent example was its ruling as unconstitutional an attempt to limit the sale of some violent video games to children as contravening the First Amendment's prohibition of any law that abridges the freedom of speech. Petty-fogging lawyers with a rush of power to their heads, the same people who ruled as unconstitutional gun control as contravening the Second Amendment, written soon after the Revolution, the right to bear arms in connection with a militia to oppose tyranny. The words now frequently appearing in American commentary is that the system is broken, and polls show that 80% of the American people have lost confidence in Congress.

Another flaw, and one that is very grave, is the power of special interests through money and lobbying to influence government. To a degree Congress is under the control of special interests, the people be damned. 'What business wants, business gets' is the subject of a New York Times article, for example preventing the introduction of anti-pollution regulations. The gun lobby has a huge influence and the Israel lobby appears to control American Middle East policy and thwart intelligent efforts to bring about a two-state solution. Indeed such factors as these prevent a so-called democracy from being genuinely democratic. The extent to which the United States is a plutocracy, not a democracy, has in recent times amazed the Western world, no one denies that quite blatantly big money from business corporations and wealthy individuals helped to determine the results in the Republican Party primaries to select the Republican candidate in the recent Presidential election. It seems that the power of money in the US political system is of long standing. Albert Einstein - yes, that Albert Einstein – wrote in 1949 of the 'oligarchy of private capital the enormous power of which cannot be effectively checked even by a democratically organized political society. This is true since the members of legislative bodies are selected by political parties, largely financed or otherwise influenced by private capitalists who, for all practical purposes, separate the electorate from the legislature' [34].

Those are American problems but democracy elsewhere may have serious difficulties, in Britain a saga is playing out, the exposure of the access that Rupert Murdoch had to the highest level of government. In the European Union the Brussels institutions lack democratic legitimacy, a subject discussed later in Chapter 14. Oh, the travails of making democracy function well! Even so, this work echoes Churchill, democracy is a bad system but the others are worse. A theme of this work is to make democracy less bad – indeed one hopes very much less bad. Easy really, in principle,: start to remember to follow faithfully the lodestar, the Social Contract, come down like a ton of bricks on any move away from this direction.

Business corporations as unguided missiles

Unfortunately, in recent years some major Western nations have strayed from this correct course, and the main reason has been a lack of understanding of the nature of the business corporation, and banks, excellent, indispensable denizens of the planet, but only if handled right. The Nobel Prize Winner, Joseph Stiglitz, tells us [35] that the crash occurred as a result of what may seem the unspeakably corrupt, greedy, behaviour of the American banking industry, under the doctrine of market fundamentalism, according to which government regulation was unnecessary. But 'bankers acted greedily because they had incentives and opportunity to do so . . . . . The basis of capitalism is the pursuit of profit; should we blame the bankers for doing what everybody else in the market economy is supposed to be doing'? Further, having just been bailed out, the banks then had the gall, Stiglitz writes, to 'blame the government for not having stopped them' . . . but 'they had successfully beaten back attempts to regulate derivatives and restrict predatory lending. Their victory over America was total. Each victory gave them more money with which to influence the political process'. The behaviour of business corporations has been marvellously explained by John Stone, the great armaments manufacturer (who in is own personal life is a model of decent behaviour), in the recent novel 'Stone's Fall', by Iain Pears:

> *Interviewer: 'I know little of your companies, Mr. Stone. . . . But I remember that you have supplied weapons to every single enemy our army and navy might face. Are those the actions of a patriot?*
>
> *John Stone: 'It is the task of a company to generate capital. That is its beginning and its end, and it is foolish and sentimental to apply morality to it, let alone patriotism . . . . Morality applies only to people. Not to animals and still less to machines . . . . If one of my torpedoes is fired, and it hits is target, many people will die. A terrible thing. But is the torpedo to blame? If it does so, it is a good machine which fulfills its purpose. If not, it is a failure. Where is there any space for morality in that? . . . . . . And a company is also merely a machine, supplying the wants of others. Why not blame the governments who buy these torpedoes and order them to be used, or the people who vote for those governments?*

'Companies are designed to multiply capital; what they make is irrelevant. Torpedoes, food, clothes, furniture. It is all the same. To that end they will do anything to survive and prosper. . . . . What if they lay waste the landscape, ruin forests, uproot communities and poison the rivers? They are obliged to do all those things, if they can increase their profits. . . . . A company is a moral imbecile. It has no sense of right or wrong. . . Any restraints have to come from the outside, from laws and customs that forbid them from doing certain things of which we disapprove. . . . But it is a restraint which reduces profits. Which is why all companies will strain forever to break the bounds of the law . . . That is the only way they can survive because the more powerful will devour the weak'.

The social commentator, Chris Hedges, puts the matter thus as regards the United States: 'The corporation is designed to make money without regard to human life, the social good, or the impact of the corporation's activities on the environment. Corporation bylaws impose a legal duty on corporate executives to make the largest profits for the shareholders . . . And, under the American legal system, corporations have the same rights as individuals. They make contributions to candidates. They fund 35,000 lobbyists in Washington and thousands more in state capitals to write corporate-friendly legislation and defang regulating agencies . . . They hold a near monopoly on all electronic and printed sources of information. A few media giants . . . . control nearly everything we read, see and hear'[36].

We must recognise that the business corporation is a magnificent, inventive, ingenious, determined, machine for making a profit. But Hedges neglected to mention that the source of their profit is producing some product for others, at which they are very efficient, and use the best technology, because the lower their costs the higher their profits. Therein lies their superiority to, for example, their former Soviet counterparts, without the spur of market competition.

Corporations have all the qualities needed to carry out with dispatch society's production tasks. But we have not properly tasked them, so to survive they run amok. In consequence, many absurd things, even wicked things, happen in our society. An article in the new York Times[37]

63

tells us that the cigarette giants are stepping up efforts around the world to fight restrictions on the marketing of cigarettes . . . They are spending billions on lobbying and marketing campaigns in Africa and Asia. . . and 'are aggressively recruiting new customers in developing nations . . . to replace those who are quitting or dying in the United States and Europe, where smoking rates are falling precipitously'. And another Times editorial tells us that 'a widespread shortage of prescription drugs is hampering the treatment of patients with cancer, severe infections and other serious illnesses . . . . The Food and Drug Administration says that more than 80 percent of hospitals delayed needed treatments, almost 70 percent gave patients a less effective drug'. One reason was that 'higher priced brand-name drugs bring far higher profits. . . . . Unscrupulous wholesalers have made matters worse by scooping up drugs and offering them to hospitals at markups that often reach 20 times the normal price or more'. Well, as Hedges writes, these corporations are obliged, by law, to maximise their profits.

Examples abound. In the continuing recession charitable donations are becoming scarce – but what sort of donation? There are donations and 'donations' and the shortfall is in the latter, the corporate social responsibility sort, the woe I discussed in Chapter 2. According to a recent report, 'Faced with an ever-increasing swell of requests, companies have raised the bar for funding . . . by focussing on causes linked to their business goals or promotion of their brands[38]'. Companies have two conflicting needs, a public relations need to show what decent fellows they are by giving money to Save the Children or Amnesty International, (and indirectly increasing their profits in the long run), and their immediate need for profits hard come by in the deep recession. Disguising CSR 'donations' as genuine donations from the heart becomes more difficult as the economy weakens.

Cui Bono?

Who benefits from many of our woes, in particular those discussed in Chapter 2? *Cui Bono'* helps us identify the perpetrator of a crime, motive, along with means and opportunity. We have just discussed CSR 'donations'.

Who benefits from the broadcasting perversion? Programmes interrupted at frequent intervals by annoying, irrelevant, tasteless commercials. Certainly it is not ourselves, the people, trying to watch the US Open Tennis tournament. No of course not, the beneficiaries are the companies promoting their product – after all, they paid large sums not only for their irritating sales pitch, but for the programmes in between, and on top of that the revenue of the broadcasting stations, and of the ad agencies they hire – and the costs of their own marketing departments – they must benefit, or believe they benefit, to dispense such huge sums. They amply pass the test of motive. And means? Of course they have the means, that is how the advertising and broadcasting system is organized. And opportunity – don't make me laugh, the opportunity is there all the time, whenever you switch on your television or radio, which is hours of watching, or hearing, daily, this annoying backdrop to, particularly, North American life.

And that's broadcasting, what about the other irksome pests – sports marketing, pestilential pop-ups, countless irritations, exasperating useless production? I've already mentioned the replacement of individual parking meters next to your car into which you slipped a few coins. Now you have to walk to a central machine, puzzle yourself about how to use it, then walk back to your car to display a piece of paper. But damn it all they might say, technology must move on – would you still want to travel by horse-drawn stage coach? Yes, one should reply, technology must move on, but it should always move on to our, the people's, benefit. The situation that our society is now in is, the people be damned, machines and the companies who make them come first, before people.

Democracy's Claim

The case made in this work is simply that our Western society has become very sick, and most particularly so, the United States, and, perhaps in lesser degree, some other Western countries. This decline is due to faulty governance related to contravention of the Social Contract and a tilt to business power, at the expense of the people and society. And, in some Western countries, more than in others, there are poorly functioning democratic institutions. The universal vote at least helps ensure that the squeaky wheel gets some grease, though even here those who squeak may get short shrift, and serious long term problems can get ignored. In the extremely rich US, for example, there remain many poor, and without health care – a situation unthinkable in, say, Sweden. And as discussed earlier, powerful lobbies distort the workings of both the US Congress and the Executive. There may also be faults in the way election campaigns are financed and then conducted with 'attack ads' instead of sober, measured debate. And populist movements can drive public policy in unfortunate directions, for example in the United States it is an objective of the extreme, Tea Party, wing of the Republican congressmen to prevent legislation requiring the cutting of carbon emissions – they deny any human cause to global warming.

The argument favouring democracy might be put as follows. If one could guarantee having an autocrat in power who is not only totally benign, but is also aware of the needs and feelings of every single citizen, and who is driven only by the desire to serve the people, all the people, all the time, then perhaps it would be less easy to argue that democracy is the best. But of course such Godlike autocrats do not exist. The only people who feel the pain from society's present arrangements are the people themselves, each and every one of them, so all must have their say before new public policies are enacted. The squeaky wheel may get some relief to its pain. And this can come about, so the argument runs, only through democratically elected representative government, or rather more broadly through the Western attributes, which include not only representative government, but also the rule of law and civil liberties. To that should be added the proviso that care must be taken to avoid faults to which democracies can be prone, including demagoguery, poor electoral practices, and the inability to deal with long term and systemic problems, climate change is one, another is the failure to act on the several contraventions of the Social Contract discussed in this work. Also, a good case can be made for adding to the political process a new agency to consider long term problems, and study the kinds of question discussed in this work. This matter is discussed further in Chapter 13.

It has been argued[39] that we must realize that in these times of upheaval in the Arab world, not all autocrats are bad and should be overthrown: 'the moral differences between one dictator and another are as vast as those between dictators and democrats', and between the megalomaniac Ghadaffi and the enlightened Sultan of Oman. And now as Libya's rebel forces have after a bloody uprising ended Ghadaffi's 41 year rule, the question being asked in the West is can orderly benign government now be brought into being or will disorder reign among disparate groups, the west-oriented, the tribal elements, and the formidable, disciplined, Islamists with their Sharia law. Post Mubarak Egypt is in the same turmoil. Often better autocracy than chaos.

Francis Fukuyama has just written exhaustively on these matters[40]. This is the gist of his argument:

'The three components of a modern political order – a strong and capable state, the state's subordination to the rule of law, and government accountability to all citizens, had all been established .... by the end of the 18th century .... England was the first large country in which all these elements came together at once. The three components were highly interdependent. Without a strong early state, there would not have been a rule of law and legitimate property rights. Without a strong rule of law and legitimate property rights, the Commons would never have been motivated to come together to impose accountability on the English monarchy. And without the principle of accountability, the British state would never have emerged as the great power it became at the time of the French Revolution. A number of other European states, including the Netherlands, Denmark, and Sweden, also succeeded in putting together the state, the rule of law, and accountability in a single package by the nineteenth century. The specific routes by which they got to this outcome differed substantially from that of Britain, but it is sufficient to recognise that once this package had been put together the first time, it produced a state so powerful, legitimate and friendly to economic growth it became a model to be applied throughout the world'.

What Fukuyama's thesis implies is that developments in political organization in the last two hundred years, in particular universal suffrage, are merely embellishments, refinements. As I wrote earlier, universal suffrage at least helps to ensure that the squeaky wheel gets grease. Besides, it symbolizes recognition of the importance and dignity of every single human being. But this does not mean that universal suffrage is not without its dangers and challenges, revealed so dramatically both in the grand farce enacted recently in Washington with regard to raising the public debt limit, and in Britain, where the hacking scandal at last brought out into the open the extent to which elected British governments kow-towed to Rupert Murdoch.

American democracy is in deep trouble, that is the subject of present leading commentators. Timothy Garton Ash[41] writes that 'in a CNN poll... 84% of Americans disapprove of the way Congress is doing its job . . Why does the system work so badly? Decades of gerrymandering mean politicians have to worry more about being deposed by members of their own party in primaries than about convincing undecided voters in elections. That is what the Tea Party did to prominent incumbent Republicans before last year's mid-term elections. . . . The undue influence of money also distorts American democracy. The US has extraordinarily divided government: the President, two houses of Congress, and the Supreme Court'. Yes, lawyers in the Supreme Court influence policy, for example, allowing unlimited private campaign spending, and recently, on the basis of their interpretation of the First Amendment of the holy US Constitution, disallowing legislation to prevent the sale of violent killer games to children – on the grounds of limiting freedom of expression. There is something most strange about treating as holy writ words written 225 years ago to suit conditions in a totally different society. 'The first thing we must do is kill all the lawyers' – Shakespeare's Henry VI – But no, lawyers will be lawyers, it is the faulty division of power and the oddity of a sacred constitution, that invites these lawyers to do harm.

How to rid ourselves of the weaknesses of fully representative democracy must be part of the New Renaissance. There is no single such weakness more malignant than the hi-jacking of the broadcast media to serve not only as an advertising and public relations medium for business corporations, but also for fighting political campaigns using sales promotion and advertising techniques, and 'attack ads'.

Wide-ranging reform is required of how elections are conducted and funded.

And the formation of a Long Term Planning Agency, to become a part of the public policy formulation process is essential. In principle upper houses might play this role, for example the British House of Lords and the Canadian Senate, but in large degree these have been used to reward party hacks, or to retire problem politicians and cabinet ministers.

However the position taken in this work is not to harp on the superiority of our Enlightenment and Western way of life, enough of high-sounding sentiments, rather we must put our own house in order, so that our Western world can pull out of its present nose dive, and thrive for many years to come, through a more perfect governance based on the Social Contract and improved democratic institutions. In the long run history will determine whether our civilization predominates, or will be supplanted by another, or whether different kinds of civilization will co-exist on the planet. But only if we mend our own society will we be able to do well in the future stakes – or deserve to do well.

My representation of the Social Contract

In mediaeval times, three 'estates of the realm' were recognised, the church, the nobility, and the commoners, all presided over by the monarch. It was only in the seventeenth and eighteenth centuries that the political philosophers Hobbes, Locke and Rousseau talked of a Social Contract according to which the interests of the commoners (the public) were paramount, the very justification of the state – otherwise why not return to Hobbes' state of nature where life was nasty, brutish and short?

Now, for our present purposes, it is useful to identify five main estates of the realm: the people, their elected government, the government departments, the business corporations, and the media. The people elect their government to assist them govern the state. The government departments and local authorities provide the publicly funded services and regulatory bodies (schools, health and welfare services, highways, justice, defence, national parks, urban planning, environmental protection and regulation in general, and others), and the media exist to provide information, enlightenment, news, and public debate, as well as entertainment, for the benefit of the people and society. These might be called the 'public' media, to distinguish them from the use of the same technologies, electronic or print, for such purposes as advertising, by business corporations. The central bank, which manages a nation's currency, money supply and interest rates, in this simple five estate division of society, is a government department. It also oversees the commercial banking industry which here are included as business corporations. The five estate division is ambiguous about where NGOs, quangos, crown corporations, and the like should be included, but that matters little for present purposes. Generally they are driven by benevolent aims rather than by the profit motive.

What role should be assigned to the business corporations? Reason suggests that their function is to produce the goods and services which their customers, consumers, government, and other corporations, select and pay for directly. They are society's 'worker bees', and excellent ones too. That is all they are paid to do, and their performance in doing this is measured in their 'bottom lines'. They should not exceed this role by providing the public with a 'free' broadcasting service as a by-product of their marketing and sale promotion activities, nor by being 'partnered' with performing arts centres in delivering symphony concerts, nor with museums, schools, and the like, in pursuance of their public relations goals. Likewise they should not engage in 'sports marketing' with huge sums, $100 million was paid annually to Tiger Woods before his fall, in order to promote sporting goods. Instead broadcasting, sporting events, orchestras, concerts, museums and schools must be paid for only by the public, directly, or by the government on their behalf, when this is appropriate.

There is a great irony in what has been the American interpretation of the Social Contract, on which the United States explicitly framed it constitution – Locke's and Rousseau's works had only recently been published. The United States has come to assign a role for business corporations larger that just defined above. One might say that

America is in thrall to business. Defenders of Calvin Coolidge's 'The business of America is business' point out that he also said 'We make no concealment of the fact that we want wealth, but there are many other things we want very much more . . . . America is a nation of idealists'. Americans must therefore somehow square the two, on the one hand, their business is business, and, on the other, they are the beacon on the hill which inspires all other nations. Clearly they have difficulty, scolding their broadcasters for delivering a 'vast wasteland'
.

It is interesting to speculate just why the United States attaches such importance to business. While one poll has just shown that two thirds of Americans believe that their standard of living is more endangered than was their parents', another poll shows a majority still believing that improvement will depend on their own individual self reliance, and that big government, not business, is the biggest threat to the country[42]. A BBC report shows some small town Americans reacting strongly against President Obama's plans, as expanding government, and local gun sales have increased by 100%. And now in the November 2010 mid-term election a Tea Party woman candidate carries a gun to show what she'll do when she gets to Washington.

What is one to make of this disparate set of facts? Here seems a likely interpretation: In the Revolution Americans rose against an oppressive British Government, and this is reflected in the famous Second Amendment of the constitution: 'A well regulated militia, being necessary to the security of the state, the right of the people to keep and bear arms, shall not be affringed'. Herein lies the opposition to gun control in the United States[43]. The state is a villain, self reliance is best. Where do business corporations fit in? Perhaps these early Americans saw business as an extension of themselves, and indeed most businesses were then small. And despite the present enormous size and power of huge corporations, it appears likely that this association of business with themselves in some degree persists.

The corporations are subjected to a severe conflict of interest, and in the following case it is easy to see which interest prevailed. The so-called Global Climate Coalition, financed by the US oil, coal, and automobile industries, has led an aggressive lobbying and advertising campaign against the idea that emissions could lead to global warming. Though disbanded in 2002, the National Association of Manufacturers and the American Petroleum Institute continue to lobby against any law or treaty that would sharply curb emissions[44].

But now in these new, vastly different times, it has become essential for the United States to reaffirm the social contract, but on correct lines: Modern business corporations are brilliantly inventive and efficient entities, but they have been left to run amok in any direction they like, to expand their sales and profit. Instead, properly harnessed, they could do great good, performing our projects to arrest global warming and meet the other great challenges of our era. But now, it is important to understand what of necessity is the motivation that drives business corporations – and *should* drive them if they are to be successful. And we need them to be successful if we are to execute the tasks of the New Enlightenment.

Guarding against bureaucracy

Bloated bureaucracies are an ever-present threat requiring good management and determined pruning. Their presence too weakens our attempts to achieve full compliance with the Social Contract. They grow up not only in government departments but within huge corporations, whenever there is lax management. Perhaps excessive bureaucracy played a part in the troubles of General Motors – continuing to produce huge cars for the American public when many were turning to small, splendidly designed cars from Japan. I'll give an example of bureaucracy that makes me fume every time I return by air to Canada from abroad. First, on the plane before landing, one must fill in a form asking many questions about any farms (yes farms) you visited when away. Then when you land you join the large queues to get through immigration – there is no differentiation between Canadians returning home and would be immigrants and visitors (in contrast, for British travellers returning home to Britain there is a separate route, and one is nodded through following a quick look at one's passport photo). When at last the returning Canadian reaches a booth, the official feels it is their duty to ask you the same questions that you've answered on the form. Finally one has to pass another official, whose only job is to take the form back from you. (What happens subsequently to the forms one can only guess – perhaps the information on them is entered into some computer program, and the forms filed somewhere for eternity).

In government the only antidote to such bureaucracy is eternal management vigilance, and determined action. For business corporations there is the added spur of market forces and the need for profit to root out bureaucracy, but, particularly in large corporations, bureaucracy can sprout. I've long suspected that the growth of CSR, 'corporate social responsibility', has had an element of bureaucracy about it – it comes to be the 'done thing', there *must* be a CSR group with its annual budget. And, absurdly, CSR groups spring up in public bodies – when we pay taxes for the provision of public services have we also delegated to some little CSR section somewhere in the sprawling civil service our donation making activity, how much to give to whom? This is just as absurd as paying more for our consumer goods so that some CSR group in the companies providing the goods can perform the giving function for us.

For the New Enlightenment, believing that business corporations operating in the free-market are the most efficient, effective, innovative producers, I have elected for a lean but highly effective government," working through improved democratic processes, to put to work society's worker bees, to do all their work for us, *only* for us, that they don't in desperation, to survive, get up to nasty pranks, making our lives more miserable than need be, and filling the atmosphere with carbon.

CHAPTER 6

Instituting the
Missing Mechanisms

And now to what we must do. The central point of our diagnosis is that our society lacks mechanisms for ensuring that the economy's productive capacity is used for the benefit of the people, their society, and the environment, and not aimlessly, or just to serve the interests of the production machine, that is, the sales and profits goals of business corporations. There are a number of institutional reforms we must make. One is simply to re-balance society in accordance with the Social Contract, so that each of the five 'estates of the realm' is playing only its proper part. This now levels the playing field, the economy will not now be driven along to serve the interests of one of its subordinate parts.

Several breaches of the Social Contract have already been touched on in our discussion. Business corporations must not exceed their proper role by providing the public with a 'free' broadcasting service as a by-product of their marketing and sale promotion activities, nor by being 'partnered' with performing arts centres in delivering symphony concerts, nor with museums, schools, and the like, in pursuance of their public relations goals. Likewise they should not engage in 'sports marketing' with huge sums paid to sporting stars, in order to promote their brand of sports equipment. Instead broadcasting, sporting events, orchestras, museums and schools must be paid for only directly by the public, or by the government on their behalf when that is appropriate.

In addition to this societal re-balancing, we need also to make some improvements in our governing apparatus. The two most vital and pressing are to replace our defective system of raising public funds through the income tax by a new 'Return to Society', and, we must change the way we manage the economy. We must – and can – end the absurdity of the business cycle, boom and bust, and unemployment, especially ridiculous when there are so many great projects we must get underway, in the Great Battle of the Climate, and to remake our dysfunctional society. Just one example is ridding cities of the traffic gridlock woe: 'Faced with maddening amounts of traffic, people just resort to leaning on the horn or unleashing a string of expletives. Around the world, cities have implemented extreme solutions to their congestion woes . . . To persuade people to end their love affair with the automobile, the overall system of public transport must be radically improved'[45]. And it is well to realize that the traffic gridlock has been due to the contravention of the Social Contract, people's excessive reliance on the automobile – indeed in North America, enormous gas guzzlers needing huge parking facilities - worked more to the benefit of General Motors, than to the people and society.

In order to make the quick restarting of the economy at the launch of the New Enlightenment, we must ignore the tenets of much of existing economics orthodoxy. Eventually a new genuine science of economics with come into being, the science of managing the economy to meet human ends and face up to the great challenges of the future. There are also a number of other reforms that we should in due time perform which will be mentioned later.

In the next five chapters I discuss the measures that we must now enact immediately. They are stopping the recession in its tracks, curing acute deficit phobia, ridding ourselves of the abomination that is our perverted broadcasting system (stated less pejoratively, 'normalising' broadcasting); implementing the 'Return to Society' to replace the income tax, and launching the mega-projects of the great Battle of the Climate. (Broadcasting will be normalised in the sense that it will now become the normal service for people that it should always have been, like all our many vital goods and services, which we pay for either directly out of personal expenditure, or collectively, through taxes).

These five great moves are inter-dependent. Engaging in the battle of the climate helps put our economy back to work, were the climate situation not so dire one might call it a blessing in disguise. Taking broadcasting away from the business corporations and placing it at the service of the people and society means that now the main means of public mass communication is on the side of the New Enlightenment. Finally, by replacing the income tax by the return to society, it will be far less difficult to find the money and resources needed to meet vital public purposes.

How to engage successfully on the Great Battle of the Climate is a subject on which our society has been singularly befuddled and inept. The Economist has editorialized thus[46]: 'How to live with climate change: It won't be stopped. But its effects can be made less bad'. Our singular ineptness in engaging in emission reduction is yet another example of a sick society – or a mad society, 'those whom the gods will destroy, they first make mad'.

After discussing the five pressing moves we shall make, we then, in Chapter 12, consider what a new, genuine, science of economics might be like. This is an essential component of the New Enlightenment: In order to manage and direct the economic system it is essential to have a discipline, founded on scientific principles, which understands the exceedingly complex social, economic, political, environmental, system, whose components exchange not only monetary but also physical and information flows. We do now have some good economists, who know a great deal about the economy, who are being helpful and offering sensible advice, people usually with a Keynesian slant, but they have been fighting with one hand tied behind their backs, lacking the extension of Keynes, which, perhaps, were he now alive, he would have himself contrived.

After that, in Chapter 13, some other improvements in our governance are touched on that we should make in due course. Then, in Chapter 14, we discuss how to extract Europe from it present morass, the broken common currency, and defective Brussels bureaucracy. Next, in Chapter 15, we briefly look at what several prominent writers have just written on our society's sick state. What they say differs from what I have written, but I do not disagree with them, there is so much wrong that several writers can focus on particular aspects and all be right. Then, in Chapter 16, we look to the more distant future: decadence and decline and what the shape of our society will be in the very long run. In the West, or at least major parts of it, at present it appears that through lack of attention to the Social Contract, society's evolution is being driven by business in conjunction with a fast-appearing new gadgetry and software. Ordinary humans, the general public, have lost control in the United States. The picture painted by the American Chris Hedges in his 'Empire of Illusion' verges on nightmarish, it looks to me like the ultimate consequence of the broadcasting perversion, and other similar perversions, in the contravention of the Social Contract. In this work we are trying to nullify the forces driving a major part of Western society into deep degradation. China is on the rise, yes, but its utter disregard of the 'western attributes' has been dramatically demonstrated in May 2012, in the airbrushing of the disgraced high official, Bo Xilai out of public life by a strategy perfected during the Cultural Revolution, and by the diplomatic crisis between the US and China on the blind activist, Chen Guangcheng.

If the West goes down, the whole world may be plunged into a terrible, long dark age. What must be done to avert this calamity is for major reform to begin very soon somewhere in the West, and for this to take hold and bring us back from the brink. How this might come about occupies us in Part Three below.

Hamlet without the Prince of Demark?

Many will be struck by what seems a glaring omission in this work, no discussion of the financial crisis and economic meltdown which have been our sorry lot in the last five years. Clearly reforms are required to prevent a repetition of these unpardonable events, sub-prime mortgages and highly leveraged banks with too many loans on their books. But given the huge attention the subject is now receiving, one can surely be reasonably confident that there will not be a repeat of this crash for a long time - or perhaps never, if our new science of economics is broad enough to include how to manage the financial system.

Were this work as complete as it might be it would also look outward, to help a suffering humanity, how to alleviate world poverty, how to respond intelligently to the Arab Spring which in Syria and Egypt has become a Nightmare, concern itself with world population growth, and also with world terror and fanaticism, and nuclear proliferation. But if we can make the radical institutional reforms that are the subject of this work we should be more capable of dealing with these other matters.

Political Stance

Inevitably, it will be asked, is not change in democracies usually brought about by political parties responding to public opinion on the issues of the day ? Sometimes great reform movements have played a part, nudging society in a new direction – for example the abolition of slavery and child labour, and universal suffrage. And nowadays the environmental movement plays some part. Where then does this diagnosis, and the remedies proposed, stand in the political spectrum? Left? Right? Socialist? Liberal? Conservative? Radical? Radical - Conservative? Party was not in the writer's mind, but if a label must be applied, then it is Radical – without radical change we are all sunk. Or even, it is a possibility, Radical-Conservative, simply because there is so much that is good in Western civilization that should be conserved, and inattention to the Social Contract has been putting much of that to risk.

Neither of the two major remedies proposed here, relieving business of its control of the airwaves and transforming the public finance system, is put forward by any party. The Left is associated with improving the position of the Have-Nots, and the Right protecting that of the Haves. Here we are advancing the position of the All, without some such action we shall all sink together. But leftists may comfort themselves, at last poverty can be banished, and business power tamed. And the right too should be pleased, government will not grow, indeed it might even be made leaner, by ensuring that it perform only its proper functions, governance of the state, redistributing income to the needy, regulation to protect the environment and prevent harm to society by business corporations pursuing their own goals. And this leaner government must also provide those services that are properly the province of the state, public education, justice, defence, health and social services, and support of cultural institutions, as well as arranging, on contract, for business corporations to improve and add to the public infrastructure. All the grand projects ahead to combat global warming will be performed by business corporations, whether additions to the publically owned infrastructure on contract to government, or on their own account under the inducement of government subsidies, tax advantages, or regulation.

This work is most assuredly not an anti-business rant – the business corporations are wondrous machines, innovative and efficient, because they prosper only if they are governed by the need to survive in the free market, and to be profitable. But we must understand that they are machines that become unguided missiles if they have been poorly tasked. The American legal fiction that corporations are 'persons' must be extirpated, they are machines to be put to work to serve society.

Business corporations, society's worker bees, will flourish, engaged in the vast new projects to remake society to be both less carbon-emitting, and a more comfortable place for human beings. And it is not fanciful to think of business corporations mobilized to perform the public's projects – the phenomenal and fast output of American business corporations to arm the allies in World War II is testimony to that.

CHAPTER 7

Stopping the
Recession in its tracks

The world economy, in particular our Western part of it, is in deep
trouble, and still, five years after the stock exchange indexes started
their deep downward plunge in October 2007, the economists are
deeply divided about what must be done. In the US, the heartland of
the meltdown, house prices had peaked in mid 2006 as a consequence
of the sub-prime mortgage, anyone can-buy-a-house-even-if-they-
can't-afford-it nonsense, and the resulting foreclosures. But in
the mad unrealistic euphoria of the times the Dow Jones Index
accelerated its upward climb, rising by a further 30% to an all time
high fifteen months later, in October 2007. At last reality set in and
unemployment increased from 4.5% to 7.3% by the end of 2008, and
the Dow sank fast, especially following Lehman Bros' bankruptcy,
when it dropped by 26% in only three weeks. It reached its low
point in early March 2009, less than half its October 2007 value. By
October 2009, unemployment had climbed to 10.1%, and since then
has remained stubbornly high. Unemployment has fallen slightly,
but the outlook remains uncertain, with a succession of good news,
bad news, good news, bad news, what will the morrow bring? And
the European Union is on a roller coaster of uncertainty, matters
made worse by the difficulties of the Eurozone common currency.
Now, a reaction is setting in against the austerity policies that have
aimed to cut deficits instead of promoting growth. Nowhere has

austerity been pursued more vigorously than in Britain, where there is now talk of 'triple-dip' recession.

Could this unhappy state of affairs have lasted so long – indeed even have come into being – had economics been a genuine science? The matter of bringing about a new, genuine, science of economics is the subject of Chapter 12 below. Here we are concerned with the immediate problem, the rational way of dealing with the present recession.

How then are we to restart the economy? Huge public funds have been spent to rescue the banks, and on spending, and for the latter Keynes has been 'in', and market fundamentalism 'out'. But deep nervousness exists that consequent increases in the public deficit and debt will endanger economies. The Tea Party movement against big government is rampant in the United States (though US government spending is one of the lowest among the advanced economies) and nowhere is deficit-phobia greater than in Britain, where the Conservative government has enacted austerity with apparently dire results, and the government's rating has plunged in the polls. Britain's deficit fear is surely excessive. Though the public debt has increased sharply from 43% of GDP to 77%, it is still tiny compared with the 238% it was at the end of World War II. Besides, the annual interest burden as a result of the debt, at about 2% GDP, is a small fraction of the levels at which nations default on their debt. It is time to proclaim that the cycle of boom and bust is an archaic absurdity. We can split the atom and reach the moon, yet we cannot keep our economies fully employed, even now when there is so much to be done. Are our economists, with their models and their equations, the modern equivalent of the mediaeval schoolmen, who debated how many angels can dance on the point of a pin? Perhaps China, having fewer schoolmen, is not so in thrall. The great world recession suddenly reduced the demand for China's exports, so its government quickly launched giant infrastructure projects and China has maintained its phenomenal economic growth, though this may now be starting to moderate.

There is no good reason why like China Western nations cannot be nimble. Our governments must immediately put their economies' idle parts to work on the mega-projects of the Battle of the Climate, and, in the United States especially, on improving defective infrastructure, spending on which was crowded out in the mad rush to acquire consumer goods, some of little or ephemeral value. And at the same time governments must be unstinting in transferring money to the unemployed and indigent.

Saying that is easy, but how is all this to be paid for? The mega-projects are capital expenditures, creating new capital assets, which business corporations pay for partly out of their depreciation allowance and their profit (net of tax and dividends), but mainly by selling bonds and issuing new shares. Government should pay for new capital assets in the same way, from its depreciation allowance, its surplus, if it has one, of tax revenue over current spending, and by borrowing, that is, by selling government bonds. If a government has instead a deficit on current account, which is the case with most governments now, that is, it is spending more on government services and health care, welfare, and unemployment benefits, than the taxes its levies, then these taxes must be supplemented through borrowing. This is the reprehensible type of government borrowing, borrowing to cover these services rather than adding to public infrastructure, but is temporarily justified when an economy is in trouble. Business corporations under these conditions, their sales revenue falling short of their operating cost, go out of business. But of course governments don't go out of business. Japan has done this to a huge extent, its public debt as a percent of GDP is more than twice that of the United States, and far from being a basket case, has low unemployment, a large balance of payments surplus, and the yen has until recently been rising against other currencies. This underlines the absurdity of the recent US debt limit fiasco. Excessively high national debt of course is undesirable in the long run, and this problem can in good time be rectified by raising taxes and/or trimming government services. (In the future, as a result of the governance changes which are the subject of this work, there will be no need for a tax increase, as there will be in operation a totally different public finance system, the subject of Chapter 10).

The only legitimate purpose of government bonds, except sometimes in the short run, or if waging war, is to pay for new public infrastructure. The total value of the public infrastructure (appearing on the government balance sheet[47]) is likely to be of the order of about 30 or 40 percent of GDP, and this is the legitimate size of the public debt for a well run country which, over the business cycle does not spend more on public services and transfers to people (social welfare, health, and unemployment benefits) than it collects in taxes. That 30-40% of GDP is a rough and ready figure, countries requiring exceptionally large infrastructures (eg they are very mountainous and need many tunnels, or they are very large with low population density, and need huge road and rail networks), may reasonably have a higher public debt. And now, prosecuting the great battle of the climate, we shall be moving into a period of abnormally large capital expenditure, part of it by governments, building new nuclear generating stations, 200 mph train networks, and redesigned cities, so we must expect our national debts, as a percent of GDP, to go up, and this will be healthy – debt to pay for infrastructure is good debt. Indeed, perhaps we need a new AAAA (quadruple A) rating for nations whose public debt is only about 40% of GDP, or whatever is the size of their public infrastructure. The present triple A rating is given to nations which, it is believed, will never default on their debt, and US treasuries have until now been regarded as good as gold, a safe haven, but the US has recently been downgraded to AA+ by the S and P rating agency as a result of the recent Tea Party anti-debt fiasco in the US House of Representatives. Despite this, funds are still fleeing to US treasury bills, despite their very low rate of interest.

(Just as we measure the public debt as a percent of GDP, the total national output, so the long term bond debt of business corporations can be expressed as a percent of each corporation's share of GDP, which is its 'value added'. The 'value added' of any economic activity is the sum of what it pays to its factors of production, Labour and Capital. The sum of the value added of every activity in the economy, both private and public, equals GDP, the Gross Domestic Product. The size of business corporations' bond debt, unlike that of government, is hugely variable, some industries require huge capital facilities, that is plant, equipment, and structures, and others, much less capital intensive, will have smaller bond debt. And of course the size of their bond debt will also depend on the extent to which they rely on equity capital, that is, new share issues).

So what are we now to do to end the Great Recession? Let us look at the situation that the large advanced Western nations are in. Their economic growth rates are low, they have high unemployment, and their public debts have risen to high levels. The US has, in 2011, joined the 100+ % public debt club, whose other advanced nation members are Japan (229%), Greece (152%), Italy (120%), Ireland (114%), and Iceland (103%)[48]. Here then is the problem we face: Given low economic growth, high unemployment, and high public debt, how can nations yank themselves out of the Great Recession?

Yanking nations out of deep recession

To end recession forthwith calls for reliance on Keynesian thinking. There are many who still froth at the mouth at Keynes, which is a shame because to think on this matter like Keynes is simply to apply logic and common sense. The anti-Keynesian view in general relies on 'Say's Law', formulated by the French economist Jean-Baptiste Say at the beginning of the nineteenth century, and soon restated by James Mill as 'production of commodities creates, and is the one and universal cause which creates a market for the commodities produced'. Latterly, according to laisser-faire economists such as Friedrich von Hayek, massive unemployment and depressions are the consequence of state intervention in the markets, which effectively blocks the natural balance between production and consumption at full employment in accordance with Say's Law.

The Keynesian view can be put simply as follows. GDP, the economy's product, can be expressed two ways, the sum of all spending to buy the product, and the sum of all income earned in producing it:

$$GDP = \text{total spending} = C + G + Ig + Ib + (E - M)$$

$$GDP = \text{total income} = L + K$$

where C is personal consumption spending, G is government spending on services, Ig is government investment, Ib is business investment,

(E - M) is exports less imports, L is wages and salaries, and K is capital income: profit, interest, and depreciation allowance. (I wonder whether an item 'X' should be added to L and K in GDP income-based, to represent the increase in the debt burden over the year – recently people have been buying goods with money beyond the income they earned – and so brought on the great debt bubble that eventually spectacularly burst. I don't know whether this item X satisfies rigorous national accounting rules – Canada's national accounts show GDP Expenditure-Based *equals* GDP Income-Based, but lacking the term 'X' – apart from a very small item which is referred to as a 'statistical discrepancy'. Perhaps a little extra thought on this matter is called for – is there in fact an item 'X' that complicates our task of yanking our economies out of recession?).

Now, if 'aggregate demand', that is, the total of what consumers, business, and government, as well as foreign importers, wish to spend is less than what the economy can produce when fully employed, there will be unemployment. For example, the recent sub-prime mortgage crisis triggered the economy to go into free fall, a hugely indebted public suddenly became reluctant to continue their profligate spending on consumer goods and services, as a result of which there were massive lay-offs of the workers who made those goods. And there were also lay-offs by the makers of the capital goods which the consumer goods producers buy to expand their capacity. What Keynes believed, which surely is common sense, is that if people's 'propensity to consume' is too low, reducing aggregate demand, businesses will have to cut down production and lay off workers. Perhaps the people have become pessimistic, they may have suffered foreclosures, they realize that their household debt is too high, or they decide they don't really need to buy that new gadget (despite the incessant TV ads screaming at them that the gadget will make them, oh, so happy).

What would a free market laissez faire economist recommend be done? Keep hands off and leave the economy to restore its own balance and return to economic growth and full employment? Perhaps he'd suggest giving it a helping hand by some QE (quantitative easing, discussed below). Ben Bernanke, Chairman of the US Federal Reserve, has launched QE 3 – his third round of QE since the beginning of the recession – third time lucky? Perhaps not, there is little sign of American economic recovery.

Another line of action is that of the 'deficit-phobic' school of thought: When the economy goes into recession and labour income and profits fall, so does government tax revenue with the consequence that there is a large government deficit. But, the phobics say, the government deficit is a great evil and must be immediately slain, and as a result, with this cancer extirpated, the economy will recover and full employment will be restored. That approach as is well known has been used with vigour and determination in Britain, government programmes have been pruned and public workers laid off, but the policy has dismally failed. Well, of course, the Keynesian says, when you lay off government workers, they won't have the money to buy consumer goods, aggregate demand falls, and the economy shrinks: GDP falls on both the spending and income sides. Now is not the time to reduce the deficit by pruning government, wait until the economy is healthy and fully employed again – and much of the deficit will go away by itself anyway, as tax revenues recover.

So what might a Keynesian approach be in the present continuing recession? This is the Keynes – inspired approach that surely is now called for: Government must immediately start to increase aggregate demand by launching the mega-projects of the Great Battle of the Climate (the subject of Chapter 11 below), and to reshape society away from its present mistaken course; and, especially in the United States, mend or replace neglected public infrastructures; at the same time, and with generosity, government must provide income for the unemployed and impoverished victims of the economy's present derailment, thereby increasing their ability to consume. Generally the propensity to consume, which is much a state of mind, pessimism or optimism, will quickly increase, here is a government that knows what it is doing, the future seems less dark. These transfers to the unemployed will soon fast decline, both on account of the new economic activity, and because of the new spirit of confidence in the air. Keynes' famous animal spirits will be reignited, and his multiplier will go to work – the chain reaction of spending through other parts of the economy.

Yes, yes, fine, but where will the necessary government money come from, to lead the process? Governments must freely borrow to fund their share of the mega-projects, and to create public infrastructure. This perhaps is where President Obama fell short, he launched so-called 'shovel-ready' projects, and they made a difference for a while, but Obama was severely hobbled by America's huge debt and taxes phobia. As already discussed, debt to pay for government owned facilities is 'good' debt, indeed there is no other intelligent way to fund these facilities. The excessively high public debt, due to past profligacy and under-taxing, can be attended to in due course. In the meantime a percent or two of GDP of additional public debt interest is the only burden suffered, and this will disappear as the economy fast revives, and government tax revenue with it.

So the government will borrow freely for its capital projects, but where will it find the money for large unemployment and welfare benefits? One way is to borrow for that as well, do not worry about the public debt now. As already observed, the acute government debt loathing of the United States and Britain is odd at a time when despite Japan's far greater public debt, that nation's state is far from miserable – it has low unemployment, a strong external balance of payments, and a yen that has until recently risen against the dollar in recent years. There is much talk of a dreaded Japanization, of sluggish growth and high public debt – but how dreadful is that when everybody has jobs, and a high standard of life?

If it is an inopportune time to borrow, for example if there are insufficient people willing to borrow at current low yield rates, the better way is surely for the government in conjunction with the central bank simply to 'print money' and transfer it to people in need, for them to spend. Printing money, which means creating money *ex nihilo*, just running the printing presses, is now accepted in the form of 'quantitative easing' (QE). The central bank uses the new money to buy up bonds held by the banks, thereby increasing their cash holdings, which it is hoped will renew their willingness to lend money to business – tight bank credit has been viewed as strangling the economy. Or if the central bank buys long term securities (the US Fed's QE3 involves buying mortgage backed securities), it seems that the aim is reducing long term interest rates, perhaps with the hope not only of encouraging business investment but also more consumer spending – the rationale for QE3 is murky, it seems something of a desperation move. You can lead a horse to the water, you can't make him drink. Businesses will not borrow if there is little prospect of sales to their customers in the stalled economy, where aggregate demand is low. Indeed that that is so has just been revealed by a survey of the chief financial officers of large companies[49].

No, surely the way forward now is for the government instead of simply trying to get the economy to reignite itself on its old sorry path based on profligate consumption, it should borrow freely to pay for the great new projects of the future – and perhaps, if borrowing becomes difficult, even use printed money. Government doesn't grow, it doesn't do the work itself, it contracts out to construction companies and industry the building of the new nuclear stations and fast train networks. And it can also print money to pay for transfers to the unemployed, so they too have the wherewithal to spend on goods and services.

It is probable that a large share of the new capital facilities that must be created are best initiated and owned not by the government but by the private sector, for example high speed train services, which are now provided by Deutsche Bahn AG in Germany and Virgin Trains in Britain. Government will induce business corporations to build and operate new nuclear stations and fast trains, through subsidies, or tax inducements – eg high taxes might be placed on fossil fuel generated electricity and on domestic air travel. And perhaps government will subsidize households to convert their heating systems to electricity.

What of the supposed inflationary effect of printing money? If restoring business activity indirectly by quantitative easing doesn't cause inflation, why should printing money to put in the pockets of people to spend, thereby directly putting business to work, be inflationary? Inflation surely arises only when 'there is too much money chasing to few goods'. In the present case we are creating new goods, the new generating stations. Without doubt we must manage the process skilfully. The total money supply should not exceed that required to suit the current level of economy activity without inflation, and one also must be sure that on the production side the capability exists to build the new generating plant and other public facilities. If we attempt to push the economy beyond its existing capacity and skills to produce, of course we will get inflation. And in any case a *little* inflation can be lived with.

The term 'vulgar Keynesianism' has been bandied about in recent years, referring to the current 'Keynesians' who apply the words of the Master without clear understanding of the complexities of actual economies. Structural difficulties, for example a shortage of particular skills and capital facilities can prevent an economy from being fully employed. An economy is an exceedingly complex physical system of interconnected parts, of which I am very aware as a result of my experience as an engineer as well has systems analyst. And further, Keynes assumed a closed economy while now it is highly globalized – it is not easy to influence the E (exports) term in the GDP equation given above. Be all that as it may, one cannot escape the iron logic that if what the buyers of an economy's output wish to buy falls short of the maximum that the economy can produce, there will be unemployment. At the same time, it is false thinking to accept the Hayek view of the natural balance between production and consumption at full employment in accordance with Say's Law – therefore government intervention must be avoided. Nonetheless physical, structural matters are important, and the input-output table which each nation's statistical agency maintains – what each industry buys from other industries – should be monitored for blockages.

There is one point that might be raised with the proposition that present structural difficulties now impede Keynesian action. Before the sudden economic meltdown four years ago, unemployment was low, so then there were no structural difficulties then. So did the structural problems suddenly invade the economy and make Keynes inoperative? As an engineer I have difficulty understanding these sudden structural difficulties.

It is interesting to speculate: Is it possible that Say's law becomes increasingly less operative by the day? When it was first formulated 200 years ago, one can understand that it might be thought that whatever the economy could produce would be snapped up – the economy's output was low then and a great many people would be anxious to acquire some of it, many were hungry. But now, assuming that productivity has been growing by 2% annually – the industrial revolution was underway – output per person is 50 times greater – or even if productivity grew at only 1.5%, it would now be 20 times greater. Superfluity becomes a problem, hence in the long run working hours per person must fall. Unless they do, one can picture people shopping daily to replace all the goods they'd scrapped in the previous day's cull – and the economy's waste disposal service would have to be gargantuan.

And now, in October 2012, the results of a huge experiment have just been announced at the IMF- World Bank conference in Tokyo. The test participants were most of the Western nations, who had adopted austerity measures to rid themselves of their nasty deficits – they hadn't realized that the fates had enrolled them, guinea pigs, in a clinical trial –, thumbing their noses at Keynes they had confidently applied austerity measures, strong medicine, but one they were confident would cure their depression. Under the heading 'The IMF game changer' an article in the Financial Times[50] tells us that Christine Lagarde, managing director of the IMF, 'has urged countries to put a brake on austerity measures . . . the IMF is becoming increasingly concerned about the impact of government cutbacks on growth . . . . It's no surprise that Paul Krugman, who warned about this being the case all along is feeling a bit smuggish right now (and rightly so)'. And further we learn that the nations which had applied austerity the most severely had suffered the worst slowdowns.

But if the Keynesian case is so airtight logically, that unless there are enough buyers for what the economy produces, there will be unemployment and low growth, why then does the austerity, deficit slaying, conviction, cling so stubbornly on? Perhaps it has something to do with the notion in some quarters that government is getting too big, inefficient bureaucracy doing unnecessary things, or things that the private sector could do better, and spewing out regulations, for example Denmark has a huge public sector, it forbids the sale of Marmite and Ovaltine – well I ask you, I won't part with my Ovaltine and Marmite! Not only that, these deficit haters don't like welfare bums, loafers battening on the public purse, the notorious 47 percent whom Mitt Romney says won't take responsibility for themselves, and therefore will never vote for him. Two things can be said about all that: yes there may be an element of truth in the charges, as I have argued elsewhere in this work, the public sector should be lean and hugely capable, and should make sure that the economy's efficient, and innovative workhorses, the business corporations do most of the work – but make sure that they do only what society really needs and wants. And this lean and capable government must also implement the institutional reforms that are the subject of this work. So yes, government can get too big and inefficient, and yes, there are some welfare bums. But as Keynes wrote, and Christine Lagarde has just repeated, you don't pick the depth of a recession to prune government of unnecessary activities and flab. Interestingly, according to the same article the IMF is 'eating crow: for generations now . . . the IMF has enforced austerity, conditionality and accountability wherever it goes. And for the most part, it's the emerging world that suffered most. . . Recanting now on some of these closely held beliefs, especially now that the bitter medicine is predominantly applied to the developed world, is awkward to say the least'.

'Stimulus'

The word 'stimulus' is now applied to the supposedly Keynesian approach which is now the subject of so much debate, but wrongly so for the Keynesian process I have in mind. The Oxford dictionary defines a 'stimulus' as 'a thing or event that evokes a specific functional reaction in an organ or tissue', or more broadly, 'a thing that arouses activity or energy or something; a spur or incentive'. The aim of what now is referred to as 'economic stimulus' is, I suggest, to make the naughty economy behave itself, be a good boy, stop throwing people out of work, or having large government budget deficits. This sort of 'stimulus' is like the spurs worn by a horse rider, or a shot of adrenalin, or catnip to a cat. What I have in mind is very different, it is, in accordance with the Social Contract, democratically to control, and to repair, where necessary, the economy so that it serves mankind, that is, not only to end involuntary unemployment, but also make human life more comfortable and fulfilling, and avert climate catastrophe.

This kind of Keynesian policy now called for has two major parts. On the one hand the government puts the business corporations to work on the giant projects to save the climate and remake society, while at the same time generously transferring funds to the unemployed so they can resume consumption, until they are quickly drawn back into the economy becoming busier by the day. The corporations either carry out the work on their own account under government inducements, including subsidies, tax advantages, and new regulations; or instead carry out the projects on contract to government, out of public funds – and remember that this new government-owned infrastructure, quite legitimately, is paid for by borrowing – that is what government bonds are really for. And if business instead owns, as well as builds new infrastructure, they too will borrow to pay for it, or, alternatively, raise money by issuing new shares.

And, on the other hand, this form of Keynesian policy requires quickly mending the underlying governance malfunctions, in particular extirpating the broadcasting perversion, and replacing our present dysfunctional public finance system by the Return to Society. This is very far from mere 'stimulus', to prod the economy to start behaving itself while continuing along its old failed path. It means, instead, mending its governance institutions so that it changes course, and starts to serve mankind. This is the kind of economic policy that is implied in the two scenarios discussed later in this chapter, and again in the simulation exercise which is the subject of Appendix 1.

That what I am arguing reflects Keynesian thinking one need only quote his words, when he expended effort, in vain, at the depth of the Great Depression, with huge continuing unemployment, to persuade the British Government to put the nation back to work: 'With men and plant unemployed, it is ridiculous to say we cannot afford new developments. . . . When we have unemployed men and unemployed plant and more savings than we are using . . . it is utterly imbecile to say that we cannot afford these things. . . . Only public works' can jolt the sluggish economy back to life. . . There is work to do, there are the men to do it. Why not bring them together' He also pointed out that by acting vast sums would be saved. 'Unemployment benefits were already costing taxpayers 50 million pounds annually (650 million in today's money), and over the previous eight years ten times as much. 'Such a vast sum could have built a million new homes, or renewed a third of Britain's roads' But Keynes was hopelessly railing against the crabby, died-in-the wool, mentality of the British Treasury. He was up against the same tight, 'waste not, want not' establishment mentality now in power in Britain that have visited double-dip recession, perhaps it will be triple-dip, on the British people. Polls show that the opposition Labour Party has a ten percent lead, and is promising a large programme of public infrastructure and homes building – what Keynes recommended – if it gets into power at the next general election.

There is another way of putting all this: as stated earlier, boom and bust is an archaic absurdity, the only purpose of the economy is to serve the people, all the people, all the time. Of course our society can devise a way to employ everybody who wants to work, especially now when there is so much to be done, as is outlined on these pages.

Ferguson versus Krugman

I am a great admirer of Niall Ferguson and his works. He is no 'poseur' as Paul Krugman has claimed. He is an historian, a very broadly engaged economic historian, who is an admirer of John Maynard Keynes, and has stated that Keynes would not be pleased with what is being proposed in his name by today's 'vulgar Keynesians'. Ferguson has written that three conditions now existing preclude Keynesian actions: the high level of debt, both government and private, structural, that is, 'supply side' problems, and globalization. I don't believe Ferguson is right. My view is that society can and must take control, and put the economy to work on its increasingly necessary projects. in accordance with the Keynesian policy, ensuring aggregate demand at full employment. In most major economies, in particular the United States, the United Kingdom, Germany and Japan, ten-year borrowing costs are extraordinarily low. And borrowing is in any case the correct way of paying for government infrastructure, that's what government bonds in peacetime are really for.

And I suggest that the government can pay for transferring money to the unemployed by printing it. It bears repeating that printing money causes inflation only if there is too much of it chasing too few goods, but there won't be too few goods because the sellers of these goods, now in the doldrums, will be more than glad to resume production. And, as argued earlier, it is illogical to believe that while printing money to restart consumer spending *indirectly,* through QE, quantitative easing, is justified, printing money for the same purpose, *directly*, by giving it to consumers, won't work, or is inflationary. When the economy falls into depression, at the root of it is that the public does not want to, or cannot afford to, buy enough consumer goods. What QE tries to do is by increasing banks' cash reserves entice them to lend money to businesses, so that they will invest in capital goods – but firms won't do that if the public's propensity to consume is low. I suggest that it may make more sense to give the printed money directly to consumers, and when the latter restart their spending, businesses will be more than willing, without the need for government encouragement, to expand their production facilities or to replace old facilities – it is reported that these have not been replaced, and the size of the usable capital stock has fallen. But though the fall-off of production when the economy suddenly crashes is due to consumers stopping buying, there are also times when that other element of aggregate demand is too low, investment in new public infrastructure. This is needed now not only for improving neglected public infrastructure, but also, in these challenging times, to reshape society through the mega-projects that will save the climate and improve the quality of life, and also bring about the new Age of Enlightenment – the mega-projects that are discussed in Chapter 11.

There is no doubt at all that Paul Krugman too is a clever fellow, and the policies he proposes in his latest book, 'End the Depression

Now' are much like what I have suggested in this chapter. (One point of difference is that the public works he recommends are only for improving or replacing neglected infrastructure, not also for the mega-projects to reshape society. More broadly I differ from him by attaching prime importance to the West's present sorry state, to the institutional faults that are the subject of this work). That Krugman may be a little narrow in his thinking is suggested by the way he heaped scorn on John Kenneth Galbraith, who revealed great truths about how the US economy behaved, and then subsequently took back his words. Furthermore, he reviewed Nouriel Roubini's 'Crisis Economics' as 'a very good primer on how finance gone bad can wreck an *otherwise healthy* economy'. But the subject of this book is how very *unhealthy* the economy, or society, is. And regarding Ferguson, Krugman has said 'I'm told that Ferguson is a very good historian, but, on economics, he's a poseur (Merriam Webster: 'a person who behaves affectedly in order to impress others') who hasn't bothered to understand the basics, relying on snide comments and surface cleverness to convey the impression of wisdom. He's all style, no comprehension of substance'. Krugman's own thinking must be a little narrow, 'there are more things in heaven and earth, Paul, than are dreamt of in your philosophy'. He had to be told, he did not already know, that Ferguson is a good historian, well-known for his masterly works not only on the terrible carnage in Europe and Asia in the last hundred years, but also on economic history. Ferguson gave the 2012 BBC Reith Lectures, on 'Civilisation', and he was preceded the year before by Aung San Suu Kyi, and in 2010 by Martin Rees – 'poseurs' are not invited to deliver the BBC's annual Reith Lectures.

But I have an agenda here in talking about the Krugman/Ferguson clash. It's the clash between the specialist and the generalist, the specialist is concerned with the minutiae, the orthodoxy, of his special discipline. The generalist instead is interested in the grand whole, embracing all the many specializations, to see how the whole bag of tricks works, why the world is how it is, how it became so, and where it is heading. No matter how brilliant he might be – and Ferguson is most certainly that – his grand view may be at odds with the particularities, the current accepted truths of particular areas of specialization, and quite wrong as I believe he now is in challenging Keynesian policies for restarting the economy. I am a generalist, I am expecting a torrent of hoots of derision if this work ever is successfully published and read. And no doubt, some of the complaints will be justified, and perhaps, I'll even have to alter my world view (though I very much hope not, it would upturn my whole personal belief system of fifty years standing!). And we should remember it is not only the broad thinkers who can get things wrong, so can even the most celebrated of the specialists. Krugman's economics by my reckoning is too narrow: For example he does not see, nor do any of his colleagues see, what is staring them in the eye: the American broadcasting system is not a final economic good serving the people, it is not measured in the national accounts as part of 'C' – it does not appear in the basket of consumer goods and services. No, you have to dig into the accounts to find it lumped under 'advertising services bought by consumer good purveyors from advertising agencies'.

That I have a slightly Ferguson way of thinking, is suggested by what I've just learned through the wonders of Google: Ferguson believes that history is not just the result of underlying forces pushing it in the direction it has taken, but can be influenced by 'contingent events, sometimes trivial', but which might never have happened. When very many years ago I read Tolstoy's War and Peace, I was struck by his view – though not fully convinced by it – that it was the underlying forces that changed the world – if there had been no Napoleon, some other person would have played his role. So I immediately wondered whether Ferguson had read War and Peace, and re-googled 'Niall Ferguson Tolstoy' just on the off-chance – the odds were long – and discovered that my guess was not only right, but that Ferguson includes 'War and Peace' among the five great books[51] that have influenced his work (interestingly one by Keynes, Krugman's hero, 'A Tract on Monetary Reform'). In the interview Ferguson says 'out of all the thinkers whom I have engaged with, I identify most with a philosophy of history which emphasizes contingencies, and represents a complex world on the edge of chaos rather than something that is nice and predictable'. Regarding Tolstoy, he says 'I react differently than I did when I first read 'War and Peace' at about fifteen. At first reading I was completely captivated by the concluding essay at the end of the book, where Tolstoy writes about political determinism. I thought that then, and it was only in my twenties that I rebelled against it'.

'Contingencies, some trivial! I've just done a little thought experiment. Say, against all probability, that this work somehow convinces a group of influential individuals, and they start the process that I describe later in Chapter 17: Driving Action, and that this actually leads to a rebirth of the West in a new Enlightenment, then, wow! Ferguson will have been proved right. Or say, another, less improbable contingency, the Western nations heeded Krugman's new book, 'End this Depression Now!', and this actually led to the West's economic recovery. That too would support Ferguson's contingency theory of history – and, wonder of wonders, 'Ferguson and Krugman' would shake hands in a short-lived truce – short-lived because Krugman's writes under the title 'The 'Conscience of a Liberal' and Ferguson is known of as a conservative, perhaps, one might say, an enlightened conservative, with which I have considerable sympathy. In Chapter 6 I asked where this work fitted in the political spectrum, and suggested 'radical conservative', because there is so much that is good in Western civilization that should be conserved, and our defective governance has been putting that to risk.

In Ferguson's recent, and most impressive, 'Civilization: The West and the Rest, he is concerned with the very long term, with why civilizations rise and decline. He further takes the matter up in his just published 'The Great Degeneration', which I discuss later in Chapter 15. This, after all, is the subject of this book.

Banishing Boom and Bust for all time

The New Enlightenment involves not only yanking nations out of the present recession, but ending the absurdity of boom and bust once and for all. There will no longer be one party shouting 'austerity' and the other calling for 'growth'. The economy will be managed, reconciling the short term with the long term, engaging in whatever grand projects are needed to improve society as well as save the planet and avert calamitous climate change. And in the long run, shortening the hours of work, because increasing productivity will make a long work week unnecessary. How will this be done? One way of saying this is by quickly bringing into being the new science of economics (the subject of Chapter 12). The principles already outlined above for stopping the present recession in its tracks will be further developed into the new science of the management of the economy for the long term. Keynesian remedies now demand government spending on public works to fill the gap in aggregate demand when suddenly consumers stop spending. But in the future managed economy, these public works won't be just any public works, to prevent idle hands, they will include the set of mega-projects required to create the better, non-polluting, society of the future. These grand projects are described later, in Chapter 11: The Great Battle of the Climate. Adopting the new public finance system, the subject of Chapter 10, will much simplify the task of keeping the economy on an even keel.

To manage the economy for the long term will require adding a new long term planning agency to government, to advise, and to communicate with the people and their elected government, on what must be done. This new agency is discussed in Chapter 13, on reforming democracy.

The Role of Intense Sales Promotion

It strikes me that both schools of economics, the laissez faire and the Keynesian, have an important omission, and that is the role in the economy of consumer product sales promotion, especially broadcast advertising, which is discussed in Chapter 12 below. Nearly half American advertising is in television and radio broadcasting, and in the last few years Americans have been watching more TV than ever, for the average American, for over five hours daily. As a result Americans are exposed to about an hour of commercial interruptions each day urging them to buy. A study shows that the share of air time allocated to commercials in U.S. television has increased from 13% in 1958 to 31% over the last four years: that is, there is about one minute of advertising for every two minutes of programme. In addition there are imbedded commercials, where a character uses, or displays, a product, in such a way that it is clearly evident, and intentional. Also there is the ever-present radio belting out frequent selling 'messages'. Surely this constant nagging to buy contributes to the propensity to consume and aggregate demand.

Americans live in an ambience of buy, buy, buy. Their whole value system must be to a degree slanted to the acquisition of stuff. As there are surely many busy, highly educated and cultivated Americans who can't abide this ambience, that means that for a great many Americans, the television or radio is on most of their waking hours away from work – it's the backdrop to their lives. For me, who loathes broadcast commercials, this is the stuff of nightmares. And perhaps it is a measure of how brutal the post-Lehman Bros. shock was for many Americans, that despite the increasing intensity of sales promotion from companies struggling to sell their wares, the US economy still refuses to rise out of its deep depression. Advertising's place in America defies belief: Mark Zuckerberg tells the world (Financial Times 23 October 2012) 'I want to dispel this myth that Facebook can't make money on mobile'. The social network's founder 'once vigorously resisted displaying advertisements that could interfere with the user experience.' but now champions it . . Facebook is delivering 'more mobile adverts to users, adverts that occupy a much larger proportion of the small mobile device screen than the slim column of adverts on the desktop view'. This is all stuff of the American Dream, that is now going sour.

Two scenarios

The following are two alternative spending scenarios for a hypothetical country with a GDP of one trillion dollars, extracting itself from the depths of a deep depression, which it does by launching the mega-projects of the great Battle of the Climate (the subject of Chapter 11 below), and also generously transferring money to the unemployed and otherwise distressed. The first scenario is a for a country that frowns on public services, for example Tea Party America, and the second for a nation without this particular phobia.

The scenarios are certainly over-ambitious, how can such huge projects get underway so fast, but they do serve their purpose of demonstrating the mechanism of economic recovery.

For simplicity, I have assumed a country with zero population growth so that the economic growth rate is the same as the average rate of increase of people's incomes, and also zero inflation. For both scenarios, in year zero, at the depth of the recession, unemployment was 9%, and in year 4 the economy has fully recovered, and unemployment is at 3%, effectively full employment. Over the four years, the economy grows annually because of both increasing productivity, and increasing employment. As a result GDP increases by about 19%, at an average annual economic growth rate of 4.4%. Both scenarios show a huge rate of capital investment increase, an average annual increase of 12.6%. As a result capital investment increases from 20% of GDP in year 0 to nearly 27% of GDP in year 4. This requires adding about 30 billion dollars annually of new capital facilities, over and above normal capital investment, by both government and business corporations – the building of new nuclear generating stations, high speed trains, and other facilities and equipment leading to a low emission society.

In the business scenario the economy emerges from recession with the fair rate of increase of consumer spending of 2.4% annually, while government services increase slowly, their share of GDP falling from 20 percent to 17.4 percent of GDP, perhaps enough to please tea-party-ites, and the British chancellor George Osborne. As for the huge programme of capital investment, business corporations are induced, by large subsidies and tax incentives, and where necessary regulation, to build the nuclear generating stations and high speed electric trains of the Battle of the Climate, and business capital investment increases by 13.3% annually. Government capital spending also increases, but at the lesser rate of 7%, engaged in public infra-structure projects – for these most of the construction work is of course contracted out to business corporations.

1 Business-Friendly scenario

	Year- 1 Economy in Deep Depression Unemployment 9%		Year-5 Fully Recovered Unemployment 3%		Average Growth Rate Years 1-5
	GDP ($ Billons)	%	GDP (Billons)	%	
Consumption	600	60	659.7	55.1	2.4%
Govt. Services	200	20	208.6	17.4	1.1%
Investment					
Government	25	2.5	2.8	2.7	7.0%
Business	175	17.5	288.4	24.1	13.3%
Total Investment	200	20	321.2	26.8	12.6%
Net Exports (exports less imports)	0	0	8.6	0.7	
GDP	1000	100%	1198.1	100%	4.6%

2 Public spending-friendly scenario

	Year- 1 Economy in Deep Depression Unemployment 9%		Year-5 Fully Recovered Unemployment 3%		Average Growth Rate Years 1-5
	GDP ($ Billons)	%	GDP (Billons)	%	
Consumption	600	60	649.5	54.2	2.0%
Govt. Services	200	20	212.8	18.3	2.3%
Investment					
Government	25	2.5	46.9	3.8	17.0%
Business	175	17.5	274.3	23.0	11.9%
Total Investment	200	20	321.2	27.0	12.6%
Net Exports (exports less imports)			8.6	0.7	
GDP	1000	100%	1198.1	100%	4.6%

One difficulty this scenario might have with tea-party type people is the huge investment in mega-emission-cutting projects. At the time of writing the contenders to become the Republican Party candidate in the next Presidential election were all affirming their scepticism on man-made global warming, so perhaps the projects could all somehow have come under the name of infrastructure-mending. But no, no, this is preposterous, in these sad times the only intelligent solution is a brave President who can stare down Tea Party Republicans, and expose their climate delusions – do they think they know more about the climate and meteorology than their own nation's National Academy of Sciences, charged with acting as 'advisors to the nation on science, engineering, and medicine'? Now, writing after the State if the Union speech, re-elected President Obama has at last taken a 'brave' stance.

The second scenario represents the same recovery from deep recession under a strongly Keynesian government. There is the same mega-project programme, though the government's share of this increases at the high rate of 17% while business capital construction grows a little less fast at 11.9%. In this scenario, though government services grow quite strongly at 2.3%, it is still possible for personal consumption to increase by 2% annually.

It will be noted that in both scenarios, whether business-friendly or Keynesian, actual mega-projects construction work is carried out by the business sector, society's work-horses. The difference is the question of ownership, who pays. In the business scenario, business is the owner, and they are induced to perform the projects by subsidies and tax incentives. In the public-friendly scenario, the government pays and is the owner – though it might eventually privatize the facilities.

Interestingly, for both scenarios, being in deep recession makes it easier to engage in the great battle of the climate. The grand mega-projects are an excellent way of speeding recovery from the Great Recession. Instead of using all of the economy's rapidly increasing output in a return to profligate consumer spending, much of the new output is spent on new low emission facilities – and also building a new, more comfortable world for people.

These two tables show only the spending side of the ledger – these figures are what are called 'GDP expenditure-based'. GDP can also be shown 'income-based', that is as the sum of the payments by industry and government to the factors of production, labour and capital. And in addition, the national accounting statistics show two other sets of money flow, 'intermediate payments' – purchases by businesses and government of materials, equipment and services from supplying firms; and so-called 'transfer payments', which include income taxes, government unemployment and welfare benefits, and government subsidies, purchase of bonds and shares, and dividends. In Appendix 1, for the 'business-friendly' scenario, I have simulated a five year period, showing all these elements of the national accounts, the first four years of economic recovery from year 0 to year 4, and the fifth year when attention switches to reducing the government deficit.

As will be seen, in the first four years, the extent to which the outlay on government current spending exceeds tax revenue, that is the budget deficit, is far from a priority matter, indeed it rises slightly from 8% of GDP to 8.9% – reducing the deficit will be a preoccupation only in later years. What is achieved in the four years is the reduction of unemployment from 9% to 3% of GDP, effectively full employment, and a huge increase in investment spending, which grows from 20 to 27 percent of GDP. Moreover in the period, government transfers to persons – unemployment and welfare benefits – fall from a huge 13% of GDP at the depth of the recession to 9 percent in year 4 (clearly with a return to full employment less unemployment benefits are necessary). At the same time labour income has grown at 4.4 percent annually, profits at 5.7%, income tax, both personal and corporate, by 4.5 percent. One other change in the four years has been the provision of large government subsidies to business in support of their action on climate projects. By year 4 these constitute 6.1 percent of GDP.

Despite the huge increase in capital spending, this has not been at the expense of personal consumption, which has grown at 2.4 percent annually. This is a larger amount than might be thought at first sight, because during the four year period a determined programme of broadcasting reform has much reduced the frantic advertising interruptions that now urge the population to purchase this or that rubbish at the expense of consumer goods of genuine value, not only that, to replace things they have still in good working order by slightly different, not always better, new models. The programme to correct the present broadcasting perversion is the subject of the next chapter. I have referred to this simulation as 'business-friendly' but clearly it is one that is nonetheless generous in transferring money to its disadvantaged and unemployed – it is 'enlightened business friendly', one that realises that a population amply provided with income can better buy its goods. The simulation shows profits over the four years as increasing nicely, thank you, by 5.75% annually.

In year 5, by which time full employment and a busy economy have been restored, a start is made to re-balance the economy by reducing the huge government deficit. As will be seen, the deficit falls from its awful 8.9% in year 4 to a considerably less awful 6%, and one can be comfortably sure that it will disappear altogether in another two or three years. One can reflect that the horrible deficit wasn't really as awful as had been thought, the sky didn't fall in. But, the simulation also shows that there is some pain in the deficit reduction, real growth, the increase in the output of consumption goods, capital goods, and of government services is temporarily put on hold – there is some belt-tightening, but really nothing serious, the people have become nicely affluent, and can readily mark time for a period.

[I am puzzled by what the 5th year of the simulation shows – that though GDP grows by 3%, there is zero increase in real output – the seeming large increase, 15% in government services, is really just a monetary transfer money paid by government to reduce its deficit. Perhaps a more elaborate version of this macro-economic model, showing balance sheets and bank accounts, could throw light on the situation].

A blessing in disguise

We can even consider the present Great Recession as a blessing in disguise – if we seize the opportunity. Our economies now have huge overcapacity. In the United States the unemployment rate if we count not only the 9 percent officially unemployed, but those discouraged and no longer seeking employment, and also the under-employed, is about 17%. One sixth of the country's capacity is lying idle. The great danger for the United States is that it will try to go back to where it was. One reason its recovery is so slow is that its people have had a great shock. They had been over-consuming, their personal saving rate was very low, they were living on debt, they owed China a trillion dollars.

The main reason for the Great Recession, and the difficulty of restarting the economy, is the underlying cause, discussed earlier, the lack of an intelligent mechanism for making use of our magnificent production system. To a large degree, and most particularly in the United States, the economy has been held aloft by profligate consumption, rather than by some means that best serves the public purpose. But now, at last the old way is unsustainable. And one part of this old way is the perverted broadcasting system, which is the subject of chapter 9. If the US, and other nations, behave rationally they will stop trying to put the clock back, hoping that all the unused labour and industrial capacity will simply return to producing what it produced before – the old sales promotion-driven profligate consumption. No, a thousand times no, much of the spare capacity must be directed to the tasks of the New Enlightenment. There probably has never been a better time for many Western governments to launch huge programmes of capital spending on giant projects and infrastructure: With economies depressed and people nervous about investing in shares, and instead preferring the security of bonds despite extraordinarily low interest rates, there couldn't be a better time to borrow to pay for giant construction projects.

George Osborne's unwarranted crowing

And just as I was completing this book, the Financial Times of September 10th 2013 tells us that the Chancellor 'George Osborne claims Austerity Victory", proclaiming that recovery was underway, and that recent "early signs" of growth were a vindication of his economic policies'.

Well really! The Guardian of April 25th 2013 provided statistics that compared recovery times for five British recessions, from the Great Depression (1930-1934) to the present Great Recession that started in 2008. For the Great Depression, GDP fell by 7% over 2.5 years, after which the economy recovered and after five years GDP was 4% above its pre-depression value. To my surprise I discovered that recovery has been much slower in the present recession. GDP fell sharply and after 15 months it was 6.5% below its 2008 value. But after that it has failed to recover - at the end of April GDP was still 2.8% below its 2008 value.

And now with a small increase in September, has Osborne anything to crow about? Of course, eventually there was bound to be some growth whatever Osborne did. No the kind of growth that there should have been was the average annual growth of 4% of the scenarios earlier in this chapter. However, in one dimension the depression of 1930 was much worse - unemployment was much higher - in the absence of present day policies of providing aid to society's unfortunates - now unemployment and welfare benefits mean that people can still buy basic living necessities, so aggregate demand doesn't suffer such a nose dive.

But of course, though depressions are no longer as nasty as they once were, in the future new Age of Enlightenment, the absurb cycle of boom and bust will be but a dim memory - of course the economy can be managed so that there is no involuntary unemployment.

---

1 National Institute of Economic and Social Research, as presented in the Guardian of 25 April 2013.

CHAPTER 8

Slaying the
Micawber Bugaboo

What are the academic credentials of those who manage the economy, and avert public deficits and excessive public debt? One would think that they were called 'economists', the doctors of the economy, who prevent it from getting sick and cure its illnesses, but perhaps that is wrong. The Finance Ministers of the major western nations graduated in the following subjects:

Timothy Geithner, US Treasury Secretary: government and Asian affairs, and international economics.

Gordon Brown, former UK Chancellor of the Exchequer: history.

George Osborne: present Chancellor: modern history.

Jim Flaherty, Canadian finance minister: law.

Dominique Strauss-Kahn, former director of the IMF (International Monetary Fund): economics.

Christine Lagarde, former French minister of finance, and now director of the IMF: law and political science.

Francois Baroin, French finance minister in the Sarkozy government: government and Asian studies, and information and library technology.

Wolfgang Schauble: German finance minister: law.

Only one finance minister was trained as an 'economist' – or one and a half if we include 'international economics'. Whatever their academic credentials – and there is no reason to believe that it would be any different if they had graduated in economics, a dysfunctional discipline – muddle and illogic are now much in the news. This is the question of the budget deficit and the public debt. If there is such confusion here among those in authority on such an elementary matter, have we leaders ready to grapple with the difficulties of reversing our society's decline?

What after all could be more simple: a deficit arises when spending exceeds income. Well apparently not quite so simple, in some channels of power, among them the drafters of the Maastricht Treaty that underpins the Euro, the European common currency, and also the International Monetary Fund. I have spent many hours searching for clarification on the matter, but all I find is ambiguity and excessive words. But in fact 'deficit' and 'debt' are easy-to-grasp concepts, and the only question is why the present muddle exists, and makes it possible for a George Osborne to strangle an economy (the British economy) with stringent austerity measures at an inopportune time.

Perhaps we can call the deficit phobia now bedevilling many governments the Micawber bugaboo. Dickens' Mr Micawber said 'Annual income twenty pounds, annual expenditure nineteen pounds nineteen and six, result happiness; annual income twenty pounds, annual expenditure twenty pounds, nought and six, result misery'. Obviously true, and if a government's annual spending exceeds its annual revenue from taxes, it will suffer a deficit, and if that is chronic and goes on for years, the result is indeed misery – *but only if one defines spending correctly.* There is a most extraordinary definition of government budget deficit in vogue which I will refer to as the 'Maastricht deficit', perhaps unjustly, perhaps the drafters of the Maastricht rules for deficit and debt for member countries of the Eurozone were merely using a government accounting terminology already widely in use.

Of course deficits correctly defined are bad, a business corporation which runs at a loss will go out of business, an individual who lives beyond his means will declare bankruptcy. Consequently it is a puzzle why the Maastricht rules for membership in the Eurozone require that national governments' deficits not exceed 3% percent of GDP. That is really profligate overspending, meaning that the government's current spending exceeds its tax revenue by, say 7.5 % (assuming government spending is 40% of GDP). Does Maastricht really mean that this huge annual loss is permissible, or is it defining the word 'deficit' differently? Over the years I have been unable to find any mention, let alone discussion, among economists of this anomaly – nor for that matter by public affairs commentators, nor by the ordinary man in the street – perhaps these quite naturally just assumed that the economists, authorities, whatever, knew what they were about. It seems unlikely that such an enormous deficit in the normal meaning of the word was considered acceptable, not least because Germany, which originally insisted on the 3% rule, is a stickler for this sort of thing. Therefore the explanation of this 3% rule must be that the word 'deficit' is defined differently from its usual meaning, and perhaps the Maastricht framers were not distinguishing between current and capital spending. In other words what Maastricht calls the deficit that will have to be covered by borrowing, is the extent to which the government's tax revenue fails to cover not only its current spending on services and welfare and unemployment payments, but also the year's capital investment, additions to the public infrastructure. This I have recently confirmed is the correct interpretation[52].

Of course the government's capital investment must be covered by borrowing, by loan capital, but to call this borrowing deficit spending is absurd. One does not pay fully this year for capital facilities which will provide service for thirty years. Business corporations pay for their capital investment, their plant and equipment similarly by borrowing, that is through corporate bonds, and also by issuing shares – governments obviously rely purely on bond issues.

And it appears that not only Maastricht, but the IMF in its 'World Economic Outlook', uses this quirky Maastricht definition, in its reports on governments' gross financing requirements, as discussed below. It was, and remains, a strange mistake of nomenclature: to treat government capital spending as deficit spending. This is an absurdity that should be immediately corrected, to put sense in the public discourse on questions of public finance.

The gross financing requirement

Government borrowing is not limited to covering current spending in excess of tax revenue, plus government capital expenditure. That is only 'net borrowing' The 'gross financing requirement' is higher. This is the total amount that governments will have to borrow in the current year, and includes the additional amount of borrowing needed to cover the year's maturing debt. The IMF reports this annually for the advanced nations, in its 'Fiscal Monitor'. Below are the values, expressed as percent of GDP, for the G7 nations from the Monitor of 14 May 2010. (I have since learned that the 2012 Monitor is much the same).

	Gross Debt (2009)	Gross Financing Needs 2010	Deficit	Maturing Debt	Average Maturity (years)
United Kingdom	68.2	20.0	11.4	8.6	12.8
Germany	72.5	15.9	5.7	10.2	6.0
France	77.4	25.1	8.2	16.9	6.5
Canada	82.5	21.2	5.3	15.9	5.6
United States	83.2	32.2	11.0	21.2	4.4
Italy	115.8	26.4	5.2	21.2	6.7
Japan	217.7	64.0	9.8	54.2	5.2

As will be observed, this table uses the Maastricht definition of deficit – what it calls the deficit is in fact the sum of the deficit correctly defined plus the additional borrowing needed to fund capital expenditure, the additions to nations infrastructures. That is usually between 2 and 3 percent of GDP. If we assume 2.5% then in the above table, the UK's true deficit is only 8.9% – still bad of course. And Canada's is not 5.3 but only 2.8% which is not horrendous in the depth of a great recession. Interestingly, the deficit of that casualty country now much in the news, Italy, is even less than Canada's, so the huge fuss about Italy's woes owes not to its government budget deficit but to something else, presumably its public debt, among the large nations dwarfed only by Japan's, and also its international payments deficit, and the dysfunctionality of the Euro common currency, described in Chapter 14. Japan's huge debt is a mystery that is seldom discussed. One notes that Japan's yield on its 10 year government bonds is only 0.8%, which seems to suggest that Japanese people or institutions are happy to receive this tiny yield. There is much mystery in the subject of finance. Switzerland 's yield is even lower, only 0.6%, and perhaps that is related to that country's highly successful economy, its high positive international balance of payments, and it's consequent aim of lessening the appreciation of its currency.

Among the G7 nations, in the minds of the public and of politicians, Britain and the United States are in the deepest financial trouble, but that appears far from true for Britain. While in 2010 the British government's gross borrowing requirement was forecast to be 20% of GDP, that of the United States government was a shocking 32% and Japan's a doubly shocking 64% of GDP. Only Germany had a lower financing need than Britain. In fact the US is saved much grief, as whatever the S and P rating index says, foreigners are happy to buy US treasury bills, despite their very low yield – the US is not suffering the current Italian woe, where to meet a financing need lower than that of the US, investors have been asking for a yield higher than 7% – hence austerity and the exit of Berlusconi.

Britain's gross borrowing requirement is low because its maturing debt at 8.6% of GDP is the lowest of the G7 countries, while that of the US is a huge 21% and Japan's a horrendous 54%. From this one can only infer that Britain has managed it fiscal affairs rather skilfully. Its average debt maturity of 13 years is double that of all the other nations, and most particularly that of the United States whose average maturity is only 4.4 years. This suggests that while Britain has borrowed in the main with very long term bonds as is appropriate to pay for capital spending, other nations have had larger current budget deficits, which they have financed with shorter term bonds. Most especially this appears true of the United States, whose 4.4 year maturity is obviously far shorter than the life of infrastructure items. Perhaps Gordon Brown has been wrongly demonised because of the sudden sharp increase of Britain's deficit in the last two years. It was surely inevitable that Britain would be hard hit by the present financial crisis, because it is a great financial centre. I suspect that if Gordon Brown, previously as Chancellor of the Exchequer, had not managed Britain's finances so well, Britain would be in a much sorrier state. The question whether Britain has allowed its public sector to get too big is a totally different issue, and some other nations have larger public sectors, notably Sweden which is regarded as an exceptionally well-governed nation. Another indicator that Britain has managed its finances relatively well is that its national debt in recent years has been below 40% of GDP, and has only shot up in 2008 and 2009 to 68%, which was the lowest of the G7 nations, while that of the US was 83% and of Japan 218%. Japan's fiscal situation as measured by national debt has been far worse for years than that over which the US and Western Europe are in such a frenzy about. Yet these nations are talking of the life and death imperative to reduce the deficit – this is the main concern of the new British Conservative government, and George Osborne, the Chancellor of the Exchequer, and in their ardour they may have choked off the reviving British economy.

(The foregoing was written two years ago, and now in August 2012 as Britain drops into severe 'double-dip' recession, both economists who originally lauded his deficit reduction efforts, and British industry, have turned against him: 'Britain's economists are increasingly in agreement . . . that George Osborne can no longer stand idly by and watch the hope of recovery crumple. And that spending on infrastructure . . . is the solution. . . If that means borrowing more, so be it. What's the point of having the cheapest borrowing costs in 300 years if you don't borrow.'[53] As for British industry, 'The outspoken attack from the director general of the British Chambers of Commerce . . . is a severe blow to the Chancellor. . . . His comments just two weeks after the head of the Confederation of British Industry tore into ministers for failing to do more to boost infrastructure[54]).

The table suggests that Britain and Germany are in the least bad financial state, and Japan and US the worst, as judged by their immediate need to borrow huge amounts. Britain is in the unique position that as its debt maturity is very long, it can run considerable deficits for several years without financing difficulties – the only annoyance for the public might possibly be the size of annual interest payments for servicing the debt, but that really is a flee-bite, compared with the huge losses that Britain and other countries will incur if paranoid action throttles their economic recovery. Indeed interest on the public debt is a mere 2% of GDP. Britain is among a handful of nations whose rating by Moody's is at the highest, AAA, level[55], and if its finances were in as parlous a state as its government claims, why (in September 2012) would Britain have an interest rate on its 10 year bonds of only 1.8%, only a little higher than the US's 1.6% and Germany's 1.5%?. In contrast Italy's is 5.3%and Spain's 6%, and Portugal and Greece very much higher. The only reason that the US interest rate is low is that the dollar is the world's reserve currency, treated by the world as 'as good as gold' despite the huge US budget and international payments deficit and large public debt.

There is a widely held view in Britain, no doubt used as justification by the government for its austerity measures, that the public debt is in reality much higher than the official value, which as already mentioned, is lower than that of other large nations. This high debt claim is based on the notion that to the official debt should be added the large obligation the British government has to pay the future pensions of retired government servants. Unlike many other nations it does not have a pension fund which its employees pay into through a deduction from salary, and so pays its retirees out of current spending – indeed this is one of the British government's largest categories of current spending, as large as its health payments under the National Health Service. But surely to say its future pension payments should be added in to give a true value of the public debt makes no sense. These future pension payments are no more debt obligations than are all the other future payments the government will have to make, rather they might simply be regarded as transfer payments to government retirees, analogous to transfer payments to people on welfare, to those who are unemployed, and to those who are sick under the NHS. All of these will be future obligations, we can be sure there will be always be people who are on welfare, unemployed, or sick, just as certainly as there will be retirees. A genuine debt, like the official public debt, is characterised by interest payments, which are absent from the present British arrangement. And these unfunded future obligations are not *our,* the present generation's, obligations, they are the obligations that the future generation will have, to support its unemployed, sick, on welfare, as well retired former civil servants.

Perhaps I am mistaken in writing that the present flap about the British debt is unwarranted, after all there appears considerable consensus that the situation is dire. So I have searched on the internet to try and find where my argument may have fallen down. But, no, I have been unable to. The matter is taken up again below, in chapter 15.

Italy's finances too are in a sorry state, with a gross financing requirement of 26.4% of GDP, and a public debt second only to Japan's. Even so, one wonders whether Italy's crisis is due more to the dysfunctionality of the euro common currency rather than to the size of its public debt. Both the US and Japan have larger financing requirements.

Regarding Japan's situation one wishes that the experts, the commentators on the present world financial crisis, would offer more enlightenment. Japanese debt and borrowing requirement are enormous, far worse than that which is causing such dismay in the United States, and Britain. But if the deficit and debt are so to be dreaded, why has the yen been until recently rising so strongly in value? The yen appreciated, up 50% over the dollar since mid-2007, up 55% against the Euro, and 90% over the pound? Japan's unemployment at 5% is not very high, exports are strong, and Japan enjoys a huge current account (that is, international payments) surplus. Japan is often referred to as an ailing nation, yet how really ailing is it? Perhaps one reason that the sky is not falling in on Japan is that only a tiny proportion of Japanese central government bonds are owned by foreign countries – the bonds are mainly held by Japanese banks and other institutions and these are clearly not unwilling to hold these bonds despite their tiny yields. In contrast to Japan, about 30 percent of British and US central government are foreign owned. The extent of foreign ownership of government bonds in the present 'casualty'

Eurozone nations is extremely high – for Greece and Portugal 63%, and for Ireland an astonishing 83%[56]. This casualty situation is shared with the lenders and banks of other countries, which own the casualty nations' risky bonds.

The borrowing requirement table above represents the situation reported for 2010, but the IMF's report published in September 2011 projects very little change right up to 2013. Throughout this period, Germany has the lowest total financing of the G7 nations, and in rising order, the United Kingdom, Canada, France, Italy, the United States, and with the much the highest financing need Japan.

The table shows only the G7 nations. According to more recent IMF statistics, outside the G7, Sweden's total financing need, already a low 10.1% of GDP in 2010, falls to a remarkable 0.5% of GDP in 2013. In that year the nation's projected (Maastricht definition) deficit will be – 1.7%, instead of the + 3% that Maastricht allows, in other words, Sweden will raise in taxes 4.7% of GDP more than it will spend on government services. According to the IMF, Sweden will have to pay 2.2% of GDP out of this 4.7% for maturing debt, which will allow 4.7 – 2.2% = 2.5% for capital spending. As Sweden's financing need will be + 0.5 % of GDP, Sweden will be spending a healthy 3% of GDP on new infrastructure. If all nations did as Sweden does, government bonds would become an extinct species – they'd vanish from the face of the earth – to re-emerge perhaps only to wage wars. But is a world without government bonds possible? – I doubt it.

Ridding ourselves of the weird Maastricht deficit

This discussion of Sweden highlights the absurdity of the Maastricht nomenclature. Just extend this Swedish huge surplus on current spending to business corporations' accounting. With large enough operating surpluses corporations could invest in new plant and equipment without recourse to new bond and share issues. Surely it is time that the strange Maastricht deficit nomenclature was discussed and brought out into the open. To put the matter baldly, why not, in government accounting, stick to the normal everyday definition of not operating at a loss? Government borrowing to build the nation's vital infrastructure is not that naughty, unspeakable thing, deficit spending correctly defined.

That the economists err so spectacularly in this matter is especially strange when one considers that business corporations and the accountants who serve them get the matter right. Have the Maastricht people never read any business corporation's annual presentation of its financial statements? A business corporation's capital assets can be stated as a percentage of its sales revenue, its equivalent of the government's tax revenue. This will vary greatly, some industries require huge capital facilities, others far less. Likewise the size of a nation's infrastructure will vary considerably. A country with a very large area compared to the size of its population (like Canada) will require longer highways and railways, and a mountainous countries like Switzerland or Madeira, more tunnels. The size of the public infrastructure will also depend on a nation's degree of privatization, whether its electricity supply, its railways, its airports, and so on, are publicly or privately owned. Another factor that might affect the size of the infrastructure would be some special vital need, for example total electrification of the economic system to engage seriously in the great Battle of the Climate. To cut carbon emissions by the huge factor needed, a huge programme is required, a great many new nuclear generating stations, high speed electric trains, and new transportation and communications systems must be built. Thus it may be that the advanced nations which will at last engage seriously in the Great Battle of the Climate are entering an era of huge government borrowing and high national debt.

But to the extent that this huge new infrastructure, for example new nuclear generating stations, is paid for and carried out by the private sector, it will not be called 'public infrastructure', it will be owned by business corporations, it will not add to the public debt. This would happen if under government subsidies and tax incentives these corporations were induced to undertake these projects. The infrastructure facilities will now appear as fixed assets on the balance sheets of business corporations, and so part of the nation's new infrastructure will have been financed through new share capital and corporate bonds rather than by government borrowing and adding to the public debt. If however the new infrastructure though built by these same business corporations is done on contract to the government, it will add to the public debt.

One must ask, were – are – the framers of Maastricht unaware of the chalk and cheese difference between current and capital spending, a distinction starkly apparent in every business corporation's annual report? Corporations' financial statements are prepared by chartered accountants, and perhaps accountants were not involved in drafting Maastricht (but if so, why not?). The corporations' operating statements show the year's revenue from sales, from which is subtracted the year's operating cost (including its depreciation allowance – money set aside to replace aging equipment,) to yield an operating profit out of which it pays income tax and dividends to its shareholders, leaving the rest as 'retained earnings'. These retained earnings, plus the depreciation allowance, are supplemented by new share issues and by borrowing, that is, by new *bond debt*, to pay for additions to the company's stock of capital facilities (whose value appears at the top of the asset side of its balance sheet).

If these same accountants prepared the government's accounts, the situation would be identical, except that there is no need to pay income tax, nor to raise new share capital. All the capital spending will be financed through the surplus on current spending, if any, the depreciation allowance, and by *borrowing*, that is, through new government *bond debt*. The accumulated value of this borrowing is the national debt. If over the business cycle, the government has managed to have a zero deficit on current account (the normal meaning of the word 'deficit'), then the national debt will reflect only past capital spending. But if a government has been consistently overspending on current account, then the national debt will be abnormally high and reflect the extent to which the government over the years has borrowed to cover its overspending – the nation might be said to be in hock to itself. 'This dear, dear land . . . is now leased out, like to a tenement or pelting farm'[57].

Maastricht set not only a 3% deficit limit (their definition of deficit), but also a 60% GDP limit to the national debt. This suggests that the Maastricht framers intended their 'deficit' to consist of capital spending, and the 60% public debt to cover only accumulated capital spending. Thus, if a country is well-managed and normally has no current deficit, then its public debt, though growing, will tend not to rise as a percentage of GDP. That is because the government's borrowing is used only to finance capital investment which enables the economy to grow. Consider for example, a 'good' country that has no current deficit, and adheres to the Maastricht rules, 3% and 60%. Say its economy grows 5% annually in nominal terms (2% real growth plus 3% inflation). If in year 1 its GDP is 100 and its debt 60; then in year 2 its GDP will be 105 and its debt 63. The debt has grown by 3% of GDP but remains at 60% of GDP.

The quirky Maastricht rule places an extraordinary straightjacket on government policy, limiting the amount it adds to its capital infrastructure. Thus if a nation is well-managed in the conventional sense and balances its current spending, it can go ahead and spend up to 3% of GDP in adding to its public infrastructure – highways, public buildings, ports, hospitals, airports, parks, and publicly owned railways, power stations, and so on. 3% of GDP spent thus is not an unreasonable amount in some circumstances, that, for example has been Canada's average amount of government investment in recent years, while Britain's has been about 2.2%. As already discussed, there are a number of factors that will determine the ideal amount for any country. That is for a well-managed country which has not overspent on current spending. Other, back-sliding, countries will be punished by having to invest less on infrastructure. If their current deficit is 1%, they are allowed up to 2% of GDP on capital spending, if it is 2%, only 1%, if they have a 3% current deficit, absolutely none on the nation's vital infrastructure. Preposterous!

A nation's needed public capital expenditure is in no way related to the vagaries of its government's current deficit or surplus. This is Alice-in-Wonderland stuff. Latterly British business has been begging the deficit-phobic British government to allow spending on new infrastructure, something which it is finding difficult to do given that its (Maastricht) deficit target is only 1.1% of GDP.

Maastricht and inaccurate GDP statistics

Only lately has it struck me that the faulty Maastricht definition implies that the published national statements of GDP may be quite wrong. Can this be true? GDP can be expressed as the sum of all spending in the economy as follows:

$$GDP = C + G + (Ib + Ig) + (E - M)$$

where C is consumer spending by households, G is government current spending on providing services, Ib is business capital investment, Ig is government capital spending, and (E − M) is net exports. As just discussed, Maastricht's 3% allowable deficit is the result of defining government spending as its *total* spending, not only in providing services, but also on its investment spending. If the nations which use the Maastricht definition of the deficit are consistent, the item Ig will be missing from the official published GDP statements, which will show a G value that may be too high by about 3% of GDP, and a capital investment value too low by the same amount. Whether, in fact, the official national accounts do contain these error, so far I have been unable to determine, so ambiguous have been the statistics that so far I have been able to access.

But one thing is quite, unambiguously true, Canada's official national accounts do not have this extraordinary anomaly. As will be seen later, in Figure 1.1 of Chapter 10, Canadian government capital spending is included as part of total capital spending. Government capital spending is shown as $37.1 billion dollars, or 2.7% of GDP. If instead Canada followed the Maastricht rule, it's reported value of G would be the present amount of $260.0 billion, plus $37.1, to give an inflated G of $297.1, or 14.3% too high.

The Economist regularly reports what it calls every nation's current budget balance, whether it is in deficit or surplus, but what definition of deficit it uses, whether true or 'Maastricht' is not clear. In a recent issue it shows the Canadian deficit as 2.8% of GDP, and those of France and Germany, both in the Eurozone, as 4.7% and 1.5% respectively. The reported Canadian value is probably correct, but France's deficit may really be only about 1.7%, and Germany may actually have a surplus of 2.5 (if the Economist is using the official Maastricht values). Try as I may I am unable to find unambiguous information on these matters. Very clearly, if we are to have credible budget deficit statistics, we must have correct definitions in use, the Maastricht definition must be banished. It is quite extraordinary, especially with the world economy in its present disarray, that this absurd anomaly persists. Recently I revisited Dean Swift's Laputo, where Gulliver was given a grand tour of that Kingdom's scientific wonders, and they were equally amazing.

Two public debts in the place of one

Given the great confusion just described on the public debt, it is surely time that it was understood that there is good public debt and there is bad public debt. And surely it would be a good idea to separate them in the national accounts. These would now show two public debts, the good and the bad. The good debt would be what has been borrowed over the years to build the national infrastructure, buildings, roads, ports, parks, public works in general, parallelling what business borrows and issues shares for, to acquire their stock of buildings, plant and equipment. The other public debt would be what has been borrowed over the years to pay for current services in excess of tax revenue – that is for government's living beyond its means, analogous to the huge personal debt that characterises the present recession. This could be implemented immediately, by first estimating the respective shares of the total debt spent on past infrastructure creation and past current over-spending. After these initial figures, in future years borrowing can be accurately attributed to each of the two categories.

Most interestingly public debt statistics provided by the IMF show, for the twelve years preceding the 2007 recession onset, that while the UK's public debt was at a low 40% of GDP, that of the US, Canada, and the Euro area was much higher, 60 to 70%, and the UK's was still in 2011 the lowest. The low pre-2007 UK figure suggests that the UK's public debt alone among the nations was mainly 'good', that is, infrastructure, debt. I suspect that this owes much to Gordon Brown's stewardship as Chancellor of the Exchequer – I clearly recall his saying that only a 'deficit' incurred for current spending is not justified (yes, he did use the strange Maastricht definition of deficit). All this makes it particularly surprising that the present British government is pursuing its savage austerity policy.

It would surely be a most valuable early step for the would-be Enlightenment nations to enact immediately this enlightened division of their public debts into two parts, infrastructure debt, and over-spending debt. One can be vigilant on the latter. If, for example, the bad debt is 30 percent of GDP, this shows that the nation has been badly improvident for a number of years – or simply that several years of deep recession has reduced tax revenue and increased unemployment benefits – nothing to panic about, it can be attended to once the economy has recovered.

CHAPTER 9

Correcting the
Broadcasting Perversion

I always wonder why what I write about here, what to me seems so obvious, is not widely so viewed in our society. That is why I often ask myself, am I suffering from an *idée fixe*? There is much written on the shopping spree, the consumer society, and of advertising's role, but none, at least that I have encountered, on the oddity, the shear perversity, of organising society's electronic medium of mass communication as part of the marketing function of business corporations. People seem to me to have developed an extraordinary mindset that blocks out reason. (I should qualify this statement, this strange mindset is most acute in North America, far less so in some European countries where there is much less advertising-funded broadcasting).

Right now is not soon enough to rid our society of this obscenity. I've just this moment unearthed a scribbling of mine written twenty years ago: 'Future historians will surely be astonished at how we, especially in North America, organize radio and television. That society's central nervous system should be distorted to serve parts of society to the grievous detriment of the whole will be seen for the obscenity that it is. Fashions in what is 'obscene' change. For Victorians it often related to sex. In Huxley's Brave new World sex is encouraged, the more sex the better, but in a society whose babies are factory-produced in test tubes, a class of school children sniggers at the naughty word 'mother'.

The obscene is that which undermines, or is viewed as undermining, society. The day must soon come when people will suddenly realize that what is now coming over the airwaves is an obscenity, a crime against humanity, and feel such deep revulsion, that they will fast replace it by broadcasting to serve them, and them only. It will at last dawn on them that what is now broadcast over the airwaves is paid for by business as a virtually round-the-clock sales promotion service, to get them to rush to buy whatever they choose to produce. They will realize that instead their broadcasting must become like all their other services, their education, their health care, their entertainment, everything else they need and buy.

Advertising-broadcasting's evils are manifold. The individual viewer is delivered a 'vast wasteland', and a preposterous forty-four[58] minutes of his time is wasted daily on commercial interruptions. The Olympic Games become a multi-million dollar advertising opportunity. Quite clearly advertising-broadcasting's programmes must be defective (except as consumer bait). Consider literature, theatre, the cinema, art, music: the writer and the artist strive to please only two parties, the public which buys his work, and himself, and his own urge to creative self-expression. In literature this has given us our great heritage, Shakespeare, Moliere, Cervantes, Wordsworth – and indeed the Bible, and at the present, everyday level not only our Nobel or Booker Prize novels, but also our marvellous suspense and detective novels, Ruth Rendell, John Le Carre, Henning Mankell, and fortunately many others. And in art we have da Vinci, Rembrandt, Renoir, in music, Beethoven, Mozart. Contrast all this, what is genuine cultural endeavour, with what commercial broadcasting, radio and television do for us. Here the writer must in addition serve a third party, his paymaster, the advertiser, which trumps the normal two. Can one imagine the writer complaining 'but that is corny', and being told 'whadya mean, boy, does it sell my cream pies – or underarm deodorant, sanitary pads, whatever'?

Just how awful is the fare provided by this travesty of a service for people is sharply made clear by viewing the contrary, the excellent programmes broadcast by TV Ontario and the American PBS, public broadcasters partly paid for by viewer donations. These broadcast many excellent programmes, among them many imported from

Britain. Perhaps the latter are good because of the presence of the BBC – even the advertising-supported British channels produce some good programmes because the BBC has educated the public to expect good programmes[59]. Genuine, good broadcasting is a great boon, once, in England I had a seat in the front row on Centre Court at Wimbledon, seven hours daily, without a single advertising interruption for two weeks – except that I was in somebody's living room.

But it is at the level of society that the most grievous harm is done. Me, me values are fostered, advertisers seek to replace citizens with a fuzzy breed of human who is a consumer, the sovereignty of parliaments, national identities, are threatened, consumption takes precedence over saving the environment, and the political process is corrupted, advertising politicians like headache pills. And lurking behind is deceit, hypocrisy, cynicism, and hidden agendas, nothing inimical to profligate consumption will be broadcast. Just how malignant advertising-broadcasting is is shown by this passage from an advertising text book[60]: 'A major mistake . . . is to destroy or seriously impair the emotional elements of the commercial by including too much copy or an appeal to reason . . . Capturing the viewer's interest is by no means an easy task, because as soon as the viewer realizes a television commercial is beginning, his guard goes up and his interest down . . [he] probably has set up defence mechanisms when the commercial interrupts a favourite program' (Observe, the writer of this was not a reformer, telling people how Machiavellian, deceitful, advertising broadcasting is, he was trying to teach students the technique of making commercials).

Some of our present global warming paralysis surely arises because the public's mind is addled by perverted broadcasting dedicated to business goals. How can this nagging backdrop to modern life not help mould people's knowledge, opinions, attitudes and values, hence public policy? Despite the rising use of the internet, and the proliferation of electronic gadgets, television and radio are a seldom-off presence, four or more hours of each daily, the major part of people's leisure time. It is everywhere, even in doctors' and dentists' waiting rooms. In Canada I recently endured root canal work with pop and ads despite my outraged protest. Broadcast advertising played a crucial role in bringing President Obama to power, and the President continues to use television to explain and defend his programme (when the President makes a speech, of course, advertising is suspended, unwittingly underlining what genuine people-serving broadcasting would be like all the time, as the BBC is in its domestic programmes broadcast in England).

'Greed, Gluttony, God, and the American Dream' is the title of a chapter in a book by the Canadian political scientist James Laxer[61] 'Never in the history of the world has there been a society with such a compulsive drive for More. . . . . I can't get over the capacity of Americans to shop, shop and shop some more, to go home and arrange their acquired treasures and then plan the next outing. . . . . Consume Now is the mantra. One way that is evident is in the evolution of the American diet. Americans are eating more and more, and that is creating a serious new health problem for them, the problem of obesity'. Laxer describes visits to restaurants: 'The portions are huge. When my chicken and potato arrived, the chicken was literally hanging off one end of the plate . . . In the mass-fast-food sector . . . the battle for customers has now become combat over quantities served . . . McDonald's has come up with an option called "super-sizing" . . . For an extra 79 cents, an order for a cheeseburger, small fries, and small Coke grows into a cheeseburger, supersize fries . . . and supersize Coke (forty-two ounces instead of sixteen, with free refills').

But Laxer makes an interesting observation. 'One exception is Martha's Vineyard, the island playground of the affluent just off the coast of Massachusetts . . . the slender, fit vacationers I saw there were like no other American crowd. Obesity, it seems, is not an affliction of the rich in America'. And no doubt many of these rich own shares in both the food companies, and the broadcasting networks that incessantly promote their food. This immediately brings to my mind Orwell's '1984'. While the ruling class has a high standard of living, the lower class 'proles' live in poverty, and are kept happy with cheap beer, pornography, and a national lottery. Or perhaps Huxley's 'Brave New World' reflects better the American Dream, with the Alphas at the top with unlimited sex and pills which give soma-holidays of bliss, and Betas and the others performing their allotted inferior functions.

While there is much discussion about the obesity problem, not only in the USA, but also in other Western countries, I have never encountered any suggestion that the intense promotion of junk food in television commercials plays a part. A surprisingly large proportion of the commercials is devoted to promoting junk food. The theme is bliss equals our stuff – in one scene of love ecstasy approaching climax, the girl suddenly disengages to cross the room to gorge on the advertised goody, and her partner immediately joins her in a happy munching duo.

A study I carried out in 1996[62] showed that in Canada as much was spent to make commercials that occupy 20% of viewing time as is spent to make the programmes that take 80% of viewing time. In other words, the commercials are four times more expensive – they are filmed with huge care, and often include celebrity endorsements – the now fallen Tiger Woods received $100 million annually from Nike and other companies.

Earlier, in the preface, I asked whether my long-held views were merely an *idée fixe,* an obsession, or whether instead, they reflected reality. In nothing have my views been more constant than in broadcasting. This is from notes I wrote in 1985:

'Commercial TV & Radio:
The Telecommunications Sociological Obscenity

- Why should TV/Radio services be financed differently from other services, as a "free" adjunct to the sale of advertising? (If we buy any consumer good or service we acquire it directly, as the "object of the deal" made).

- It could be argued that it is vital for modern society to have broadcast advertising, and that the only way to induce people to watch it is to tack on "shows" and "entertainment". But if so, what about other successful Western countries, eg. Switzerland?. What about our own society before commercial TV and Radio? (I have confirmed now, in 2011, that Switzerland still has the least advertising-funded broadcasting among advanced nations, it is one of the most affluent, and has the lowest unemployment. And the Scandinavian nations and the Netherlands also have little advertising-broadcasting and also have high living standards and low unemployment).

- Orwell's 1984: Sales Promotion is for the people "on the wrong side of the tracks" – the masses. (Shoddy products and shoddy entertainment) – Orwell didn't actually mention sales promotion, but it would fit.

- The idea of a society partly built on deceit: Both sales promotion and PR are deceitful: Their aim is not to give the truth' (I should have added 'unless it so happens that telling the truth also helps selling the product advertised).

For the American model of broadcasting I use the term 'advertising-broadcasting' as distinct from plain 'broadcasting', which would be a service for the public, akin to education, health care, highways, national parks, the armed services, and so on, all paid for by the public, either collectively, or through personal expenditure. (I suppose it would be possible for a particularly zealous disapprover of public funding to propose an education system run by and paid for by business corporations that would school the young in the three Rs, and even sciences and other subjects to acquire the training to become their future employees. Perhaps giant corporations would each have their schools, and the parents of little girls and boys would decide whether they will go to GM School, or Walmart School, or Kraft Foods School. Each school might have its own school uniforms, with the appropriate logos).

The extent to which people tend to believe that advertising-broadcasting is normal and reasonable, and as fixed as the laws of the Medes and the Persians, is illustrated by a recent complaint by a Canadian politician about the government grant to the Canadian Broadcasting Corporation which gives it an unfair advantage over competing broadcasters who are not similarly subsidised. The CBC oddly supplements its government funding by the same share of advertising as the 'commercial' broadcasters, and if one assumes that the true purpose of broadcasting is advertising, then it is quite logical to view the CBC as unfairly subsidised.

Some history

Our splendid free market system is always developing brilliant new products to sell to consumers, for example the new gadgets that in the last few years have resulted in the much talked of 'social media'. Turn back the clock to the 1920s when new radio technology made it possible to broadcast to the public. There are a number of ways a new industry might have developed. One civilised way would have been that companies could have seen a wonderful opportunity to sell a new service to the public, news and entertainment which people could buy without budging from their living rooms. That would have been the start of pay radio broadcasting Alternatively, or in addition, a new public broadcaster could have been formed which people could pay for through their taxes. The latter was the method used in Britain, when the BBC was formed – a new service for the people, provided publicly, and paid for by a license fee levied on houses with radio receivers.

But pay broadcasting was not the route followed in the United States. There the advertising industry and marketing arms of business corporations saw, instead of pay broadcasting, a wonderful opportunity for a new advertising medium, and to make this idea attractive to the public, who would have to buy themselves a new product, a radio, to receive the advertisements in their homes, the advertisers added the inducement of accompanying their advertisements with 'free' news and entertainment programmes – not really free of course, because the advertisers would have to raise the price of the goods they were advertising to cover the added cost. And that is the explanation for the existence of the 'American model of broadcasting' – in the United States, what business wants, it often gets. This then is the origin of that extraordinary animal, now increasingly dominant world-wide, advertising-broadcasting, the hand-maiden of the sales promotion and advertising industry.

Even in the United States the advertising-funded route was not adopted without argument, President-to-be Herbert Hoover, then Secretary of Commerce, said that it was `inconceivable' to allow 'so great a possibility of service... to be drowned in advertising chatter'[63]. The fact that Hoover was a Republican suggests that opposition to advertising-broadcasting is no left wing notion, it is plain common sense. And it was soon quite evident that Hoover was right, how badly the public was served. The extraordinary American mindset is revealed by the 'vast wasteland' scolding given to the broadcasting industry, nearly fifty years ago by the Chairman of the Federal Communications Commission:[64]

> 'Your license lets you use the public's airwaves as trustees for 180 million Americans. If you want to stay on as trustees, you must deliver a decent return to the public – not only your stockholders. Instead, you are delivering a vast wasteland'.

But how could he expect otherwise, putting the fox in charge of the hen house and then scolding him for eating the chickens? The American broadcasting industry is paid huge sums, 130 billion dollars in 2008, to promote consumer products, and any service to the public is incidental. For the 2009 Super Bowl, advertising was sold for $3 million for 30 seconds of air time, and the Budweiser beer company alone bought $30 million for just five minutes of advertising time. Does anyone think Budweiser paid that amount altruistically in order to provide the public with good television, and not to sell more beer?. And as for reducing carbon emissions, just imagine this twisted message: "Buy! buy! our SUV, and save our climate!". Such are the motivations driving American broadcasting. And bear in mind that the economists, our doctors of the economy, have never, as far as I know, railed against the absurdity of this American-model broadcasting. The dysfunctionality of our present discipline called 'economics' is the subject of Chapter 12 below. Economics should be tied to the Social Contract that should be the governing principle of the economy, and which the broadcasting system so obviously breaches.

The national accounts and the Social Contract

The national accounts from which GDP is calculated implicitly reflect the Social Contract, our lodestar in launching the New Enlightenment. As already discussed, each country's national accounts are organised to reflect the fact that the economy's proper purpose is to serve the people:

$$\text{Gross Domestic Product, GDP} = C + G + I$$

where C is what people spend on consumer goods and services, G is what people spend collectively on government services, and I is what industry and government must spend on capital facilities in order to produce both sets of goods and services for the people [65] (for simplicity I have omitted net external trade E (exports) less M (imports)). C, G, and I are referred to as *final economic goods*. But the companies and government departments that produce these final goods must purchase the materials, equipment, and services they need from another set of corporations, the producers of *intermediate economic goods* (though this inter-company trade is vast, it only appears in GDP as part of the costs of the producers of final goods). Commercial broadcasting, what I have called 'advertising-broadcasting,' is one of these intermediate goods, an advertising service purchased by business corporations from advertising agencies and advertising-funded broadcasting stations and is identified as such in the national accounts. According to their official national accounts, nations which use advertising-broadcasting (nearly all broadcasting in the United States) do not give their citizens a broadcasting service at all – they are exposed to a *form* of broadcasting, but as the advertising target, not as the customer who selects and pays for it, via pay-broadcasting or public service broadcasting like the BBC. More than half all advertising in the world is American, and nearly half of that is over the airwaves [66], mainly[67] commercials with so-called programmes attached to serve as consumer bait.

In Canada there is a great pretence that the Canadian Broadcasting Corporation's Television service is a genuine public broadcaster, serving Canadians, and Canada. Certainly it is paid for largely out of taxes, only about 40% by advertising. But if it barks like a dog, looks like a dog, acts like a dog, then that is what it is: It has the same 20% of air time for irrelevant commercial interruptions as the private broadcasters, wasting the viewer's time, and robbing the programs of dignity, desecrating them, and trivialising the business of the nation.

As the report of the Juneau Commission justly stated, the CBC is no more than a highly subsidised commercial broadcaster. And what a subsidy!. Normally subsidies are a relatively small amount from government to help ailing companies, or as a public policy measure to encourage certain types of production – for example 'green' energy and nuclear power may be subsidized in order to reduce carbon emissions. But in the case of the CBC the subsidy is the major source of revenue. This absurdity can only come from a lopsided mind set, and nowhere is this more evident than in the CBC annual financial statement, which has the same form as that of private commercial broadcasters whose revenue comes from advertising. The following is the statement of 1998:

Revenue (from advertising)	$ 525 million
Less Expense	1281
Operating Loss	756
Parliamentary Appropriation	760
Surplus	4

The government grant is seen as offsetting the loss, an incredibly large subsidy for any company. A mind-set suitable for a public broadcaster would arrange these same figures thus:

Revenue (grant from Parliament)	$ 760 million
Less Expense	1281
Operating Loss	521
Supplementary Advertising Revenue	525
Surplus	4

The meaning of 'commercial'

According to the dictionary, 'commerce' is 'the activity of buying and selling, especially on a large scale', and its adjective 'commercial' means 'making or intending to make a profit' – or metaphorically, 'having profit rather than artistic or other value as a primary aim'[68].

Advertising-funded broadcasting is often called 'commercial broadcasting', but the buyer here is the business corporations paying for advertising time, and the seller the broadcasting company which provides it – and often very dearly, as already noted for the Super Bowl. In this type of commerce the public isn't the buyer, the public is the advertising target.

But an entirely different type of commercial broadcasting would be one where the public was the buyer, there would be no advertising, the term 'commercial broadcasting' would refer to what is now called 'pay' or 'pay-to-view' broadcasting. Once what is now called 'commercial broadcasting' is banished in the New Enlightenment, another large scale commerce would come into being – billions of dollars paid by the public to receive their favourite television and radio programmes. For those who anxiously await the recovery of our society from its present degradation, the day that commercial broadcasting acquires its entirely new meaning will be a day of celebration.

A new development

A recent development I have noticed is the emergence in North America of 'infomercials'. Some American networks now broadcast these, all advertising without intervening programmes at all – the advertisers believe that they can dispense with the added cost of consumer-bait programmes. One I have seen was odious, I stuck it out for twenty minutes, concentrated high pressure instant selling, the purveying company's phone number on the screen. It reeked of deceit, 'experts', doctor with stethoscope round his neck, backed up by an earnest nutritionist, prostituting themselves, (or perhaps they were actors playing a part, no doubt well-paid), explaining to the assembled audience of eager, earnest, overweight, seekers after health and a cure for their obesity, how, if they bought *this* fresh fruit and vegetable juicer-cum-blender they would lose vast amounts of weight and become healthy and beautiful. And all this for – wait for it – one quarter of the price of other blender-juicers!. To me this appeared as the apotheosis of the American Dream/Nightmare – the shopaholic, easy credit, shop-till-you drop nirvana.

An interesting thought: If advertisers believed that infomercials, that is advertising, plus an array of hired fake experts and audience, were generally more successful than advertising plus the present consumer-bait programmes, at promoting their products, would not what I have called the American model of broadcasting, that is, perverted broadcasting, just disappear and sink without trace? Whether that is true we shall have to wait and see. But Budweiser's huge outlay for the World Series suggests that it will need a lot of convincing before it replaces the Word Series with an infomercial, non-stop expert explanation of what marvellous things Bud does for you, things that no other beer can possibly do. But set against this view, I observe that CBS may run three hours of infomercials without consumer-bait programmes, and would not do that if did not yield them high advertising revenue.

What is however very clear indeed, CBS and other US broadcasters are *advertising* companies first, and a *broadcasting service* for the public and society only secondarily, and therefore imperfectly – one cannot say often enough, what an extraordinary method the United States has adopted to provide its citizens with a broadcasting service – in America, what business wants, business gets. And there is nothing left wing, or 'socialistic' about saying that, it is plain, conservative. common sense and plain speaking – a splendid, dynamic, great nation, but one unfortunately hobbled by a hideous, deceitful, broadcasting system, and a strange interpretation of the Social Contract.

But at least there is a positive side to infomercials, they are pure advertising, they don't depend on consumer-bait programmes, they are not the 'broadcasting-perversion' that I have been railing against. If these informercials are a perversion, they are a lesser perversion, and one can imagine them being reformed to become a civilized shopping service, scheduling by product category, cars, wrist watches, blenders, life insurance policies – people wanting to buy a new car could watch the appropriate infomercial and listen to the rival sales pitches of different companies. Perhaps there would be a master of ceremonies, maintaining order and minimizing absurd claims – 'do you *really* mean that?' This of course will never come about without public intervention, discussed later.

Why correcting the broadcasting perversion is particularly important

No intelligent defence of advertising-broadcasting has ever been offered. It is there, *ergo* it must be there. But the truth is that this is the very symbol of our society's breach of the Social Contract, of its misgovernment that has failed to harness our brilliant corporations to serve the public good instead of profligate consumption. One of the consequences has been to hinder Western nations, but most particularly that great engine of growth, the United States, from emerging from the present Great Recession. I can not be repeated often enough, it helped to create a giant buying bubble of often inessential consumer goods, which, when people panic, they stop buying, throwing millions out of work. Shopping mania and easy credit are obvious partners – shopping facilitated by easy credit, easy credit spurred by the huge demands for it, stirred up by frenetic, ubiquitous advertising. The present crash was a disaster waiting to happen, the old sick way was unsustainable.

And despite the continuing intensity of broadcast advertising, the economy has difficulty restarting, people no doubt have realized that they can well survive without endless shopping, especially with their high debt. Even with the help of Facebook, the hugely popular social network, to add further advertising, the US economy continues to stagger. Facebook's revenue comes from selling Facebook users' personal profiles to advertisers who can then target their advertising according to each individual's characteristics. Perhaps Facebook too should be viewed as a social obscenity, here we have a vast population of Facebook users, 850 million people worldwide (as of early 2012), and exposed to targeted advertising – but there is one important difference from advertising-broadcasting, users can ignore the advertising at the sides of the screen. But perhaps Facebook is just one more symptom of a society that is very ill. The American social commentator, Chris Hedges, already quoted earlier, writes in his 'Empire of Illusion'[69].

'America, the country of my birth, that formed and shaped me, the country of my father, my father's father, and his father's father, stretching back to the generations of my family that were here for the country's founding, is so diminished as to be unrecognizable . . . . The words *consent of the governed* have become an empty phrase . . . Our nation has been hijacked by oligarchs, corporations, and a narrow selfish, political and economic elite, that governs, and often steals, on behalf of moneyed interests . . . . The government, stripped of any real sovereignty, provides little more than technical expertise for elites and corporations that lack moral restraints and a concept of the common good. America has become a facade. It has become the greatest illusion in a culture of illusion'.

If as Hedges believes America has become an 'empire of illusion' surely the perverted broadcasting system has played a part. Illusion, that is what the barrage of commercials is about, leaping, disconnected, absurd, deceitful, images discombobulating the mind, selling a revolting paradise of acquisition of stuff. It is not unlikely that Hedges may have a particularly jaded view of his society, there certainly remains much that is admirable and enlightened in America, indeed the existence of the progressive website 'Truthdig', to which Hedges contributes a weekly article. Also freedom of expression remains in the United States. But even if Hedges is only half right, nonetheless a great correction, a new beginning is called for in this great nation whose ways have so much influenced the rest of the West.

It is urgent to reform advertising- broadcasting not only because of its hideous qualities just described, but also as a signal, an opening shot in the rebalancing of the economic system to serve the people[70]. It will be the long-overdue correction of the tragic public policy error in the United States, at the dawn of broadcasting, which assigned what was to become the main means of public mass communication to the business corporations. And this will be a *ringing* opening shot, for example, in Canada, if the first step in normalising broadcasting will be to remove the CBC's advertising, people will notice the sudden absence from their so-called public broadcaster of the interruptions now filling 20% of airtime, and they will be told that these will progressively disappear throughout all Canadian broadcasting.

Some words on advertising

People may assume that I am attacking advertising in general, not just broadcast advertising. Absolutely not so. The modern economy needs a great deal of advertising, but it is just that a country's broadcasting system is an inappropriate place to put it. There are other such inappropriate advertising places – even in the homeland of advertising-broadcasting such limits exist, billboards may not be permitted to desecrate the scenery along highways, nor is advertising permitted on Washington's public buildings.

Broadcast advertising is unique, it must interrupt the programme. In contrast in the print media there are no such interruptions, one may be scarcely aware of the advertising, the article one is reading is 'continued on page 23'. That is a huge difference – this is not to say that in some magazines nowadays it may be difficult to find page 23 among pages of advertising. There are no tricks that the advertising industry will not get up to, 'pop-ups' often totally block out what one is reading on some websites. The absurdity of financing broadcasting through advertising was especially obvious in Canada at the depth of the recession when broadcasting stations had difficulty surviving their loss of advertising revenue. Does this not underline the irrationality of providing a crucial public service as an adjunct to the advertising industry?

The present huge tilt to business power is especially pronounced in North America, but it is also evident in Britain. The late Anthony Sampson wrote 'The Anatomy of Britain' in 1962, and updated it over the years. His last edition written in 2004 he named 'Who Runs this Place? The Anatomy of Britain in the 21st Century'. There had been a huge transformation, the power of business corporations and financial institutions was greatly magnified, that of Parliament shrunk. Even so, there are still large differences one notices in Britain, one in particular being the BBC's domestic services, not only radio but also television, which remain free of advertising. Another sign is the absence of bill boards and prominent outdoors advertising – and that makes a big visual difference.

The only possible challenge to my argument

Surely the only possible serious objection to converting the broadcasting system into a normal service for people, is that in its present form as an advertising vehicle it is essential for the functioning of the economy and to keep it fully employed[71]. Given this necessity these defenders of the status quo must then go on to explain that regrettably the people must be hoodwinked into believing that the broadcasting system serves them. Hence schedules are published in newspapers and by the cable companies, setting out the forthcoming programmes (but not mentioning the 'commercial breaks' between them). Likewise the critics review the programmes without mentioning the commercial interruptions. And the bluff works so well that the public is willing to pay for its television sets and radios and cable subscriptions, though arguably the business corporations should pay for these television sets – they pay for everything else, the broadcasting stations, the commercials, and the programmes designed as consumer bait, between the commercials. Even so, the notion lingers, that commercials are not quite nice. The presenter uses euphemisms, 'this programme will continue after these messages' or even more circumspectly, 'after this' (everybody has to go to the bathroom, we just don't talk about it). And underlining that commercials aren't very nice, the American television networks suspended them for three days after the 9/11 attack – no poo, sorry, no commercials, came over the air.

In rebuttal of the notion that broadcasting with advertising is essential for the economy, Switzerland which has one of the world's most successful economies, without a hint of recession, has little broadcast advertising, but relies on other advertising media. In only slightly less degree the same can be said of the highly successful Scandinavian nations. Besides, it should be evident in itself: it is an outrageous notion that society's major means of mass communication should be a sales promotion service rather than a normal service for the public.

The Structure of Future People-Serving Broadcasting

A future good broadcasting system might have three components:

1. Genuine public broadcasting, free of commercials.

2. Genuine pay broadcasting, also without advertising.

3. A separate new consumer information system.

The public broadcaster will be modern society's equivalent of the ancient Roman forum, where the public's business is discussed, people are virtually present at parliamentary debates, at summit conferences, witnessing state occasions, watching history being made. On the public broadcaster, all segments of society could argue their case, and their views on public policy, and so could business representatives. And the public broadcaster could also have heritage programmes, acquainting people with man's long struggle which bequeathed us Shakespeare, Leonardo, Beethoven, the sciences, free democratic government and the rights of man. But business could no longer use it for touting its products.

The pay-to-view component of broadcasting would provide sporting events, concerts, theatre, comedy series, movies, educational programmes, history programmes, whatever people like to see without budging from their own living rooms. Sports would no longer be perverted, prostituted, as a sales medium for peddling sporting goods, automobiles, Rolex watches, and for awarding sports stars' stratospheric incomes beyond avarice.

The third component, the new consumer information service, might have two parts, one paid for by corporations parading their products – a reformed version of the present infomercials – the other by people seeking product information, perhaps in the 'enquiry-mode', or consulting broadcast equivalents to the 'Consumer Reports' periodical.

Implementation

Funding broadcasting through advertising is so ingrained in people's minds as normal, and there are so many vested interests in the present system, that change will require the most determined action. There may even be some temporary dislocation of the economy. Heads of government must first explain to the public why the change is vital. So much can be said, and briefly, about how perverted and irrational advertising-broadcasting is. Implementation can then come about in three ways: by exhortation, by relying on the free market, or by edict.

Relying on exhortation will require that the government first arrange for alternative broadcasting to which people may transfer their allegiance. Pay-broadcasting services must be launched, for example, by subsidizing advertising-funded broadcasters willing to convert, which many might perhaps do, suffering from falling advertising revenues in the current recession. Experience in Britain shows that people willingly subscribe to pay television. The falling advertising revenue of BskyB, the British satellite TV broadcaster, has been offset by strong growth in its subscription pay TV service. BskyB's annual subscription revenue, at about nine billion US dollars now far exceeds the BBC's revenue of $ 5 billion which comes from a householder's license fee. Surprisingly, BskyB householders are not deterred by the large annual fee of about $800. And BskyB's profitability was surely made clear in the great hacking scandal and the failed bid of its parent corporation, Rupert Murdoch's Fox, to become BskyB's sole shareholder. The future of broadcasting has been in some ferment in Britain with vigorous public debate, and perhaps conversion away from advertising-broadcasting may be easier than one might suppose. There appears to be no such fluid situation in North America yet.

But exhortation may be too slow for ridding ourselves of pestilential advertising-television. Another method that doesn't *compel* people to switch would use the free market but transfer the role of customer from the advertiser to the public. People preferring advertising-television (and many people may now be addicted to the commercials, often perhaps more appealing than the wasteland between) would now have to pay for it *directly*, as they do for everything else they want, and they would find it very expensive, as already observed[72], as much is spent on making the commercials, which use 20% of air time, as on making the programmes that take 80%. A practical way of transferring the cost to the public can readily be devised. For example people who elect not to receive advertising-broadcasting might have their radios and TV inactivated for the receipt of advertising-funded stations, qualifying them for a large income tax credit. Another way might be to make advertising-broadcasting a form of pay-broadcasting, the payments being made to the government, who might use them for public broadcasting. At the same time the public will be lured away by the new superior broadcasting service available, which would surely soon become the 'in' thing. Advertising-broadcasting would surely not take long to disappear.

The third way of broadcasting reform, implementing by edict, is certainly defensible, and also sure. While the modern economy needs a great deal of advertising, there must remain advertising no-go areas as discussed earlier. Why should not the airwaves be a no-go area for unsolicited broadcast advertising interrupting programmes as deeply perverting society? It is not unusual for nations to prohibit what is considered as undermining health, decency, and the public interest, for example, the US's 'War on Drugs', or for that matter the prohibition of many things the public thinks are disgusting: there is a need for the public to begin to realize just how disgusting the broadcasting perversion is.

As each day goes by, the more convinced I am that advertising-broadcasting must go. Nothing more symbolizes the contravention of the Social Contract than placing the broadcasting system at the service of the business corporations to peddle their wares. As I have already noted, no good argument in favour of advertising-broadcasting has ever been produced.

Society's main means of public mass communication must become a no-go area for advertising. People must pay for all their broadcasting just as they do for all their other great services. The American model is a tragic anomaly that must without delay be corrected.

What BBC World Television News should immediately do

The BBC World Television news service is seen in more households world-wide than any other broadcaster, and it is a brilliant broadcaster not only of news but other programmes of interest. Unfortunately, since its Thatcherite 'rebranding' as a commercial broadcaster it now carries advertising (though not as frequent or tasteless as other broadcasters).

Few measures would be a better opening shot for a world-wide decontamination of broadcasting than a new BBC World rebranding as its former, and still deep-down, self. Imagine in America, the home of advertising-television, how this BBC change might be explained in full page statements in America's leading newspapers. It would be explained to the American public that the BBC is bringing its overseas television broadcasting into line with its domestic broadcasting, and its World Service radio broadcasting. As a result BBC TV will no longer be an advertising vehicle for business corporations, but will now be solely a service for the people, and for its large world audience. Americans have a strong idealist streak and perhaps many high-minded Americans would take up the cry: The Airwaves for the People – get those nauseating, insincere, lying commercials off our screens!

The Broader Principle

Ridding society of the broadcasting perversion is only one, if the most important, instance of our society's neglect of the distinction between final economic goods and intermediate economic goods, which was discussed earlier. To repeat: the former are paid for by, and serve, the public, and the latter are paid for by business corporations, the materials and services which they must have and buy from other corporations, including their advertising and public relations services.

These two forms in a good society must remain distinct and separate, a good must be either a final people-serving-good, that is a consumer good, or it must be an intermediate good serving business, and ne'er the twain shall meet. The broadcasting system's aim must be service to the public. Charitable giving must be aid directly given by people to their fellows who are suffering hard times – faith, hope, and charity, and the greatest of these is charity, so spake Jesus. Spectator sports must be solely for the pleasure or reward of us the people, it must be directly paid for by ourselves, not paid for by the advertiser. Yet, especially in North America, these vital services have been hi-jacked for sales promotion and public relations purposes by the corporations. This makes them unclean things, lacking in decency and sincerity. This is at the heart of, the propagator of, the consumer society, of shopping mania.

Advertising will use, and appropriate anything it is permitted to get its hands on, and you can't blame this on the business corporations, it is for us, the people, to decide what are permissible advertising media. The social media are now prominent in many peoples' lives. Not surprisingly, there is a very long article on Facebook in Wikipedia – one in seven people are chatting with each other on it. But in this long article one finds only a single sentence on where its revenue comes from: from business corporations, not from it's billion users – they merely have to provide their 'profile' and the Facebook corporation then analyses these profiles, and then sells information to advertisers who can then target advertising to each user's tastes. But this fact is barely touched on in the article, so normal and proper it is considered to be to use advertising to provide a 'free' service to the world, which of course is not really free. The corporations recoup the money they pay to Facebook (Facebook's revenue in 2011 was $3.1 billion) by raising the price of the consumer goods they sell. So it is we, the public, who have to pay, and not fairly, but everybody, not only Facebook users. What a lopsided way of arranging things in a society. It is not only Facebook, but also the others, Twitter, MySpace, LinkedIn, all rely on advertising: this from an article[73] I have just found on the web: 'Apps, programs, networks appear to be free, since you don't actually pay to use them. But it seems as if everything that's "free" in the online world comes with a catch. It's called advertising'.

Of course, in the no longer lopsided world of the New Enlightenment, instead of services for the public being an appendage to the advertising industry, people will have to pay for them, just as they pay for their groceries or to go to a cinema, or to make a phone call. Thus instead of Facebook's $3.1 billion revenue coming from advertisers it would now come from it's billion users, or $3.10 per user – not an exorbitant price for something that so many people now seem to like very much. Just a thought: Say the US government ordered Facebook to replace its present source of revenue by selling it to each of its users for $3.10 a year, would most of its present users immediately subscribe? True, they would no longer have ads to read on their screens, but one gathers most people are more interested in chatting with their Facebook friends than looking at the ads.

What the New Enlightenment will do is to put the lopsided world the right way up.

CHAPTER 10

Transforming our
Public Finance System

Not only must we re-balance our society so that the people are in charge, we must also deal with another great flaw in its governance, how we extract funds out of the economy for public purposes, politicians promising to reduce taxes when a world in crisis needs much public spending. Not only is the present method dysfunctional, it is our annual pain in the neck – nothing is inevitable but death and taxes. Well that can be changed, leaving only death to face. We can replace the income tax by a more effective, fairer, and more democratic system, one that was foreshadowed by items (viii) and (ix) of my 1969 diagnosis, discussed in Chapter 4, a way of 'bleeding public funds out of the productive processes'. Below I discuss a new approach which I suggest should be called the 'Return to Society'.

Consider how fair the personal income tax really is. It is called 'progressive', because higher income people are taxed at a higher rate, but how progressive is it really? Surely what the free job market tends to determine is *net* incomes, *after* income tax, and the progressive income tax simply pushes up *gross* salaries. Limiting this one might expect corporate management to resist having to pay these higher gross salaries, but it seems not, as their own scandalous incomes now in the spotlight show. As my diagnosis of 1969 shows, my notion of the failings of 'progressive' income tax is of long standing.

The income tax started in Britain on a graduated scale of 0.8% up to 10% of people's income, to pay for waging the Napoleonic wars, and later in the US similarly to pay for the Civil War. There it was not progressive, everybody whose income exceeded a certain amount paid the same percent, and though in recent years it has been progressive, it has been much noted that Americans appear to mind large income inequalities less than other nations. In its origins the income tax was a reasonable idea, pass the hat around so that everybody can chip in and support the cause. But now the income tax is very much not a good idea, for two reasons. First, as has already been discussed, its progressivity is a farce, and does not address income inequality, and also that it is a poor basis for deciding, especially in these tumultuous times, what proportion of the economy's output should be assigned to personal spending (some of it on useless fripperies that add little to the quality of life), and what proportion for public purposes, a proportion that now needs to grow to meet the challenges of our times. No, a far more reasonable, as well as more democratic, way is to settle in parliament, X% of the national income will be spent on personal spending, and Y% on public spending, and on the great projects needed to make a better society, and to save the climate. Thus the new 'Return to the Third Factor of Society' is needed in our times. And one thing the decent society demands is that no one any longer should live in abject poverty, as so many now do in the 'affluent society'. Adequate money must be transferred to them. It does not matter that one small section of society may be spongers, malingerers, or mentally challenged, mostly they are an unhappy lot. Let them be, and let them eat. America is very religious but it seems to ignore what Christ said: 'Faith, hope, and charity, and of these the greatest is charity'.

Our taxation system could be totally replaced by recognising a new third factor of production, 'Society'. It is not only the two traditional factors, Capital and Labour that make production possible, but also the parent society, its institutions, its education system, its store of knowledge built up over many years, its stability and health, its people. These are the ultimate source of all production. Society, not only capital and labour, should be remunerated. Every single economic activity, in both the private and public sectors, would now pay the same percentage return to society, the remaining part being divided between labour and capital, depending on the activity's labour intensity. In Canada, for example, as a proportion of total government revenue, income taxes provide about 52%, people's health and welfare contributions 9%, and the goods and services tax 17%, together 78 percent of all government revenue, or 22.5% of GDP. These would now disappear, and be replaced by the Return to Society set at 22.5%. (The goods and services tax is essentially an extension of the 'value added tax' which is a prominent feature of European taxation).

In this new regime indirect 'sin' taxes, whether on cigarettes and alcohol, or on gasoline and gas-guzzling vehicles – yes, it will be sinful to drive a gas guzzler when the world is trying to prevent catastrophic climate change – would continue be levied as now from the companies involved. And for the various personal income tax credits now allowed, for dependent spouses and children, health care and charitable donations, a separate system could readily be devised, resulting in automatic payments by the government to the public. Subsidies, the reverse of indirect taxes, might be used to foster economic effort that supports the new climate change goals, for example building nuclear generating stations.

For the individual, farewell the drudgery of the annual tax return, one's gross salary is also one's net salary – what you get you keep. And no longer the tedious campaign promises to lower taxes, the public debate would now be what share of the national income needs to be used for public purposes, including ensuring for the first time in history that no one lives in penury, and to arrest climate change. If it is decided once and for all to eliminate poverty, the appropriate funds would be transferred to all poor citizens, and this would be enabled simply by raising the return to society from its present 21% to, say, 24%, gradually over a period of say five years. Also now there would be the funds to pay for our cultural institutions without resorting to the absurdity of 'corporate social responsibility'.

A demonstration of the 'the Return to Society'

It is all very well to talk in broad-brush strokes of dispensing with the income tax, but is it practicable? To be sure that taxes could be made to disappear, I drew macro-economic flow diagrams using Canada's national accounts, and found that indeed this is possible, though quite an adjustment is involved, requiring it to implemented gradually over, say, five years.

The study's aim was to learn how the economy's financial flows would be changed as a result of replacing income taxes and various personal taxes by the new Return to the factor of production Society. Using Canada's national income and expenditure accounts for the year 2005, macro-economic flow diagrams were constructed for two cases, the present situation, and the equivalent situation using the R to S (Figures 1.1 and 1.2 below[74]). I have included these diagrams here to demonstrate that far from being incomprehensible to the layman, the national accounts are easy to understand (if presented in this way), thereby clarifying the discussion of the important economic issues of our times.

The diagrams show the economy divided into three major sectors, 'Households' (We the People), whom the economy is supposed to serve, and two production sectors, 'Government Production' and 'Business Production'. Together these produce the 'gross domestic product' (GDP) which 'Households' want and pay for. Each of the two production sectors has two components, 'Production', that actually makes things and provides services, and 'Capital', which accumulates the stock of plant and equipment, which, allied with labour (provided by households in their role as workers) makes production possible. There is, in addition, another entity (abstracted from the Government Production sector for present expository purposes), the 'Government Transfer Function,' which receives taxes and redirects the money, on the one hand to pay for government services, and on the other hand, to redistribute money to households - unemployment, old age security, health care, pension payments, and other benefits (the 'social safety net').

GDP can be shown two ways, as the sum of all spending, on household consumption, C, on government services, G, on capital investment by both business and government, I, and net exports, M (exports less imports). It can also be shown as the sum of all income earned in producing it, wages and salaries paid to labour (L), and capital payments, (K), the sum of profits, interest payments, and depreciation

Figure 1.1: Canadian National Accounts 2005 ($ billions)
The Present Situation

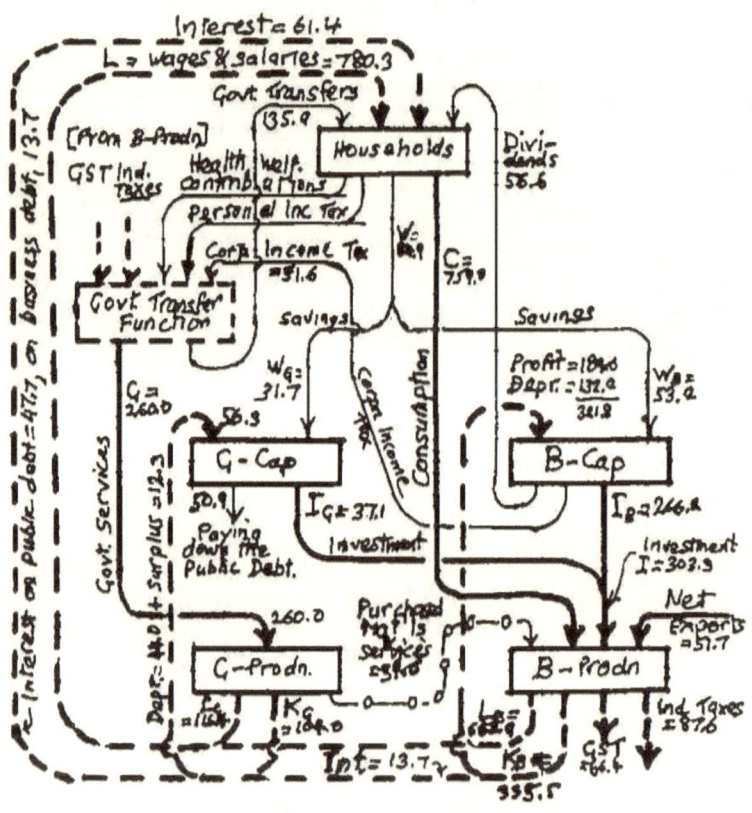

GDP Expenditure-based		GDP Income-based		Flow Categories
$ billions	%	$ billions	%	GDP Expand →
C = 759.0	55.2	L = 780.3	56.8	GDP Income ⇒
G = 260.0	18.9	K = 439.5	32.0	Transfer payments
I = 303.3	22.1	Ind. Taxes = 87.6	6.4	Intermediate purchase of
E = 51.5	8.8	GST = 66.4	4.8	materials & services
GDP = 1373.8	100%	GDP = 1373.8	100%	

**Figure 1.2: Canadian National Accounts 2005 ($ billions)
Replacing the Income Tax by the Return to Society, 'S'**

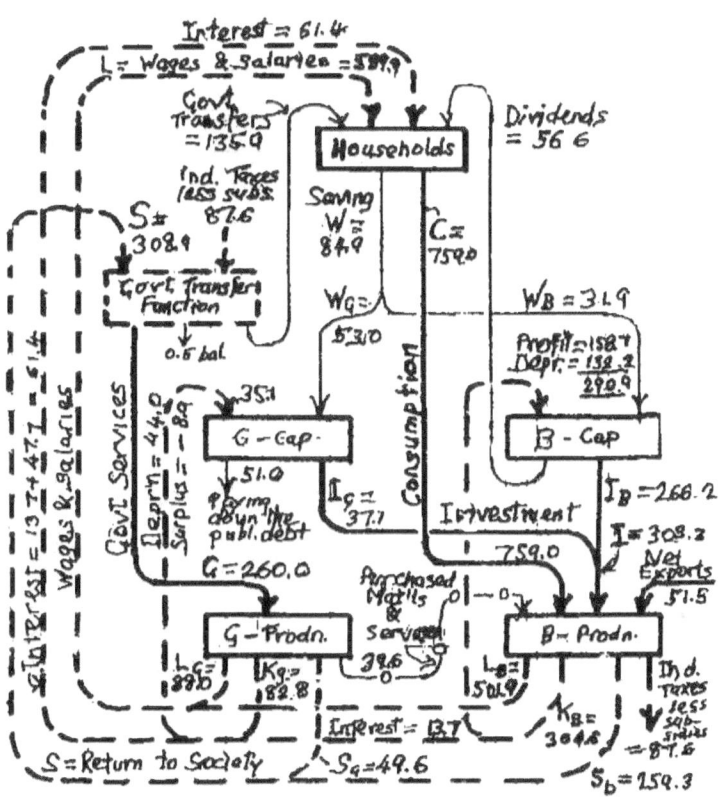

GDP Expenditure-based		GDP Income-based		Flow Categories
$ billions	%	$ billions	%	GDP Expend.
C = 759.0	55.2	L = 590.0	42.9	GDP Income
G = 260.0	18.9	K = 387.3	28.2	Transfer payments
I = 303.3	22.1	S = 308.9	22.5	Intermediate purchases of
E = 51.5	3.8	Net Ind. Taxes = 87.6	6.4	goods & materials
GDP = 1373.8	100%	GDP = 1373.8	100%	

allowances - money set aside to replace old capital assets, and also payments to government, indirect taxes and the goods and services tax, GST (similar to other nations' value added tax). In the two diagrams, the heavy solid flow lines are the GDP spending items, and the heavy dotted flows are the GDP income items. The tables show that in the year 2005 GDP was 1373.8 billion dollars both expenditure-based and income-based.

Two other types of flow are also shown on the diagrams, money transfers between sectors, represented by light flow lines, and intermediate payments, purchases of materials and services by producing components from each other, that is by government from the business sector, and also by business corporations from each other, not shown in this highly aggregated model. (The American model of broadcasting discussed in the last chapter is one of these intermediate payments, an advertising service bought by consumer goods producers from broadcasting stations and advertising agencies – it is not a consumer service, it is not a part of C).

The present and the future

Figure 1.1 shows the present situation represented by the national accounts, and Figure 1.2 represents what the effect is of replacing all present taxes on household and business (except for the indirect or 'sin' taxes), by the new Return to Society, 'S'. As can be seen, households will no longer be required to make any payments to government, and the only payments by business to government will be 'S' and the indirect taxes. The sum of all the discontinued taxes, 22.5% of GDP, will be the size of 'S' that replaces them.

Thus Figure 1.2 shows the Government Transfer function as receiving only two items, indirect taxes and 'S'. The total amount received will be the same as now, on Figure 1.1. $ 395.9 billion, or 28.8 percent of GDP.

Under the new regime, the total of wages and salaries, L, is reduced, as no longer need personal income tax and health and welfare contributions be paid ('what you earn you keep'). Similarly corporation profit is reduced as a result of the disappearance of the corporation income tax.

The Return to Society is 22.5 percent of the *value added* of every economic activity of the economy, in both the private and public sectors. The value added of any economic activity, for any period, is its revenue (whether from sales or from public funds), less the total amount it purchases from other activities. The aggregate of the value adds of all the individual activities in the economy equals GDP. Thus, in addition to the two ways of breaking down GDP already discussed, by expenditure and by income, there is a third way, by value added. It's value added is the true size of every activity in the economy. The Return to Society may be viewed as a rationalisation and extension of the European Value Added Tax.

There will of course be many details of the new regime that will require fine tuning in the light of experience. For example, now new firms starting up may expect to run at a loss for several years until successfully established, and therefore during this period do not have the burden of corporation income tax. The equivalent under the new regime might be to excuse these firms from paying the Return to Society at start-up, and allow them to increase it gradually to the general level over, say, five years.

How would that age-old curse of poverty be banished under the new regime? The diagrams show that government now transfers $135.9 billion annually to persons (unemployment and welfare benefits, old age pensions, and the like). Say we wish in future to transfer $ 200 billion instead, we must raise the Return to Society from its present 22.5% to 27.2 %. There is no ducking the matter: Banishing poverty by definition means that the now over-paid in future must be less overpaid. The gulf between the top income and bottom income groups is now far greater in the United States, Britain, and Canada than in continental European nations, and most especially Sweden. In the future it need not be so.

The three great reforms

To launch the New Enlightenment, action must be started immediately on the three great reforms that have just been discussed, changing the way we manage the economy to rid ourselves of boom and bust, placing our main medium of mass communication, broadcasting, at the service of the people, and replacing the income tax. This process should be complete in, say, five years. This will make an enormous change in the functioning of our economy. Ours will no longer be a bubble economy held aloft by a barrage of advertising from ever-present radio and television, stampeding us into acquiring the latest gadget, Galbraith's affluent society of fifty years ago still struggling to stay affluent, enmeshed in mounting debt, and stunned by foreclosures. People will now be able to become genuinely affluent, poverty will be abolished, and there will be ample funds for the mega-projects to combat global warming, for relieving third world misery, and other important missions. And so affluent can society eventually become that shorter working hours and earlier retirement will be necessary, and new ways of living will need to emerge. This question is discussed later in Chapter 16.

And the three great reforms will quickly bring good cheer, people will begin to feel they are waking up from a bad dream. Or most people will – yes of course, old ways die hard, many who profit from our present way of doing things may be less happy. And of course there is no such thing as heaven on earth, this is a vale of tears, A hurts B, B hurts C, D is incurably miserable (just how horrible is the hurt wreaked by people on other people is marvellously described by Niall Ferguson's 'The War of the World', how the world's nations murderously dealt with each other in the twentieth century). But all told there will be a new excitement, a new buzz, in the air: At last we have a new government that seems to have some wonderful ideas, and seems to know what it's doing. And wow! No more income tax! And the economy is going to get going again. And there is no need for a sudden brutal cut in public service jobs, and paring back welfare. Yes, perhaps government has grown too big, and eventually we can cut some of this flab and bloated bureaucracy. But that's not our priority, one thing at a time, and the first thing to do is mend our dysfunctional economy, and while we do so make sure that everybody has enough money to live on. And not least, there is a new atmosphere, more truth in the air, less people trying to sell you something, now there are so many lies flying around that one does not know whom, or what, to believe.

CHAPTER 11

The Great
Battle of the Climate

The planet is in huge danger, there is a possibility of calamity which might destroy civilization, but the world has acted only perfunctorily, its heart hasn't been in it, and all that can possibly be done now is mitigation and adaptation. There are three main reasons for this ghastly situation. First has been a failure to put before the public the incontrovertible evidence for human-induced global warming; second has been a failure to see just what measures are needed to arrest this warming; and the third is the shortcomings of our institutions which are the subject of this work – a society without these failings would not have set itself on its present doom-directed road, or would by now have fast changed direction. Nor would it be in a state of confused perplexity about the precise physical measures needed to arrest warming, which are obvious, any qualified engineer – if he puts his mind to it – can see this. And it has nothing to do with despoiling the world's lovely landscapes with wind turbines – as already observed, a thousand square miles of these monsters generate as much electricity as one nuclear station, and only when the wind blows. Each of the three reasons will be discussed in turn.

The first reason: the failure
to lay out the evidence clearly

The failure to put clearly before the public this evidence is quite extraordinary, as it is readily available and very convincing. One consequence has been scepticism or disbelief on the part of even highly intelligent individuals. Thus one of Canada's most read newspaper columnists writes regarding the Copenhagen gathering, that 'the talks collapsed in a smouldering heap of wreckage. The only surprise was that . . . so many intelligent people . . . actually seemed to believe that experts and politicians have supernatural powers to predict and control the climate. They believed that experts know how fast temperatures will rise by when, and what the consequences will be, and that we will know what to do about it[75].

Much of this global warming scepticism and denial surely exists because the incontrovertible evidence for human-induced climate change has not been clearly presented. Some people of course are unconvincible, whether they are of a contrarian nature, or believe that there is some conspiracy, for example some Tea Party politicians in the United States. But these groups can be reduced to a harmless minority once the unequivocal human-induced climate change evidence is presented to the public. Below are two sets of observations from such sources as the NASA Goddard Institute for Space Studies and the British Meteorological Service. The first set of observations, Figure 2.1, provides the evidence that global warming is happening, and the second set, Figure 2.2, the evidence that we humans are causing it. (The diagrams, though essentially reliable, require updating with the latest more authoritative information – for example in September 2012 we learn that this summer the Arctic ice has retreated by a record amount).

Figures 2.1.(1) and 2.1.(2) show the world's average surface temperature rise, respectively the reconstructed temperature for the last 2000 years, and the instrumental temperature record since 1850. No worldwide record of directly measured temperature, by thermometer, is available for the years before 1850, so for these years the temperature must be reconstructed from proxy measures such as tree ring variation.

As will be seen, the world's surface temperature has risen since the start of the Industrial Revolution, but the pace of rise has accelerated in about the last forty years.

Temperature rise has been very uneven over the planet as Figure 2.1.(3) shows. It has been particularly pronounced in the Arctic which no doubt accounts for the rapid shrinkage of the Arctic floating summer ice just referred to. The Arctic was originally forecast to be virtually free of ice in summer only by 2050, but the actual retreat has been much faster, and it will now likely be ice-free within fifteen years.

Feeding the views of global warming deniers is the fact that the world's surface temperature is increasing in fits and starts, because the earth is an incredibly complex interconnected system. The highest annual temperatures ever recorded were 1n 1998, 2005, and 2010 and there were similar, but much lower peaks around 1940 and 1880. But the last decade has been on average by far the hottest since records began 160 years ago. In fact the inexorably increasing heat the earth is absorbing from the sun is expended in a another way, the rise in the level of the vast ocean that covers 70% of the earth's surface. As Figure 2.1.(4) shows, this has gone up more regularly than the average surface temperature, and is, in fact a more accurate indicator of global warming. This is because it has only two main causes, the water entering the sea from the melting glaciers on land, and the expansion of the ocean as it warms[76].

To the world temperature rise should be added an increase in extreme climatic conditions, such as retreating glaciers, heat waves and drought, wild fires, tropical cyclones, and high seas causing flooding of coastal areas.

Compared with the forecasts made in 1990, at the start of the Kyoto process, the actual rise of both surface temperature and sea level, is 60-70% greater than predicted – little wonder then the growing world alarm among those who are not sceptics or deniers.

As we have seen there can be little doubt that warming is happening, but are our emissions causing it? Here is the scientists' explanation of why they are. The earth's atmosphere has an effect analogous to that of the glass that traps the sun's heat within greenhouses, and is a simple consequence of the laws of physics. It is this greenhouse effect of the earth's atmosphere that makes life possible on the earth, otherwise the world's surface temperature would be intolerably cold, near to that of outer space, and of planets unblanketed by an atmosphere. But in recent years we have changed the composition of the atmosphere by increasing the concentration of greenhouse gases, in particular carbon dioxide, CO_2, and this has intensified the greenhouse effect.

Figure 2.1: The Evidence for Global Warming

(1) Reconstructed Temperature last 2000 Year

(versus 1901 - 2000 mean)

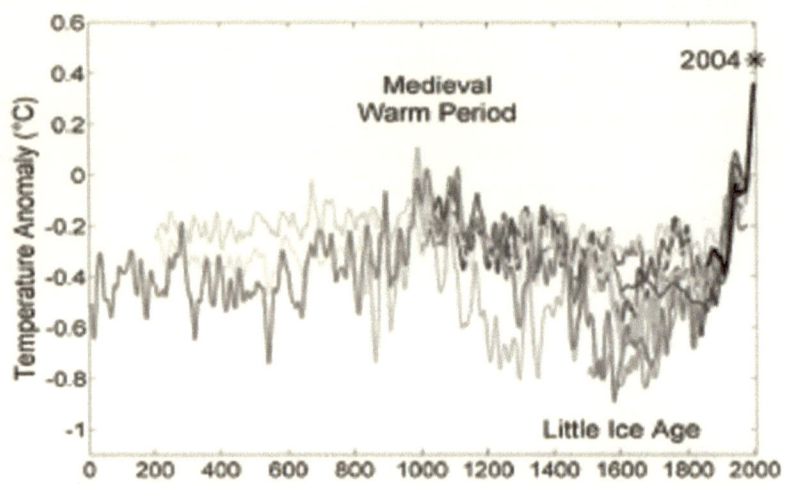

(2) Directly Measured Temperature Since 1850

(above 1901 - 2000 mean)

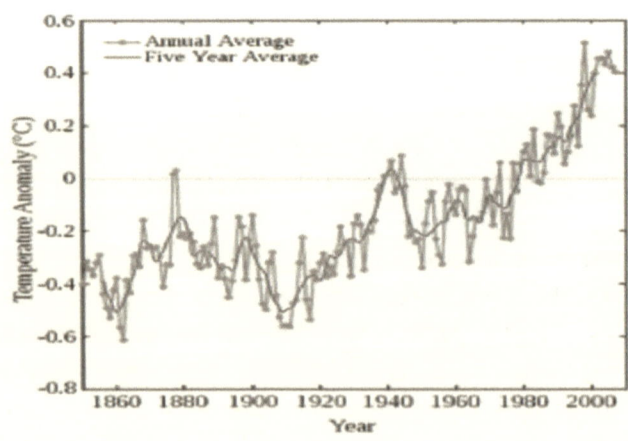

(3) Variation in temperature rise

(1999 - 2008) mean over 1940 - 1980 mean)

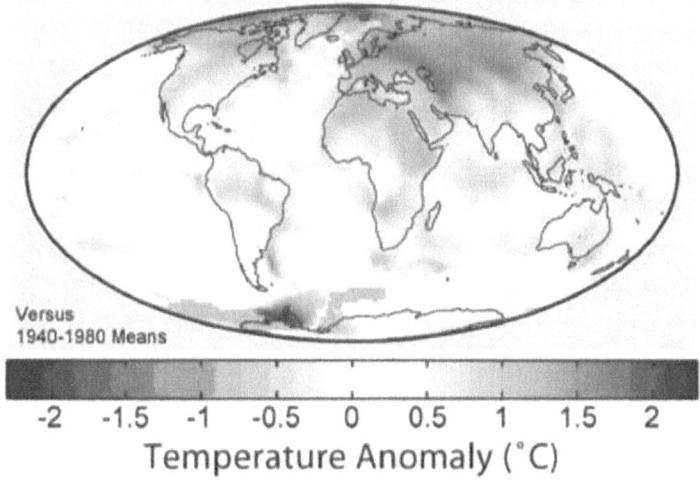

(4) Sea Level Rise since 1880

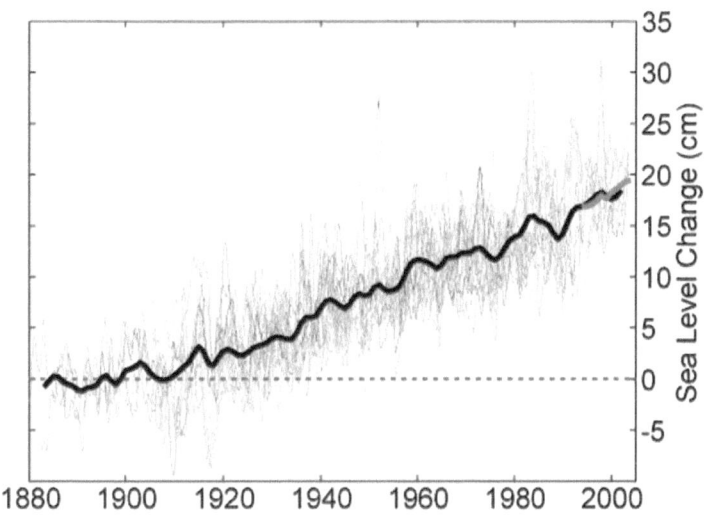

Figure 2.2: The Evidence for Human Agency

(1) Carbon dioxide concentration for 400,000 years

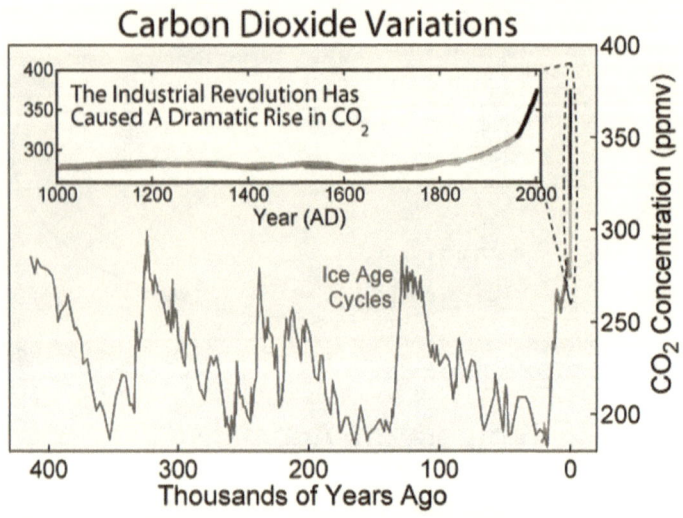

(2) Carbon dioxide concentration since 1880

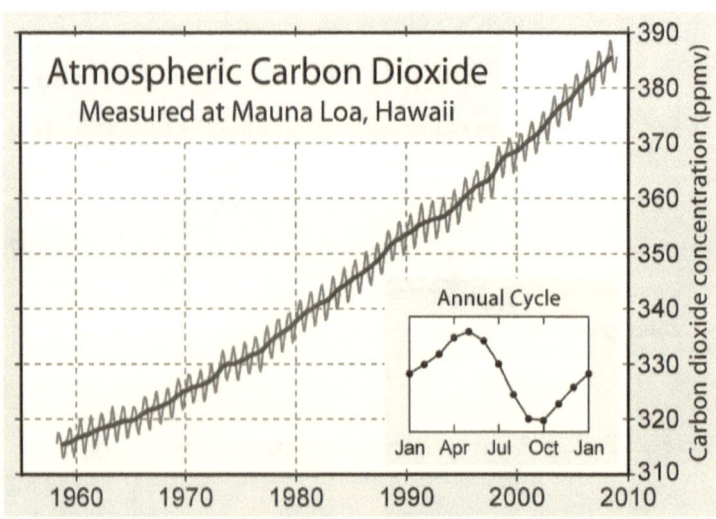

(3) Global Fossil Fuel Carbon Emissions

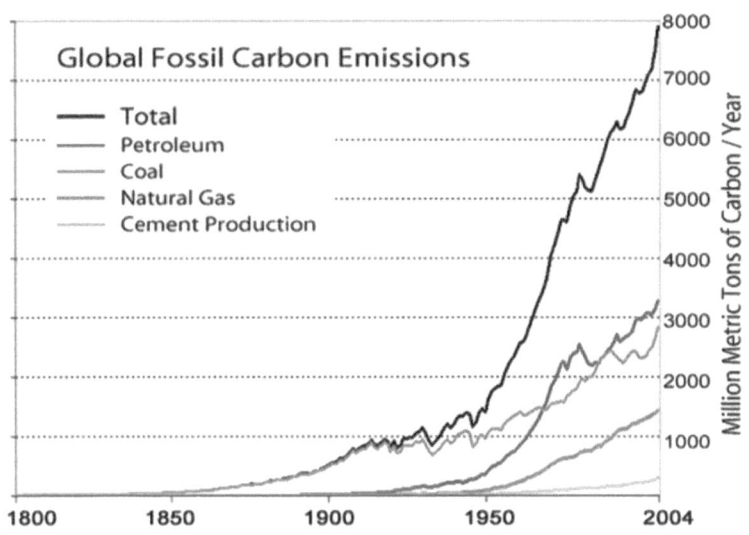

(4) Climate change Attribution

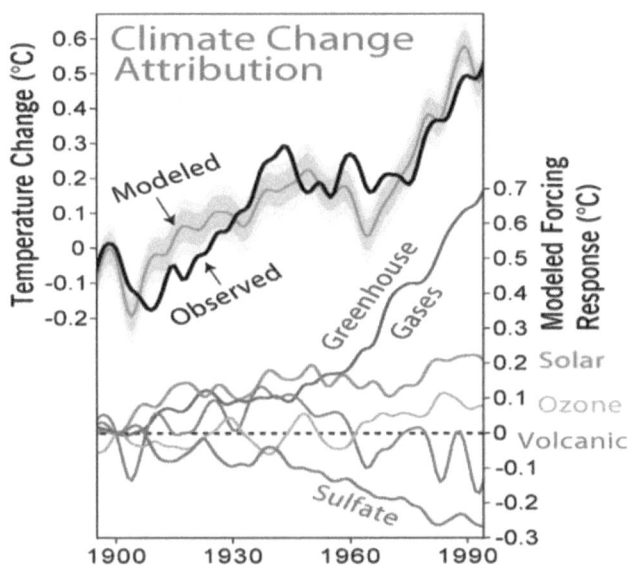

Figure 2.2.(1) shows the CO2 concentration over the last 400,000 years. Over approximately 100,000 year ice age cycles, the concentration fluctuated between about 190 and 290 ppmv (parts per million by volume) and then it started to rise above 290 with the industrial revolution. Figure 2.2.(2) shows its accelerating rise in the last fifty years to nearly 390. And this rising concentration is not surprising when we look at Figure 2.2.(3), which shows that by 2004 we were dumping eight billion tons of carbon annually in the atmosphere, an enormous increase from only one billion tons at the end of World War II, and comparatively very little 150 years ago.

And of course scientists have done the elementary calculations to determine that the eight billions tons of carbon we are adding annually to the atmosphere has been enough to produce the measured increase in its carbon dioxide concentration; and that this in turn, through its greenhouse effect, to produce the world's recent temperature increase. Hence the alarm in the 1980s which led the world's nations to meet at the 1993 Rio Earth Conference, which led eventually to the Kyoto Accord which came into force in 2007.

Reflect a moment on human collective thoughtlessness and irresponsibility: The earth's atmosphere is the source of all life on the planet. Yet with no thought for the possible consequences, we humans have extracted huge amounts of coal, oil, and natural gas from the earth, and recklessly dumped it in the air that we, and all creation, breathe. We have taken action to ban CFCs to protect the ozone layer, that was easy, fewer huge interests were affected, nor was our total way of life.

The terrible complexity
of the climate threat

It is not only our greenhouse gas emissions that affect global temperatures. Figure 2.2.(4) 'Climate change Attribution' shows an estimate of the different factors that have been in play from 1900 to about 1993. It is bad enough that world temperatures are fast rising, but there is also an element of dangerous instability. There are so many forces in play that if we proceed carelessly, dangerous feedbacks could bring catastrophe[77]. The fossil fuels we use produce not only the carbon emissions, but also the aerosol pollution haze that blankets the earth.

By reflecting some of the incoming heat from the sun back into space, this haze has an offsetting cooling effect, but for which global warming would now be about one third greater. Much of the aerosol output is due to the fast-growing Asian giants, and the British meteorological service reported in December 2011 that there has recently been a slowing of world temperature increase, probably owing to Asian aerosols, and volcanic activity. So in the short term we should rather moderate our criticism of them (and of the American coal miners whose supporters have blocked President Obama's plans), until we, in the West get our act together.

When eventually we take serious steps to reduce our use of fossil fuels, the aerosols will fall out of our skies far faster than does the accumulated CO2, and there could be a dangerous upward climb in world temperatures. We must therefore, according to James Lovelock, adopt stopgap measures to offset the loss of the atmospheric aerosols. There are several possibilities, one being to plant sulphuric acid droplets in the atmosphere to reflect heat from the sun back into space, as do the aerosols now.

Apart from greenhouse gases and aerosols other forces affect world temperature. Figure 2.2.(4) , shows three of these, variations in solar activity, volcanic emissions, and ozone changes. So-called ENSO, 'El Nino Southern Oscillation', also has some complex role, contributing to its short term variability, shown in Figure 2.1.(4), perhaps even to the record high temperatures of 1998, 2005, and 2010.

Of all the forces in play, those which might be called natural and beyond human control, solar radiation, volcanic activity, and El Nino, are fluctuating and over time are as likely to cool as to heat the globe. The controllable ones are our greenhouse gases and aerosols.

Methane Peril

To add to our alarm there have been recent reports that as a result of rising temperatures, methane now trapped in the northern tundra may be beginning to leak out. As Figure 2.1.(3) shows, global warming has been particularly pronounced in northern regions. This is disturbing: methane is a greenhouse gas 20 or more times worse than carbon dioxide, and was the source of the 'runaway warming' danger warned of in 2004 by Martin Rees, in his 'Our Final Hour'[78]. Until recently he was President of the Royal Society, and a leader of the British scientific community. He gave humanity only a 50/50 chance of surviving this century, not only from global warming, but also from terror and weapons of mass destruction in the hands of rogue nations or groups.

The Scientific Consensus

Many of the deniers believe that there is a great conspiracy, that the climate scientists have a vested interest in claiming that our emissions are causing global warming – their research funds will be cut off, or that they would lose huge face if they now reversed their views. But consider: There is a consensus not only among the small minority of the world's scientists who are climate and earth scientists, but also among all scientists, including the American Association for the Advancement of Science, and the academy representing all the European scientific bodies. There is not a single scientific academy of standing in the world that rejects the evidence – and it is not surprising which scientific body's acceptance of human agency in global warming has been equivocal, the American Association of Petroleum Geologists and it was obliged to change its stand because some of its members had resigned in protest.

In fact, it would be extremely difficult to organise and execute a global warming conspiracy, considering the many millions of worldwide observations of temperature, sea level, arctic summer ice, fossil fuel combustion, atmospheric carbon concentration, and shrinking glaciers, observations by thousands of people around the world. It is these hard facts that provide the evidence for global warming and rising atmospheric carbon concentration. It would take some conspiracy to bring about the mutual support given each other by the diverse sets of data represented by the seven graphs.

If there is indeed a conspiracy we can better establish who the conspirators are by the *cui bono* test – who benefits? We know as an absolute fact that the so-called Global Climate Coalition, financed by the US oil, coal, and auto industries, has led an aggressive advertising campaign against the idea that emissions could lead to global warming. Though disbanded in 2002, the National Association of Manufacturers and the American Petroleum Institute continue to lobby against any law or treaty that would sharply curb emissions[79]. It is not fanciful to suggest that such efforts as these may have contributed to the United States' lack of enthusiasm for tackling global warming.

The second reason: the failure to explain the 'Great Transformation' ahead

The second reason for the major nations' perplexed dithering on global warming has been the unaccountable failure of both leaders and the public to grasp what must be done to achieve the necessary reduction of our carbon emissions.

First we have failed to explain the magnitude of the task, hence not a 'waste not, want not approach, switching off lights, people primly telling one not to idle one's car. The task the world's major nations face is huge. The advanced western nations must aim to cut their emissions by, say, 80% below their 1990 level, by 2050 (1990 is the base year assumed under the Kyoto Agreement, and has been used in most nations' targets). The Obama administration originally set a target of 80% emissions reduction below their present level but since then Obama appears to have retreated, and the forces of Global Warming denial have gathered strength in the United States. (Note added in February 2013: President Obama, just reelected, has at last taken a strong stand on climate change).

The 80% cut below 1990 is an even greater task than it may appear at first sight. The developed economies, growing at, say, 2% annually will in 2050 be 2.12 times larger than they are now in 2012, but must produce at least five times less emissions (that is, if their emissions are not now above their 1990 level, but in the case of Canada whose emissions are 30% above 1990, 6.5 times less). This means they must emit 11 times less per unit of GDP by 2050 or 4.15% less each year, one might say un-doable, but with grim resolve such targets can be achieved. And the common symbol of factories belching smoke is misleading. True, they should belch less smoke, but the real task to be achieved is to convert those factories to produce different products, high speed electric trains and little electric town cars instead of emission-producing SUVs. Our society went down the wrong road, and must quickly come back and go another way. How absurd our use of huge contraptions, weighing 25 times their often single passenger, just to go down town. The Daimler

Smart car weighs only 11 times a person's weight, and thee Smarts are designed to fit into a single parking space. And the average bicycle weighs only one quarter of an average human being's weight, and now in Ottawa, bicycle routes have been set out on main city streets, and many youths are bicycling to work: Just think: add a tiny auxiliary motor to the bicycle and even oldies will delight in bicycling when the weather is clement. There is no mystery to the sudden near-demise of General Motors, a huge unguided missile of a corporation that has long courted disaster in the absence of good public governance.

It is important to realise that changes in people's lifestyle will have a knock-on effect down through the layers of the economy. Not only will the remade transportation system, based on small electric town cars, and expanded electric train and bus services, as well as greater use of the old bicycle, produce less emissions, less fossil fuel will be needed in the manufacture of these facilities, and to make the necessary steel and other materials, and to extract the necessary ores, and oil, coal, and natural gas from the earth.

An even bigger task for the fast growing developing giants

Absolute necessity requires an even larger degree of emission reduction by these nations. China is adding coal fired generating stations at a great rate, and has overtaken the United States as the world's biggest emitter. India is growing nearly as fast, and Brazil and Indonesia are coming up. These nations argue that the rich West caused global warming and hence should bear the brunt of emission-cutting, as well as help pay for their own emission-cutting programmes. But the West's transgression occurred long before the West's scientists even observed that global warming was taking place, and it was only by their urging that the Kyoto Accord eventually came into force, in 2005 . Besides it is illogical for the emerging nations to repeat the old ways that were responsible for global warming.

But a formula can be reached for emission cutting that will not unduly impede China's fast economic 'catch-up' growth. The goal set earlier for advanced nations, which implied an annual 4% emission cut per unit of GDP, assumed a GDP growth rate of 2% until 2050, requiring that their emissions fall by 2% each year. Assuming China's economic growth rate to 2050 will average 6%, applying the same formula of 4% less per unit of GDP, their emissions can actually *grow* by 2%. But that is not quite good enough, they might be held to zero emissions growth, that is 6% lower than their economic growth rate. While the already advanced nations have some range of choice between the extremes of total fossil fuel replacement and conversion to a low energy society, less such choice exists for the growing giants, they must proceed faster to the future low energy society. Thereby they can leapfrog the high-energy mess that the West has built itself – a blessing in disguise.

So what measures are necessary?

What actions are necessary if the advanced economies are to produce 11 times less emissions per unit of GDP by 2050? Simple logic gives them a three-way choice: eliminate most of their fossil fuel use, convert to an exceedingly low energy-intensive society that needs less energy of any kind, or some intermediate solution. Two intermediate possibilities are offered here, one for nations without anti-nuclear phobia, and the other for the phobic, which might be called the 'German Case'.

These four alternative cases can be understood with the help of energy flow diagrams of the economy. Figure 3.1 depicts the economy as it is now (in 2012), and Figure 3.2 depicts the same economy in 2050, for each of the four cases. Figure 3.21 depicts substitution of fossil fuels while retaining our present highly energy-intensive lifestyle. Figure 3.22 depicts the other extreme case, maintaining the present energy mix, but reshaping the economy to become exceedingly low-energy-intensive, with a transformed lifestyle. Figures 3.23 and 3.24 depict the two intermediate cases, respectively the nuclear reliant one and the 'German' one.

Each diagram shows two energy supply sectors, fossil fuel supply and electricity supply, and two energy use sectors, the one that must use fossil fuels, such as aircraft and ocean transport, freighters, oil tankers, and cruise ships. The other energy use sector is the rest of the economy, one might say the whole of the economy, less only the small part that cannot be electrified, and the sector that provides the energy needed to drive the entire system.

The diagrams are for what might be called a typical advanced economy, the values shown are very approximate – the diagrams are merely illustrative, but do show just how huge the task is – just as Churchill mobilized Britain for total war, (we shall fight on the beaches – we'll never surrender) the world's major nations must mobilize for the Great Battle of the Climate – a stand very far, in May 2012, from the rhetoric of the American presidential campaign, which is careful to omit any suggestion of climate change. (And now, in November, one might ask, is Superstorm Sandy that's just devastated New York an expression of the wrath of the gods?). It will be necessary for teams of engineers and planners, with the aid of the national income-output models maintained by each nation's central statistical agency, to refine the results illustrated by the present diagrams. Each of the diagrams is explained in turn.

THE PRESENT SITUATION (Figure 3.1)

Of the world's present electricity supply, about 67% is fossil fuel generated, 16% is Hydro, and 13% is nuclear. Only 1% is wind, and the remaining 3% is other renewables and biomass (just a glance at these figures alone is enough to suggest that the more extreme greens are living in a fantasy world). The major energy use sector is now 25 percent electric, and 75 percent fossil fuel dependent. In the absence of good data the crude assumption was made that only six percent of the economy cannot be electrified. About 2-3 percent of the world's emissions now come from aircraft and the remaining 3 - 4 percent is an allowance for sea transport in freighter, tankers, and cruise ships. If the six percent assumption is too low, and the figure should be, say eight percent, then our task becomes slightly more difficult. The electricity supply system is a surprisingly large producer of the world's carbon emissions, from mainly coal-fired, but also natural gas - fired, generating stations. In the present example 27% of emissions come from electricity generation. In the United States the figure is 33% and one supposes that the Chinese value is considerably higher – we read that China is adding one new coal generation station weekly. It is not surprising that France, whose electricity is only 10% fossil-fuel-fired, has much the lowest emissions of the large advanced nations. Nearly 80% of France's electricity is nuclear. In sharp contrast, for the United States, Britain, Germany, and Japan, about 70 to 80 percent of electricity generation uses fossil fuels.

The target we shall set ourselves for the present exercise is to reduce our emissions to 20 percent of what they were in 1990, by the year 2050. (This is the most ambitious goal yet set by any nation). Here we assume that because of the feeble efforts so far at serious emission reduction, these are still at the 1990 level, they have been cut only sufficiently to offset economic growth. The four diagrams depict each of the four alternative ways of achieving the goal.

The following assumptions have been made: the average economic growth rate over the next 38 years will be 2%. In the past, total energy use has increased at about 1% less than the energy growth rate[80], and this trend is assumed here to continue in the absence of action. Taking GDP and total energy use values now at 100 units, then in 2050 GDP will be 212, and total energy use will be 146. We assume here that in the absence of action the energy mix in 2050 will be unchanged, so that the amount of fossil fuel use and the consequent carbon emissions, will also be 146. Therefore to meet our target of only 20, we must shrink our fossil fuel use by a factor of 7.3 by 2050. Since we cannot appreciably reduce fossil fuel use for aircraft and ships[81], we must reduce its use in the other parts of the economy by more than 7.3 times. If in fact the economic growth rate turns out to be greater than 2%, we will have to reduce our emissions by an even greater margin. However, it is possible that the type of economic growth of the future, with its multitude of electronic gadgets will be less energy-intensive and make our target somewhat easier to meet.

Now we shall look at each alternative approach in turn. In all four diagrams the number to the right of each sector box is the amount of emissions in 2050 in the absence of any emission cutting action. The total economy value is 146. And the four sectoral values have the same relative shares as in 2012. The number to the left of each sector box is what the sector's emissions must be in 2050 to meet the target, and the sum of the four values must equal 20. As will be seen, there is no reduction in the 'air and sea' sector – its emissions are unchanged at 8.76. That means that the sum of the emissions of the three other sectors must be only 11.24, if the 20 target is to be met. This requires that the major energy use sector, and the electricity supply sector must each reduce their emissions by a factor of 13 times in 38 years[82].

Figure 3.1: Energy Anatomy of the Economy
The Present Situation

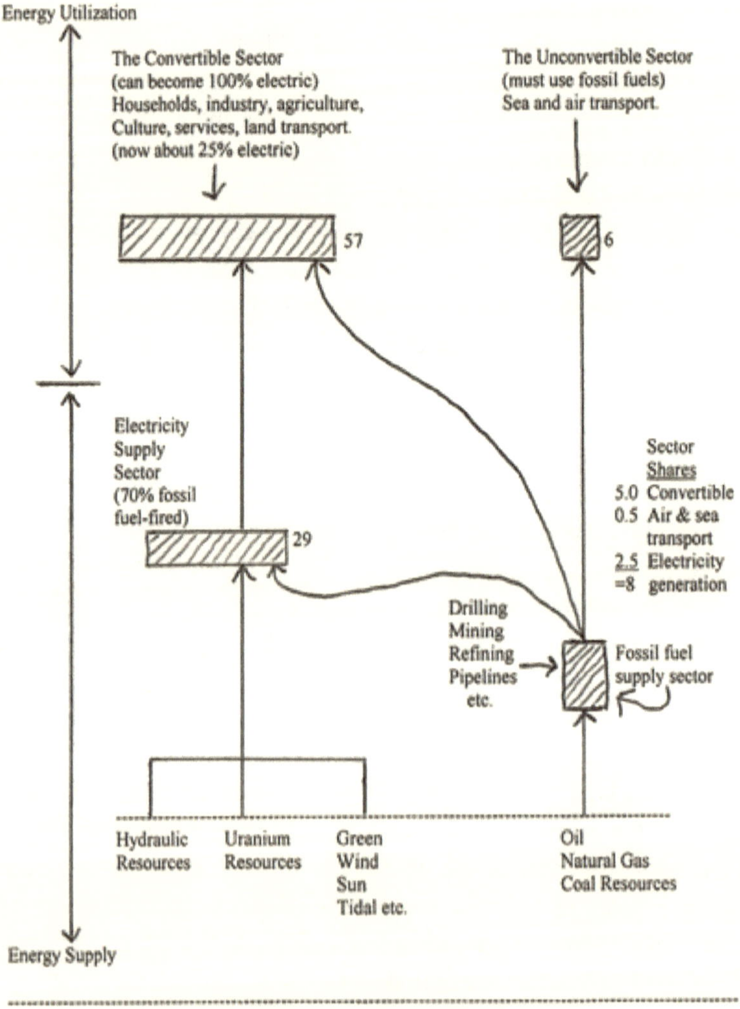

Energy Utilization

The Convertible Sector
(can become 100% electric)
Households, industry, agriculture,
Culture, services, land transport.
(now about 25% electric)

The Unconvertible Sector
(must use fossil fuels)
Sea and air transport.

57

6

Electricity
Supply
Sector
(70% fossil
fuel-fired)

Sector
Shares
5.0 Convertible
0.5 Air & sea
transport
2.5 Electricity
=8 generation

29

Drilling
Mining
Refining
Pipelines
etc.

Fossil fuel
supply sector

Hydraulic
Resources

Uranium
Resources

Green
Wind
Sun
Tidal etc.

Oil
Natural Gas
Coal Resources

Energy Supply

The Carbon Dioxide Emissions = 100 in 2012
Sector emissions are shown at the right of each box.

Figure 3.2: The Energy Anatomy of the Economy
The Situation in 2050

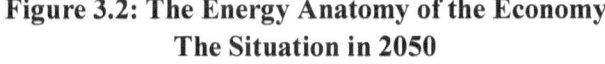

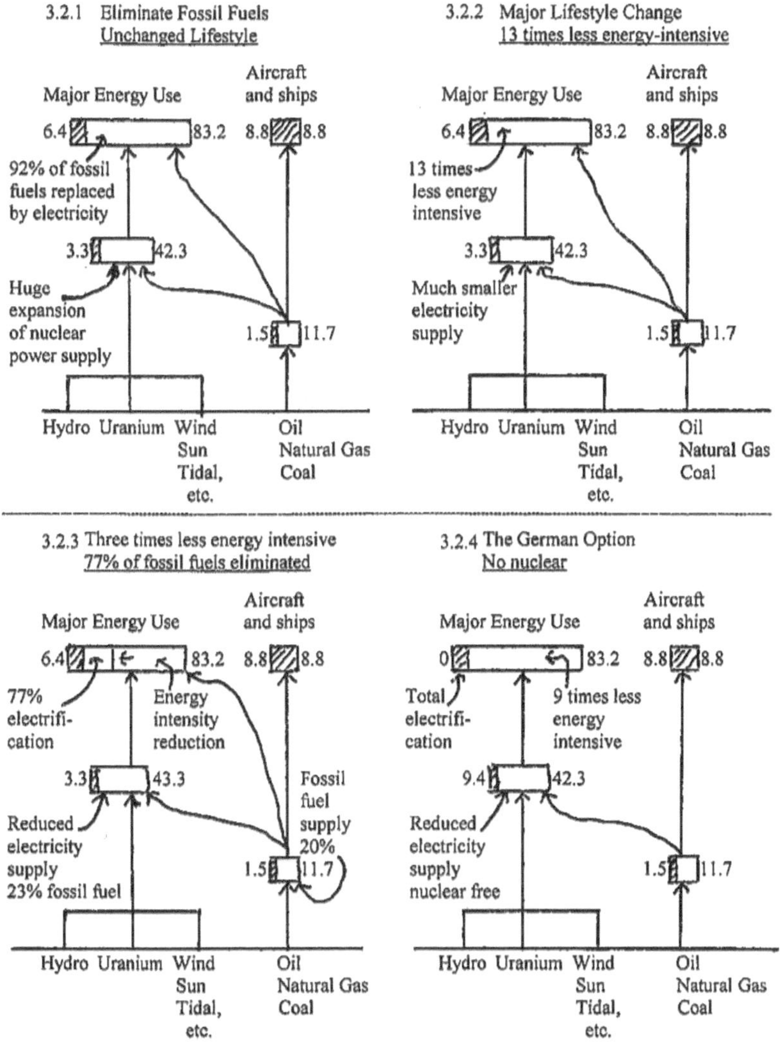

3.2.1 Eliminate Fossil Fuels
Unchanged Lifestyle

Major Energy Use

Aircraft and ships

6.4 | 83.2   8.8 | 8.8

92% of fossil fuels replaced by electricity

3.3 | 42.3

Huge expansion of nuclear power supply

1.5 | 11.7

Hydro Uranium Wind Oil
Sun Natural Gas
Tidal, Coal
etc.

3.2.2 Major Lifestyle Change
13 times less energy-intensive

Major Energy Use

Aircraft and ships

6.4 | 83.2   8.8 | 8.8

13 times less energy intensive

3.3 | 42.3

Much smaller electricity supply

1.5 | 11.7

Hydro Uranium Wind Oil
Sun Natural Gas
Tidal, Coal
etc.

3.2.3 Three times less energy intensive
77% of fossil fuels eliminated

Major Energy Use

Aircraft and ships

6.4 | 83.2   8.8 | 8.8

77% electrification

Energy intensity reduction

3.3 | 43.3

Reduced electricity supply
23% fossil fuel

Fossil fuel supply 20%

1.5 | 11.7

Hydro Uranium Wind Oil
Sun Natural Gas
Tidal, Coal
etc.

3.2.4 The German Option
No nuclear

Major Energy Use

Aircraft and ships

0 | 83.2   8.8 | 8.8

Total electrification

9 times less energy intensive

9.4 | 42.3

Reduced electricity supply
nuclear free

1.5 | 11.7

Hydro Uranium Wind Oil
Sun Natural Gas
Tidal, Coal
etc.

For
each]→
case

- At left of each sector are its emissions in 2050, total emissions = 20 (2012 = 100)
- At right of each sector are its emissions in 2050, if no action taken, total = 146
- Emissions reduction factor = 146/20 = 7.3

The four cases are the 'logical alternatives' without getting into discussing the technology and physical nature of each. These will be discussed later.

EXTREME FOSSIL FUEL ELIMINATION (Figure 3.2.1)

The diagram depicts maximum fossil fuel elimination while retaining essentially the same lifestyle, which is possible only with a very high degree of electrification of the major energy use sector – all energy to drive, heat, cool, or light nearly every activity in the economy must be electrified. At the same time the electricity supply sector must be not only vastly expanded, the new generating stations must produce few emissions, and most existing fossil fuel generating stations must be replaced.

What are the alternatives to fossil fuel electricity generation? The most obvious is nuclear power generation which already provides a considerable part of most large nations' electricity. But nuclear power is now much under challenge, Fukushima was like an adrenalin shot to the Green movement. What are the alternatives to nuclear power? Most hydraulic sources have already been exploited, and wind turbines can provide only a small part, and in any case must be backed up by nuclear or fossil fuel stations for when the wind doesn't blow. Much of Germany's landscape is now despoiled by giant wind turbines, which still only supply less than 7% of the country's generating capacity.

There is one other possible way of using wind power that until very recently I haven't heard discussed, and that is in conjunction with pumped storage reservoirs. Many years ago, such a reservoir contained within a many miles long earth dyke was built at the Niagara Falls, not for wind power, but for off-peak hydro power[83]. Water in the river above the falls at off-peak electricity demand times (then at night) was pumped up into the reservoir. Then later this water was used to generate hydro power when needed. For wind power, such a huge reservoir must be constructed near each cluster of wind turbines. When the wind is blowing, power from the wind turbines will pump water up into the reservoir with water from some adjacent water source. Then the water in the reservoir can be drawn down to generate hydroelectric power when needed. These facilities might be clustered in remote areas so as not to spoil landscapes, and the power delivered to where needed by high voltage transmission lines. This is obviously a very expensive solution, but that would matter little if like Germany, in its present mindset, it were resolved to be non-nuclear at any cost. Germany's mindset seems to ignore the fact that its neighbour, France, has been 80% nuclear with no serious difficulties – clearly France has a different mindset. Perhaps the logic of the Battle of the Climate needs to include a mindset factor.

Other 'green' sources such as harnessing tidal flows are still at the talking stage. The eminent scientist and environmentalist, James Lovelock has stated that 'only nuclear power can now halt global warming' and 'I am a Green and I entreat my friends in the movement to drop their wrongheaded opposition to nuclear power'[84]. One of the founders of Greenpeace has also switched to the nuclear camp. Already there are about 440 nuclear stations in the world, and as already mentioned France's electricity generation is 80% nuclear, and it is planning to add more nuclear stations. There are undoubtedly matters still to be resolved on waste storage, and the possibility of uranium supply depletion, but on that both the International Atomic Energy Agency and the OECD claim there is a virtually limitless supply.

What lessons can we draw from this German drama for the New Renaissance? And not only nuclear-phobia, but other phobias that can grip societies, for example, the Tea Party bogeyman of big government, no more taxes, even for the super-rich. One might wonder whether Germany's aversion to nuclear power has anything to do with wishing to avoid anything so symbolic of horror as nuclear fission, which reminds then of the calamity of the Third Reich, and the savage destruction of the country as a demented Hitler in his bunker refused to capitulate[85] though total defeat had long been certain, and Germans had the extraordinary mindset of absolute obedience to what Hitler decreed.

The foremost lesson to be learnt here is the importance of getting the public's support in a strong democracy for a government's plans, and also how strong, even irrationally strong, particular attitudes, beliefs and phobias can be with sections of the public. It was for this reason that above I have placed such emphasis on convincing the public with clear evidence of global warming. And also this is another reason for levelling the public opinion playing field by placing the broadcasting system at the service of the public, and no longer a service to wealthy special interests and business corporations.

So for this case, represented by Figure 3.2.1, we have no alternative to nuclear power, we have to build a great many nuclear power stations. To meet the 2050 target of reducing emissions by a factor of 11 per unit of GDP, given that air and sea emissions cannot be reduced, the major energy use sector and the electricity supply sector must produce 13 times less emissions per unit of GDP than they otherwise would.

In the absolute extreme of this case, with total replacement of fossil fuel in the major energy use sector, and total replacement of all fossil fuel electricity generation by non-emitting forms, the fossil fuel supply sector shrinks even further, so that now its only customers will be air and shipping lines. Total emissions in this future will be 9.5, half our target value of 20.

The task that society must set itself in this extreme case is immense, probably impossible, two enormous programmes, one of nuclear power station construction, the other, in parallel, conversion of all energy use to operate on electricity.

EXTREME REDUCTION OF ENERGY INTENSITY (Figure 3.2.2)

This is the other extreme case, reshaping society to need very little energy of any kind, but retaining the same energy mix. The economy grows at the assumed 2% annually, but it becomes far less energy intensive. People's lifestyles will radically change, to require thirteen times less energy. Figure 3.2.2 has exactly the same form as Figure 3.2.1, but the emission reduction comes about because the major energy use sector now uses much less energy of any kind. In this case there is no need to expand the electricity supply sector, indeed it will become smaller – some existing fossil fuel stations will progressively be shut down.

This like the other extreme option may be beyond possibility – to change lifestyle to require thirteen times less energy per unit of

GDP. So as either of the extreme options will be virtually impossible to bring about, some intermediate will be required, part fossil fuel replacement, part energy intensity reduction.

THE FAVOURED OPTION:
PART FOSSIL FUEL ELIMINATION, PART
ENERGY-INTENSITY REDUCTION (Figure 3.2.3)

In this case the major energy-use sector becomes three times less energy-intensive, and it can still retain 23% of its fossil fuels. The electricity supply sector will probably not need to expand – it might even be reduced in size – and some fossil fuel stations can continue in service. Fossil fuel electricity generation produces a surprisingly large proportion, about one third, of all the emissions of major nations. The single act of replacing these stations with nuclear generation makes a huge contribution to winning the battle of the climate – it really is wake-up time for the leading nations, not least Germany with its dream of sugar-plum fairies – correction, windmills. In the whole world only Switzerland, Sweden, and Norway have lower emission intensities than France, whose electricity generation is nearly 80 percent nuclear, and Switzerland is fortunate, on account of its terrain it has extensive hydraulic resources.

Some variant of this is likely to be the favoured option for the advanced nations. The effort that will be required of China and other emerging giants, will have to more stringent. Or rather for these nations they may adopt a different route to modernity, avoiding the highly energy-intensive and fossil fuel reliant path that was adopted by the Western nations.

THE 'GERMAN' OPTION (Figure 3.2.4)

This is the far more stringent variant of the intermediate option, the one that Germany has forced on itself as a consequence of its recent decision to shun nuclear power. The diagram shows no fossil fuel flowing to the major energy-use sector – all the country's fossil fuels will flow to the electricity supply and aircraft and shipping sectors. To keep total emissions down, the major energy use sector must become 9 times less energy-intensive, a little less difficult than the 13 fold energy intensity reduction of the extreme case. The huge reduction in energy requirements means that though the electricity supply sector will remain fossil fuel-fired, it will be much smaller. As a result, that sector's emissions will be 9.4, which added to those of the air and sea sectors, and of the fossil fuel supply sector will meet the emission target of 20. Germany's task will be somewhat eased if it converts its present coal-fired generating stations to use natural gas – natural gas emits about half as much carbon dioxide as coal.

The present analysis, represented by the four diagrams, shows only the emission reduction from *using* coal as distinct from *extracting* coal – there is probably a significant further emission reduction because of the reduced need to mine coal – the coal mining industry is energy-intensive.

AMORY LOVINS' SOLUTION

Recently Amory Lovins, the prominent American physicist and environmental scientist, has published an article on the questions discussed in this chapter[86]. His analysis of energy policy and carbon emission reduction has much in common with the approach I have used. In particular it relies on total electrification, and major reduction in the economy's energy-intensity. One might say that the policy he puts forward is much like the 'German option' discussed above. It eschews nuclear power, and instead relies on renewables, in particular solar and wind power. He describes great advances being made not only in their technology, but also in their application, which is mainly outside the United States, primarily because of congressional gridlock and powerful special interests. The advances are not only in European countries such as Germany, Sweden and Denmark, but also in China. 'No treaty compelled Beijing's leadership – just enlightened self-interest'.

As already mentioned, the Fukushima disaster has had a traumatic effect on new nuclear station construction in some European countries, but according to the World Nuclear Association[87] 'nuclear power capacity worldwide is increasing steadily but not dramatically', indeed Germany may be the only major nation in the world not planning or building new stations. It is difficult not to conclude that the only realistic path to major emission reduction lies through nuclear. Fukushima was a freak and probably an avoidable freak. It was the result of a terrible earthquake and tsunami, but the terrible radiation leaks occurred only because the nuclear station reactors were by unacceptable negligence constructed too close to sea level, in a seismic region subject to tsunamis[88].

Failure to meet the '20' Target

Whichever option is chosen, the '20' target, though probably achievable by determined effort, will be far from easy, especially if like Germany some nations reject nuclear power. If for example, the attempt to follow the 'favoured option' falls short, and energy intensity is only halved instead of being reduced by a factor of three, and the use of fossil fuels only halved instead of being reduced by 77%, then 2050 emissions will be, say, 40 instead of 20, this will still be a good contribution to the Battle of the Climate.

Immediate tasks to show willing

While planning the specific actions that must be carried out in accordance with the logic set out above, there are some elementary actions that every nation must immediately set in train – some European nations have already done so. Progressively, over, say, four years, each nation must place prohibitive taxes on gas guzzlers, while totally exempting small fuel efficient cars, and at the same time expand urban public transport to the extent possible with available equipment. Train services between city centres must be extended with existing rolling stock, and quickly augmented by new, faster, trains. As already mentioned, these steps will have a knock-on effect throughout the economy. Not only will the smaller cars and increased use of train and bus produce less emissions, less energy will be needed to make transportation facilities, to make the necessary steel and other materials, and to extract the necessary ores, coal, oil, and natural gas from the earth. Countries – in this the US has long been recalcitrant, indicative of its highly defective governance – must progressively raise the price of gasoline over a number of years at least to the European levels. Another immediate action is, through whatever inducements and subsidies are necessary, to start the economy's electrification, and the conversion of home heating to electricity, to the extent that present electricity supply facilities allow, and plans must immediately be set in train to increase this capacity. In parallel with these actions, as discussed earlier, the effect of the loss of the world's aerosol pollution haze must be offset, by temporary measures.

The Great Transformation ahead

We have stated the broad engineering logic of what nations must undertake, but what concrete actions will be required?. Let us say we have decided on an intermediate course, a life style change of 2.5% less energy annually per unit of GDP, while still retaining one quarter of our fossil fuels. There will thus be two giant programmes proceeding in parallel, replacing most of our fossil fuels, and reshaping society to use far less energy.

The first of these involves not only creating vast new electricity generation capacity, but also the even larger effort of re-equipping the economy to use the electricity. Building heating, urban transport, the railway system must be fully electrified. Inter-city trucking will be replaced by freight trains, small electric trucks will feed these trains.

An innumerable variety of equipment must be replaced or retrofitted, throughout agriculture, forestry, mining and quarrying, materials processing, energy supply, water supply, manufacturing, and construction. Air transport alone cannot be electrified, nor to any appreciable degree can shipping transport – nuclear powered ships are technically possible, but would face far greater safety and environmental risks than for electricity generation. Emission cuts, though of a far lesser magnitude, can in addition be achieved through higher energy efficiency in all equipment and processes, including more fuel efficient motor vehicles, better building insulation, and low energy light bulbs and television sets, those sort of fiddly things.

A large proportion of overland aircraft travel can be replaced by high speed electric trains. It is reported that France's super-fast electric trains have replaced most inter-city air travel within the country.

There has been much talk of electricity generation by 'clean coal', carbon capture and storage. Present evidence is against its feasibility, no generating stations using it have yet been built. In contrast, France which at the time of the 1973 oil crisis, relied mainly on imported oil for its electricity generation, converted its power supply from only 8% nuclear to 75% nuclear in only seventeen years[89], and is now nearly 80% nuclear after 25 years. But if in fact the uranium supply does turn out to be limited, there will be no alternative but for the world to rely more on the other huge programme, racing in haste to a remade new society. In this parallel programme to remake society, much personal and business travel will be replaced by the 'virtual workplace', through telecommunications, the so-called 'multimedia', and most intercity travel by super-fast trains which will whisk people, hourly, between urban centres. Personal small 'town cars' will be battery driven, and this will also reduce highway and parking area requirements.

Cities will be refashioned through the notion of the 'three dimensional elevator', extending the concept of the building elevator to urban transportation, but in three dimensions instead of one. Cities will be cris-crossed by frequent underground trains, small electric buses, and moving pedestrian walkways. In the now uncongested city streets bicycles would now be fast, healthy, and a pleasure.

Both programmes, especially changing our lifestyle, will require huge construction projects that produce emissions, and it will be necessary to pace construction so that the emissions of transition do not nullify the overall aim of emission reduction. The two programmes must be coordinated to avoid the possibility of converting some activity from fossil fuel to electricity, that will soon become redundant in the reshaped society.

Two other requirements that must be met are to have the determination to bring to an end the shameless cutting down of the world's rain forests, notably in the Amazon basin, which serve as a carbon sink, absorbing the world's emissions; and also to ensure that population growth soon comes to an end: huge populations serve neither the world nor individual countries: adequate living space is a great gift.

The role of the market

In these times of market fundamentalism, there is excessive reliance on the free market to combat global warming – economists in charge, where engineers are needed. The talk is of 'cap and trade' or 'emissions trading', and taxing the users of fossil fuels, the more they use, the higher the tax. Undoubtedly the market can help, and North American participation in the world's battle of the climate cannot be taken seriously until it fast increases its gasoline and gas guzzler taxes.

But while the free market can nudge individuals and companies in the right general direction, alone it cannot get us to the particular place we must get to. This is total war, the market alone could not win World War II, no more can it win the Battle of the Climate. Government direction is required to launch the mega-projects that will be needed, of nuclear station construction, transportation system transformation, and urban redesign.

Precise planning of the
great transformation

The precise choice and timing of each nation's set of measures can only be determined using the national income input-output tables of each nation's central statistical agency. These tables divide the economy into several hundred parts or industries, and show what each part sells to, and buys from, other parts. When any part changes its equipment to make it less carbon emitting, it starts a chain reaction through the parts of the economy that contribute to making the equipment. The net effect of every possible combination of measures must be estimated, not neglecting the 'emissions of transition', from the mega-projects required, which otherwise could render our overall programme futile.

The third reason: Our deficient governance

And now some words on the third reason for our society's failure to act, its dysfunctional institutions of governance. Three major defects have been discussed in earlier chapters: the misappropriation of the broadcast media, our faulty public finance system, and our pseudo science of economics. I have long believed that business's ownership of the broadcasting system to use as a sales promotion medium has contributed to our society's blindness to the threat of climate catastrophe. The defective public finance system, along with the hi-jacked broadcasting system which encourages excessive consumption of items of often dubious utility, have together deprived us of the needed public funds to engage in the Battle of the Climate. Finally, the shortcomings of our economic science permits our economy to be idle when there is so much to be done. To put the matter another way: A society that did not have these defects of governance would not now be under the threat of climate catastrophe. It would already long ago have backed away from dependence on fossil fuels – 'oh, oh', it would have said, 'that's not the way to go' – and built the kind of economy that we must now belatedly bring into being, and one that will in fact give us a better quality of life, without traffic gridlock and nasty urban sprawl.

Many will be curious why I so harp on the perversion of the broadcasting, long my pet peeve which makes people roll their eyes and say 'there he goes again'. The other two governance defects are not in the same way malign and in breach of the Social Contract – crimes against humanity – but are merely needed reforms whose time has come, and as Galbraith put it, overcome the obstinacy of the conventional wisdom. Our present way of raising public funds is defective and fails to serve the public interest, and our discipline called 'economics' has grave shortcomings. We can most certainly, by using our little grey cells, stop the recession in its tracks. It is utter rubbish to believe that cutting our greenhouse gas emissions will cut jobs, and harm the economy. There must quickly be jobs for all, building the infrastructure for the fossil fuel free electric society, and one using new transportation and communication systems, and urban redesign. And there will be much retraining of people required for new jobs, and while this is happening, income for all.

But the broadcasting obscenity is not merely outdated and no longer up to the job, it is a defect different in kind. There is a huge conflict of interest here, business corporations pay billions of dollars for the U.S. broadcasting system *not* with the purpose of altruistically serving the people and the public interest, but to increase their sales and profits. This matter is as plain as day, but our society continues to ignore it at its peril, the modern business corporations are efficient and innovative producers of goods and services, and a major reason for this is that they must make profits to survive in the competitive market. But it is essential that we arrange for them to make their profits only by serving us, the people, providing only the goods and services that we want and need from them, which we pay them for *directly,* through personal spending, or out of the public purse.

If properly used these splendid producing machines will make it possible to prevail in the Battle of the Climate. Consider the brilliant effectiveness of the US business corporations when after Pearl Harbor they were switched from consumer goods production to become the arsenal of democracy, at racing speed. And it is well to note that this great effort put America back to work from the Great Depression. Now let them, again using public funds, build at equally racing speed America's needed nuclear stations and networks of 250 mile an hour trains.

To repeat, the broadcasting media must not, through the people's thoughtlessness and inattention, be permitted to continue to serve what are *not* their functions, but are the functions of the people, of their governments, and of various institutes and think tanks concerned with public policy. According to an article in the New York Times of 20 October 2010 the fossil fuel industries 'have for decades waged a concerted campaign to raise doubts about the science of global warming. . . . They have created and lavishly financed institutes to produce anti-global warming studies, paid for rallies and websites to question the science . . . and to show that policies to reduce emissions . . . will have a devastating effect on jobs and the overall economy'. Here indeed is ample confirmation of John Stone's explanation given earlier of the behaviour of business corporations. As I have already noted *ad nauseam*, no good reason has ever been given for why society's main electronic mass communication system should be an adjunct of the advertising industry serving business corporations.

The vital question never put

There is a question that is never put, that must now be brought into the open: Many of the great and good regard nuclear power with horror, but thereby they are making it far more difficult to cut our emissions. This is the question that must now be asked: 'Granted there is a risk with nuclear power, which in any case is small, should not this be set against the very much more terrible risk of world climate calamity, and the end of civilisation'? This is one way of putting James Lovelock's appeal to his fellow greens to shed their anti-nuclear stance, and indeed some of them have come to agree with him. This is a crucially important question that must be put on the world stage.

A Joint Statement of the Scientific Academies

A major hindrance in taking effective action to slow down and limit global warming has been, as already discussed, widespread ignorance about what must be done. There can be no question but that certain easy-to-describe actions must be taken, that great projects must immediately be planned, and a construction programme started. There is surely no better way to end the present perplexed inactivity, and stir society out of its inertia than a joint statement by the scientific academies of the world's major nations, laying out an authoritative and unchallengeable statement of what must be done (much along the lines of what has been written above). And this statement must be not only delivered to every head of government, but must also be published in all the major newspapers, as well as broadcast by the major television stations.

Adding a terrible note: Climate disaster may now be inevitable

In August 2012, just as I near completion of this work, a doom laden statement appears in the press, by two prominent British scientists[90]. Doom is upon us, is it too late to take action to reduce our emissions? The carbon dioxide concentration in the atmosphere is now increasing fast and 'is set to reach 550 parts per million by mid-century, double the pre-industrial concentration'. As a result the average temperature rise will be about three degrees – in some regions, for example, the Arctic, the increase will be greater. 'Weather changes and volatility . . . could cut staple crops significantly . . . 'we may be very hungry in a few decades time . . . damages and human displacements from extreme flooding will add to the stresses . . . this could take us beyond adaptation into the realm of crumbling civil order . . . . Modern economies are built on fossil fuel growth . . .humanity is locked into a course that it has limited capacity or appetite to alter'.

Though we must continue our efforts to reduce our carbon emissions 'we must prepare for the challenging times ahead'. Consequently these two scientists plan 'to create a forum for the public to discuss the issues with leading climate scientists . . . We must begin to discuss the risks and impacts of a climate disaster, since our institutions and processes appear incapable of preventing it'.

Does all this mean that this present work is futile? By no means. These scientists blame our faulty institutions that have brought us to impending disaster, and are also preventing us from reducing our emissions. This work has in fact only one aim, that is to correct our dysfunctional institutions. We must redouble our efforts in that direction, not only to reduce our emissions a great deal – the subject of this chapter has been how to do that – but also to plan for, and reduce the scale of the climate disaster ahead.

CHAPTER 12

The New Science of Economics

This work of many diverse parts could, with only some rearrangement, have been named 'The New Economics' (or indeed, as mentioned in the preface, some other titles were possible). Were economics a genuine science like physics, chemistry, physiology and medicine, those referred to in the will of Alfred Nobel, our society would not now be in deep recession or be endangering the climate, or suffering the other woes discussed in Part One. The first Nobel prizes were awarded in about 1894, and it wasn't until 1968 that the Bank of Sweden, on its 300th anniversary, established the 'Bank of Sweden Prize in Economic Sciences in memory of Alfred Nobel', now commonly referred to as the Nobel Prize in Economics (I wonder what he would think were he alive). Earlier I wrote about the oscillation of economics between the extremes of market fundamentalism and Keynesianism. Both extremes have won the prize, once in the same year, 1974, by Friedrich Hayek and Gunnar Myrdal, and it has been reported that Myrdal was not happy about that.

In the preceding pages I have written of the serious difficulties of our society arising out of its lack of attention to the Social Contract, and the absence of a mechanism to ensure that the contract is fulfilled. The economy must not just be a balance of competing forces, or dominated by a particular force other than that exerted by the people. Were economics a genuine science with the Social Contract its lodestar, the present perverted broadcasting system would not have been permitted to exist, we would long ago have ended the oscillation between boom and bust, and in all probability, the income tax would have been superseded by something like the Return to Society. And we would have been better able to use our magnificent, innovative production machines, the business corporations, to meet the daunting, frightening, challenge of our times. The Arctic melting is increasing its pace, but that is now scarcely mentioned in the news except as the arena for a new scramble for its oil, supposedly nearly a quarter of the world's remaining supply, lying under the ice.

Another reason why in seeking a new Enlightenment we need to reform economics is that economists are hugely influential in determining public policy, in Keynes' so often-quoted words, 'Practical men, who believe themselves to be quite exempt from any intellectual influence, are usually the slaves of some defunct economist. Madmen in authority, who hear voices in the air, are distilling their frenzy from some academic scribbler of a few years back'. The economists are the doctors of the economy, who know – or should know – how it works, and can fix it when it is sick. It is a *sine qua non* of the New Enlightenment that we must be able to control the economy to achieve the people's, and their society's, purposes and avert climate calamity. And as already discussed, how to put an end to boom and bust. This, our existing pseudo science called 'economics' is manifestly unable to do.

In talking of the need for a new economics it would be unfair, indeed seriously inaccurate, not to acknowledge that some prominent economists, usually Keynesians, are very able, and know a great deal about the economy, and are giving good advice on how to deal with the present great recession. Examples coming to mind are Paul Krugman, Nouriel Roubini, and some writers in the Financial Times. Lord Skidelski, on the other hand, the biographer and interpreter of Lord Keynes, was trained not as an economist but as an historian, and that says something about economics – that a non-economist can write on the intricacies of economic theory. Perhaps these brilliant individuals are particularly to be lauded as they are hobbled by a defective economic 'paradigm', to use the term employed by Thomas Kuhn in his 'The Structure of Scientific Revolutions'.

One reason economics is defective is its method, its tendency to rely on deductive reasoning rather that on induction. Inductive reasoning is based on experience and careful observation and uses statistics, and then formulates hypotheses which may be expressed mathematically, which are then proved by further observations. This is the method of physics. In contrast economists are relying on deductive reasoning from certain axioms, for example through so-called DSGE (for dynamic stochastic general equilibrium) modelling to predict the economy's future behaviour, and as a result they failed to anticipate the current financial crisis. 'The belief that models are capable of yielding comprehensive and universal descriptions of the world blinded proponents to realities that had been staring them in the face. That blindness made a big contribution to the present crisis[91]'.

One ignored reality that I believe has been staring the economists in the face for decades has been the part played by advertising, and most especially the 'broadcasting perversion'. To repeat what I wrote earlier 'It helped to create a giant buying bubble of often inessential consumer goods, which, when people panic, they stop buying, throwing millions out of work. Shopping mania and easy credit are obvious partners – shopping facilitated by easy credit, easy credit spurred by the huge demands for it, stirred up by frenetic, ubiquitous advertising. The present crash was a disaster waiting to happen, the old sick way was unsustainable. And the economy has difficulty restarting, people no doubt have realized that they can well survive without endless shopping'. Perhaps this is the explanation, suddenly prominent in the financial press at the end of 2013; '......economic activity across the developed world remains remarkably depressed. The language of recession and recovery no longer seems relevant. Instead we are faced with persistent, economic stagnation. (Stephen King in the Financial Times, 25 November 2013).

Nouriel Roubini is one of the few who warned that the present great financial and economic meltdown was coming and in his book 'Crisis Economics', he explains most convincingly how the economy, in its present form behaves and how it should be managed. But that is where his work falls short: *in its present form*. In his review of the book[92], Paul Krugman writes 'A very good primer on how finance gone bad can wreck *an otherwise healthy economy'*. That is where present economics goes wrong, it wasn't a healthy economy, to repeat, it was a disaster waiting to happen, the old sick way was unsustainable. A healthy economy is not held aloft by a blitz of selling ads propelling a frantic, endless, shopping spree – a blitz of selling ads as unhealthy for the economy as a blitz of 'attack ads' and the oxymoron 'political commercials' are for the health of the democratic process.

The clear and obvious Keynesian fact is that if aggregate demand, the sum of spending in the economy, by households on consumer goods, by government for public services, and by both business and government on new capital goods, is too low, there will be unemployment and low economic growth. But against this obvious fact lies 'deficit fundamentalism', the same doctrine that caused the Great Depression, that there is a categorical imperative, thou shalt have no government budget deficit – cut that evil thing out and the economy will rebound. Government workers in Britain have lost their jobs, and the British economy refuses to grow. At last the austerity that Europe has espoused is on the back foot, the cry now is for growth – which of course means greater effort to increase aggregate demand.

Giant Goofs of Current Economics

The following is a list of eight 'giant goofs' of economics that I have reflected on over the years.

- Continuing poverty though each worker is producing twice as much.

- The cycle of boom and bust.

- The Great Broadcasting Perversion.

- The Shortcomings of the income tax.

- The weird Maastricht deficit.

- The crisis of the Eurozone common currency.

- Absurdity in the measurement of economic productivity increase.

- The gross inaccuracy of the measurement of the stock of fixed capital.

The first five I have already discussed above, and suggested remedies. The other three merit discussion here. If we wish for a rebirth, or a re-enlightenment, of the West, then the travails of its historic European heartland calls for our attention, and that is the subject of Chapter 14. The final two items, though they are technical matters of little general interest, are included here just to give further evidence of how defective present economics can be.

Absurdity in the measurement of the Economic productivity growth rate

'Total Factor Productivity' is a way of measuring economic progress that takes us into the realm of grand farce, reminiscent of the technological wonders of Gulliver's Laputo. Economies are obviously growing more productive over time, a nation's gross domestic product per unit of labour may grow at 2% annually through advancing technology, the increasing use of ever better machines. If on average each worker's output increases 2% annually, output per worker doubles every 35 years. That is clear and logical, and accords with the laws of physics, and plain common sense.

But then the modern schoolmen enter the lists with a curious notion called 'total factor productivity growth' (TFP growth), which appears to be synonymous with so-called neo-classical 'technical progress' (the Solow disembodied residual – 'disembodied', really!). Using TFP, the economist Dale Jorgenson claimed he had explained the economic slowdown in the US and Japan in the wake of the OPEC oil embargo in 1973, when the oil price suddenly increased fourfold. For Japan he compared post embargo TFP growth (1973 to 1979) with pre-embargo TFP growth (1960 to 1973). Pre-embargo TFP growth was 3.0% per annum, but this switched to negative, minus 1.2% post-embargo, Japan's rate of technological progress declined by 4.2% annually (defying the laws of physics). According to Jorgenson 'production reverted to vintages of technological development that existed before the energy crisis . . . These earlier technological strata were appropriate to the new energy price situation'. Quite extraordinary! Somebody waved a wand and the nation's stock of plant and equipment was converted to outdated vintages. Or alternatively the present capital stock was operated using the methods of a decade earlier. Even if this were possible, what was to be gained? Labour costs would have risen – the older vintages required more labour.

Management, rather than converting to outdated technologies or methods, in the real world responds to higher energy prices through investment in more energy-efficient (and expensive) equipment. And in fact that is what happened. Using Jorgenson's data, while Japan's output grew at 3.8% a year, the physical capital input grew at 6.0%, while labour input increased at only 1.5%. In six years labour per unit of output fell by 13%. The inverse of the latter is the nation's aggregate productivity growth. Each worker employed produced 2.3% more each year (so that although there was a slowdown in GDP growth, and unemployment increased, the nation's capital stock did not suddenly become 7% less modern. One wonders what conception the Jorgenson, Solow neo-classical, school of economics have of the real world, with their so-called 'disembodied technical progress', which remains the dominant orthodoxy in the United States, in contrast to the Cambridge, Harrodian, Joan Robinson view.

An example of the oddity of the total productivity (TFP) growth rate is that the 'Asian Tigers', whose economies were growing three times as fast as those of the advanced nations, had very low increases in their TFP. This state of affairs was explained by many complicated mathematical calculations and strange language, for example that the fast economic growth was due to 'the free gifts from externalities and scale effects'. But it was said, the Tigers' technology was not advancing. Although this doctrine continues to hold sway in the US, many other economists cannot swallow it. A 2001 paper by a prominent Canadian economist and a New Zealand colleague was entitled 'What does total productivity measure'?, and concluded 'every TFP measure should carry the caveat: there is no reason to believe that changes in TFP in any way measure technological change'.

Since a good alternative, straightforward, measure of productivity increase is available one wonders why the TFP measure continues to be used. This other measure is the labour productivity growth rate. If for example the economy grows at a rate of 3% and its employed labour force grows at only 1%, then it's productivity – that is, its labour productivity – is increasing at 2%. Just how straightforward this is the fact that the weighted average of all the individual component industry labour productivity growth rates is also 2%. Weighting is by industry 'value added', that is, its share of total GDP[93]. Value added is the sum of each industry's labour and capital inputs (its so-called 'factors of production'), and the sum of all the industry value addeds is GDP.

The gross inaccuracy of the measurement of the stock of fixed capital

All production occurs through a partnership of people and machines. In highly mechanized mass production, workers are mere operators and controllers of machines, but with other activities such as the skilled trades – carpentry, brick-laying, plumbing, gardening, hair-dressing, and the professions – doctors, lawyers, teachers, musicians, writers, and the like, the people are the producers, skilfully wielding the tools of their occupation, the drill and saw of the carpenter, the stethoscope of a doctor, the violin of a musician. One of the sets of statistics assembled and calculated by nations' central statistical agencies is the estimate of the capital stock, that is, the amount of plant, structures, buildings, equipment, and tools. The national total is estimated, broken down by type, and by industry. Nations with large capital stocks have large outputs, that is high GDPs. And the more capital stock they have per worker, the higher is their output per worker, that is, their productivity, and the greater the nation's affluence.

It is easy to estimate the amount of labour, simply counting the number of workers of each type, farm labourers, lathe operators, airline pilots, doctors, pianists. With fixed capital it is vastly more difficult, as the capital stock is hugely heterogeneous, innumerable types and designs of equipment and structures, bought over many years. Of a particular industry one cannot simply says it has 20,347 pieces of equipment. So how do statistical agencies estimate the capital stock? They use what they call the 'perpetual inventory method' (PIM). It is incredibly simple. Each year a survey determines what each company and government department spends on new capital assets (the aggregate of which is the item I, investment, in determining gross domestic product: (GDP = C + G + I + net exports). The agencies then 'estimate', as they call it, the capital stock of each industry, and each category of investment (buildings and structures, machinery and equipment), using a very simple formula: K = Sum of I for each the last L years, where L is the assumed life of that category of capital good[94]. This method would be accurate if any accurate data existed for lives, but there's the rub. For example until about 15 years ago the Canadian capital stock was estimated using American life assumptions established in about 1920, and then a new set of lives were somewhat arbitrarily adopted. Worldwide, the estimates of nations' capital stocks are highly unreliable.

One could just shrug and say it can't be helped, it's very difficult to measure capital stocks short of taking a hugely expensive physical inventory of each company's stock of buildings, structures, and equipment. But the fact is it *can* be helped, and very easily. There is only one source of data from which lives can be determined, companies' fixed asset accounts. From these accounts, through suitable equations and with the help of a computer, it is possible to infer precisely accurate lives for calculating equally accurate capital stocks. When I was an employee of Statistics Canada about 20 years ago I published in the journal, the Review of Income and Wealth, a paper showing how it could be done, by a system called FAASM (Fixed Asset Accounting Simulation Model). I then developed the computer program, containing the complex equations by which lives, and the consequent capital stock, could be calculated with great accuracy. The model even inferred the variation of lives over time, and the distribution of lives within each category of capital good.

And I provided proofs of this accuracy. But all to no avail. Current orthodoxy plus bureaucracy can be an insurmountably strong force to oppose. Internationally capital stocks continue to be estimated inaccurately[95]. And now there is the accurate method to which I have just referred sitting in a drawer somewhere, that could be placed in service and accurately measure the capital stock.

The New Economics and Keynes

The New Economics is not a negation of Keynesian economics, it is a large extension of what Keynes believed. Indeed I suspect that something not unlike it is what Keynes himself would have arrived at were he living in today's world. That his view of the nature and purpose of the economic system and its part in society is like that discussed here is suggested by what he wrote in essay 'Economic Possibilities for our Grandchildren', from his collected writings.

I don't think that Keynes', in the General Theory, makes any reference to the Social Contract as such, and how it is now being contravened by the misappropriation of the broadcast media system to serve business corporations as an advertising medium. As I noted in Chapter 4, the eminent economist, Paul Samuelson, virtually ignored advertising, and didn't even mention the broadcasting sort. Also lacking is any discussion of other similar misappropriations of what should be public functions.

J. K. Galbraith, who was a Keynesian, is the only economist I know of who has expressed views with any similarity to those expressed here, in his 'The Affluent Society' and 'The New Industrial State'. In particular, he wrote of the huge power of the business corporations, which through advertising could create 'wants' and so be sure of being able to dispose of whatever they produce. He also talked of private affluence and public poverty, in the deficiencies of the United States infrastructure, and talked of the 'revised sequence', whereby the consumer is no longer king, though he did not write of what I believe to be the hugely important perversion of the broadcast media. Galbraith described how the American economy actually works, the primacy of the business corporations at the expense of the public, but

I believe that he wrote little on what should be done to change the situation, except to improve vastly the education system, to institute consumption taxes on certain categories of consumer goods, and to set up new public authorities to mend the crumbling infrastructure. (And writing in November 2012: How it crumbles: notable in the reporting on Superstorm Sandy was the dilapidated state of the infrastructure).

Some discussion of Keynesian precepts

Classical, pre-Keynesian, economics had assumed that the free market, uninterfered with, would automatically lead to full employment. Keynes argued otherwise. This matter has already been discussed in Chapter 7, on restarting the economy, and bears repeating. An important element of his system is 'aggregate demand', the total spending in the economy, what consumers and government want to buy, and how much business and government want to invest in new capital facilities. If total aggregate demand is too low then there will be unemployment and idle plant. A crucial factor in aggregate demand is Keynes' 'consumption function', which determines the proportion of personal income people will choose to spend on consumer goods, while saving the rest. What in aggregate the public may choose to consume may not be enough to keep the economy fully employed. In his view the consumption function was not a readily changeable entity – hence, for example, the stubborn unemployment of the 1930s following the 1929 market debacle. And now we have been witnessing the huge failure of the US economy to reignite and take off again. Hence Obama's humiliating rout at the midterm election, though it is probably true that the recession would have been even deeper but for his Keynesian-inspired stimulus policy and the Federal Reserve's quantitative easing (though one can have doubts whether the latter can make much difference).

I suggest that broadly there are three sorts of stimulus. One is transferring money to the unemployed and other casualties of the recession, so that they can resume their consumer spending. Another way is 'quantitative easing', printing money and using it to buy bonds held by the banks, who now, with large money assets will, it is hoped, be glad to fund vigorous business activity, lending to businesses on easy terms to encourage them to expand their activity. A huge such quantitative easing, $600 billion, was launched in November 2010 by the US Federal Reserve to little avail. The American consumer, angry, fearful, with vast personal debt, is saving rather than spending. The once very low US personal saving rate is now starting to climb. Absent the great shopping spree so commented on in recent years, Keynes' aggregate demand – or the lack thereof – is very much in evidence in the American economy.

There is also a third totally different sort of stimulus, and that is spending by the government itself, for improving and adding to the infrastructure, which in the US is in a sorry state, and on major projects to construct highspeed trains and nuclear generating stations for serious reduction of greenhouse gas emissions. The government will not for the most part itself build infrastructure and nuclear stations, it will contract the work out to the private sector. The government itself need not become bigger, but it will have to find the money to pay contractors.

As discussed in Chapter 8, the normal, correct, way for paying for government capital investment in infrastructure is by borrowing, by the sale of government bonds. But given present high public debts (in the US it is 105% of GDP, and in Italy considerably higher), these countries may be reluctant to borrow. In that case it is difficult to see why they shouldn't use printed money for infrastructure spending. If printing money is regarded as acceptable for quantitative easing just described, to lead, it is hoped, to new business spending, why should there be any objection to its direct use to fund spending by the government?

As new infrastructure is correctly funded by borrowing, the public debt quite legitimately should go up. If nations are to engage seriously in the great battle of the future and launch a new renaissance, they will have to increase their public debts, as a proportion of GDP.

It is very much this latter form of stimulus that is now called for, not only to end unemployment, but to engage in the Great Battle of the Climate, and to meet other challenges of our times. But I wouldn't call this kind of spending 'stimulus' but rather one of the normal forms of spending when the other forms of spending are low – though in the future world of the New Enlightenment, without boom and bust, and no longer driven by profligate consumer spending pumped up by frenzied advertising, whether of the perverted broadcasting sort, or other pernicious forms, there will be far less need for 'stimulus' of any sort.

In our programme for a new enlightenment, there are two matters pertaining to Keynes that need discussion. On the first, government stimulus, a few words have just been said. The other is an examination of the fixity of the consumption function, which is blocking US recovery. Just how fixed is the consumption function? Can it, in fact, contrary to Keynes' view, be budged? What role might advertising play? Now, accepting Keynes' fixity of the consumption function, Keynesian economists appear to assume that advertising cannot increase aggregate demand in the economy – advertising, no matter how frenzied and insistent, affects only market share, 'our soap is better than other soaps'. But does not plain common sense lead one to suspect that a sustained advertising blitz (including seldom-off American-type radio and television) might help to turn people into compulsive shoppers? Can't populations be swayed by sustained propaganda?. Might this not be partly responsible for the present consumerism and shopping mania that our social commentators bewail? Surely orthodoxy's rejection of this notion as a matter of faith, defies reason. (Mind you, there may come a time, as now in the United States, when a traumatised population is not budged by even frantic advertising – their animal spirits are at a low ebb).

But it is not surprising that Keynes left advertising out of the equation. When he died in 1946, what may be called the misappropriation of the broadcasting system would hardly have been evident to him. Television as yet scarcely existed, and radio broadcasting in Britain and Europe was free of advertising. Keynes after all had matchless common sense, no unmoveable attachment to dogma or theory however hallowed. It seems reasonable to suspect that if Keynes were writing now, his consumption function could be budged by the continual advertising Big Brother.

Is it total coincidence that the United States with its particularly intense advertising assault is also the nation which has had a very low personal savings rate in recent years[96]? While the wealthy would certainly save part of their income, this is offset by others spending more than they earn through massive credit card and house mortgage purchasing. And the extent of this private indebtedness is an alarming feature of the present Great Recession – once bitten, twice shy, desperate consumers are now staying at home, discovering they don't really need to go on their weekly shopping spree, and at last the American personal saving rate is beginning to climb – but herein lies a cautionary tale – what a weird way of managing the American economy, kept aloft by advertising-induced shopping, while the national infrastructure goes untended, and the cry is amplified, cut our taxes – shrink tyrannical, spending government, return to the Constitution, give us more guns.

The structure of the New Economics

What will be the structure of the New Economics? We must appreciate that society has no separate 'economic system' concerned with monetary flows that can be manipulated through mathematical and econometric models, but is a hugely complex, living, social-economic-political-physical-environmental system. Forty years ago I developed what I called the 'Society System Model[97], which depicted society as made up of components exchanging physical, information, and monetary flows. In the ten following years I refined it, and in a 1982 paper[98] I proposed 'a design for a model of the Canadian economy' which 'seeks great fidelity by, in effect, "miniaturising" the economy into model components very like their real counterparts"; . . . 'it is fundamentally dynamic as a result of portraying capital stocks; its component sectors are goal-pursuing; it has a well-developed financial sector; and represents not only the usual variables in monetary terms, but also the underlying physical phenomena'. Perhaps one might refer to it as a living organism, as it includes goal-pursuing humans as well as inorganic parts. Therefore it is less of an exact science than physics or astronomy, more like biology or medical science.

At the end of this chapter are several items from these papers which will give an idea of the nature of the new economics. Figure 4.1 is the basic form of the society system model, and Figure 4.2 depicts the major flow categories, physical, informational, and monetary, between the people-as-people (that is people in their personal lives rather than as workers in the economy), on the one hand, and organizations (the economy, broadly defined) and the physical environment, on the other.

These are the 'ultimate' flows, that affect the people's quality of life. Other flows, between the components of the economy, are called 'intermediate' to use the term of macro-economics.

I concluded the 1982 paper by writing that 'within the broad philosophical framework of the Society Systems Model . . an ultimate consequence may be that economic science is broadened to become part of a unified social science, which will permit the coordinated study of all aspects of the societal system, social, economic, political, monetary, technological, attitudinal, geological, environmental, and so on. The concepts of the economist and other social scientists can be brought together with those of the engineer and the systems analyst'.

The society system model in detail

Readers uninterested in the more detailed levels of the society system model should skip this section. Figure 4.3 shows the monetary flows between the people and each of the major sectors of the economic system: government, consumer goods industry, capital goods industry, intermediate and raw materials industry, the banking system, the unions, the mass communications media, and the general physical environment. The monetary flows shown are in fact the elements of the national accounts system, and are the components of GDP. This is a macro-economic model in flow chart terms. Not shown here are the two diagrams portraying the counterpart physical and information flows between the sectors.

Figure 4.4 represents exactly to same information in the form of a national income input-output table – I have adapted the standard Leontieff table to represent the people as the paramount sector of the economy which exists to serve it. Finally Figures 4.5 and 4.6 show the detail for Sector 5, materials production sector, in the form of accounting statements, respectively the annual operating statement and balance sheet of the sector. Underlying all these diagrams is the notion that society and the economy exist to serve the people.

It is worth noting that all these exhibits together represent the integration of company financial statement accounting – the annual operating statement and balance sheet, and the source and application of funds – and the national accounts. I do not know whether other researchers have used this same integration, but it is surely probable. The need for this new science of economics is especially pressing when the world's economies must be managed and reformed in order to mitigate calamitous climate change. As already discussed earlier, economists play a huge part in advising governments. The New Economics involves not jettisoning present macroeconomics, whose substructure, based on the system of national accounts, is essentially sound, but greatly broadening it to embrace the following fundamental requirements.

1. The new economics is the science of the monetary dimension of the total societal system social, political, economic, environmental. Its other dimensions are physical and informational.

2. The Social Contract is the overriding principle governing the societal system, and its economic dimension. The system's sole purpose is to serve the people and protect the environment.

3. Modern society is organised in a set of 'estates', or sectors, each with its particular function in order to fulfill the Social Contract. It is useful to recognise at least six estates, respectively: the people; their government which helps them govern; the public services; the business corporations, the monetary and financial system; and the mass media.

4. Society must be on guard to prevent the misappropriation of roles among the estates. Among our society's grievous ills has been the hijacking of the people's functions, most notably, the misappropriation by the business corporations of society's main

system of public masscommunication. Other such hijackings are the function of charitable giving, and paying for sports ('sports marketing') in order to serve their sales promoting and marketing objectives. It is the function solely of the people to select and pay for their broadcasting service. Charity is solely the function of the people, who alone must decide what are worthy causes and donate to them. Sports stars, and sporting facilities must be paid for solely by, and serve, the people.

5. An effective and fair system must be installed to decide what proportion of the gross domestic product should be paid for by personal spending, and what proportion by collective spending. The present system of the income tax, both personal and business is fundamentally defective, and needs to be replaced by a new 'Return to Society'.

6. Full employment and the provision of adequate income for all must be ensured. The absurdity of cyclic boom and bust has no justification in a sane society.

7. Civilised society has an overriding requirement to protect itself and the environment, and to address impending calamitous climate change.

It will be observed that this statement of the New Economics resembles the set of nine elements of my 1969 statement given in Chapter 4, on the deep disorder of our society. How an economy is structured is inseparable from the purpose of the society itself. Society might be described as having two major parts, the People, and the Economy. The people are tied to the economy a large part of their day as workers in it, and as receivers of the goods and services it provides for them. In accordance with the Social Contract, they should as much as possible fulfill themselves in satisfying work, in pleasant surroundings; and the economy should produce the mix of goods and services designed to maximise their enjoyment and self realization during their sojourn on earth, and also to protect their physical environment. For example, the economy should not impose on them the waste of part of their day in traffic gridlock, and it should not so load the earth's atmosphere with greenhouse gas emissions that future life on the planet is threatened.

The accuracy of the new science of economics

The new economic science, like medical science, must lack the precision of physics and chemistry, which deal with inorganic objects. The trajectory of a missile can be exactly calculated, space ships can be accurately sent to Mars, eclipses of the sun can be exactly predicted. Medicine deals with an enormously complex organism, the human body, and there have always been controversies among medical scientists. For example, regarding breast cancer, should simple lumpectomy, or total mastectomy be used, and more lately, there is a controversy regarding the use of the PSA test in the treatment of prostate cancer. Moreover there may be giant industries, including the pharmaceutical industry, which have a vested interest in huge reliance on their products to maintain the status quo. Even so medical science progresses, human life expectancy increases.

The new economics will also be dealing with an exceedingly complex system, of wayward, sometimes noble, sometimes merely happy to be alive, sometimes wicked, human individuals, and at the helm other individuals, some marvellous, some awful, supposedly in charge, but in fact often obstructed by giant corporations, profit-making machines which may each be pushing in a different direction – the whole a huge array of interacting physical, informational, and monetary entities. The News Economics will not be an exact science. But it will make sure that all these entities together observe certain unbreakable ground rules, there will be no boom or bust, no people will ever be in penury or unemployed against their wills for very long, science and technology and innovation will continue, but always with the proviso that they improve people's quality of life, according to their own considered wishes, without brain-washing. And those ingenious, innovative. efficient, machines, the great business corporations, will continue to thrive and make profits, but always to serve only the interests of the people.

Figure 4.1: The Basic Form of the Society System Model

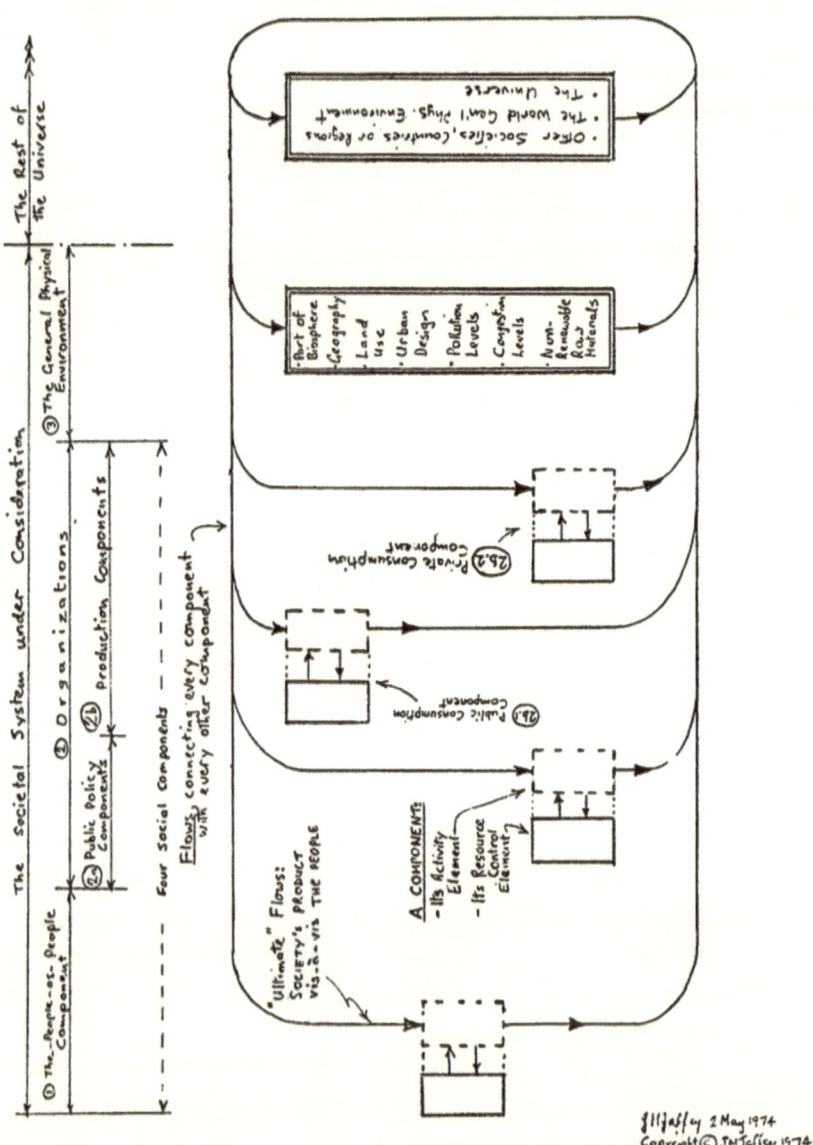

**Figure 4.2: The Flows of the Society System Model
Physical, Informational, and Monetary**

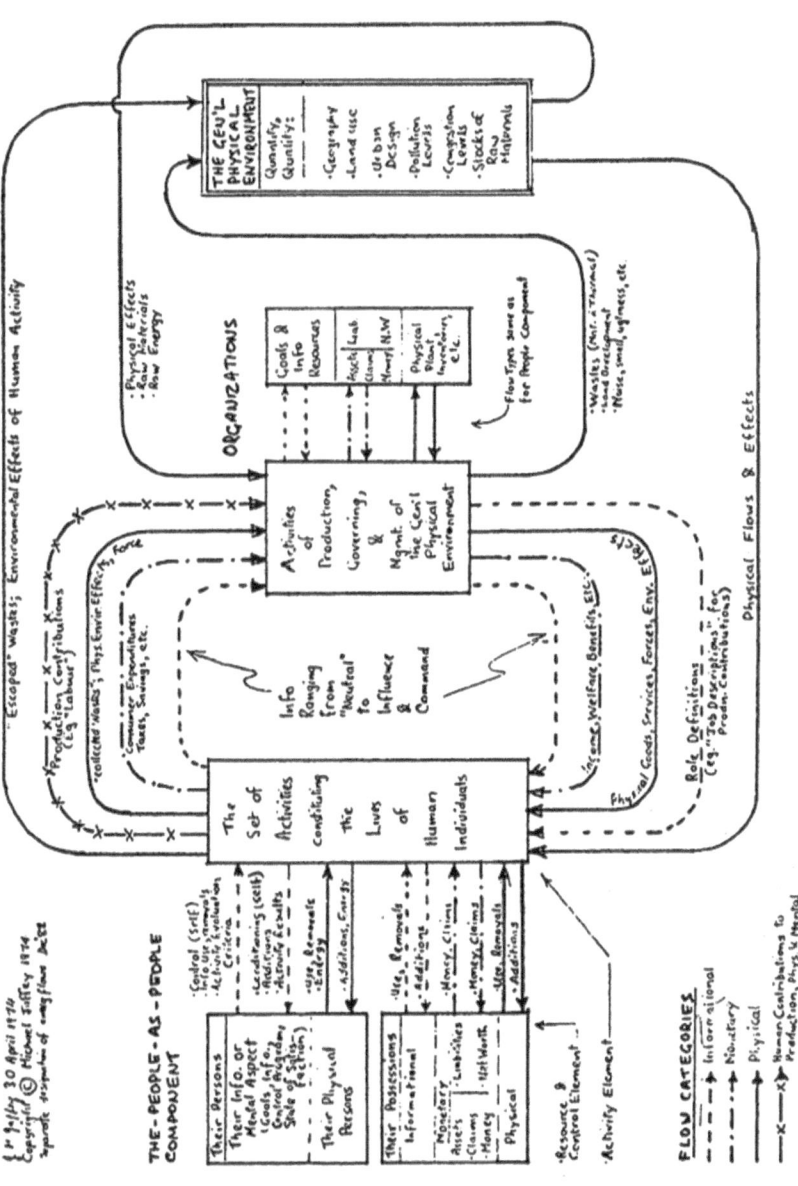

Figure 4.3: The major inter-sectoral monetary flows

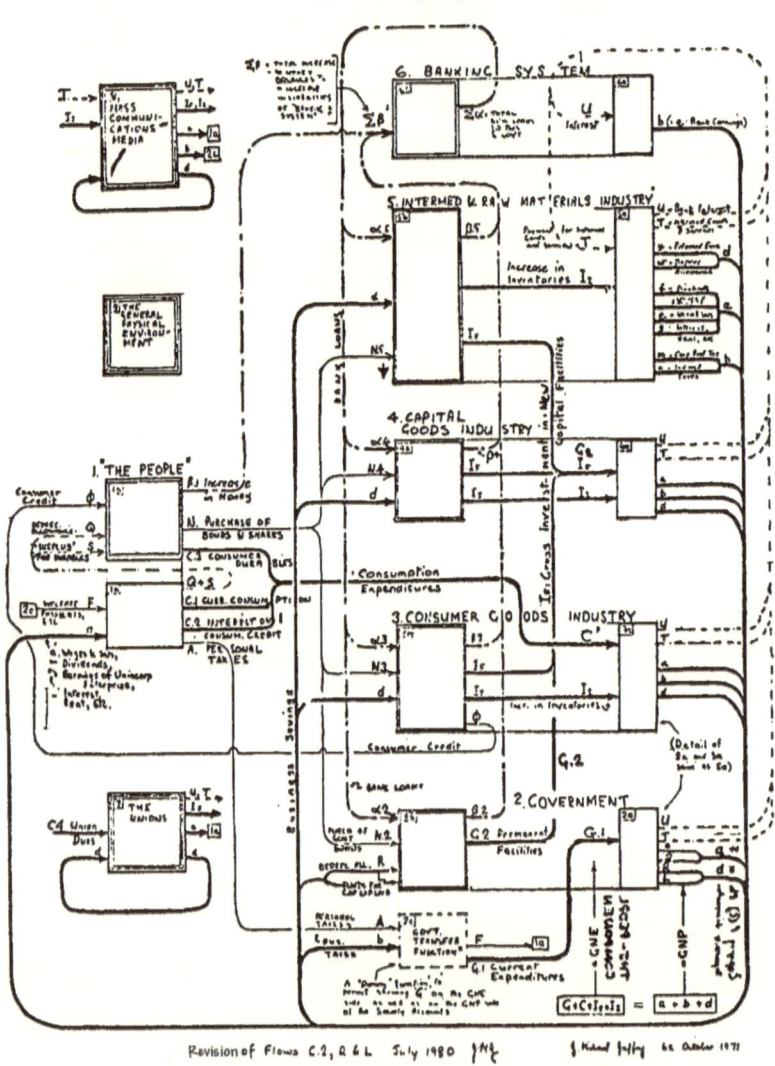

Figure 4.4: The major inter-sectoral flows in the form of a macro-economic input-output table

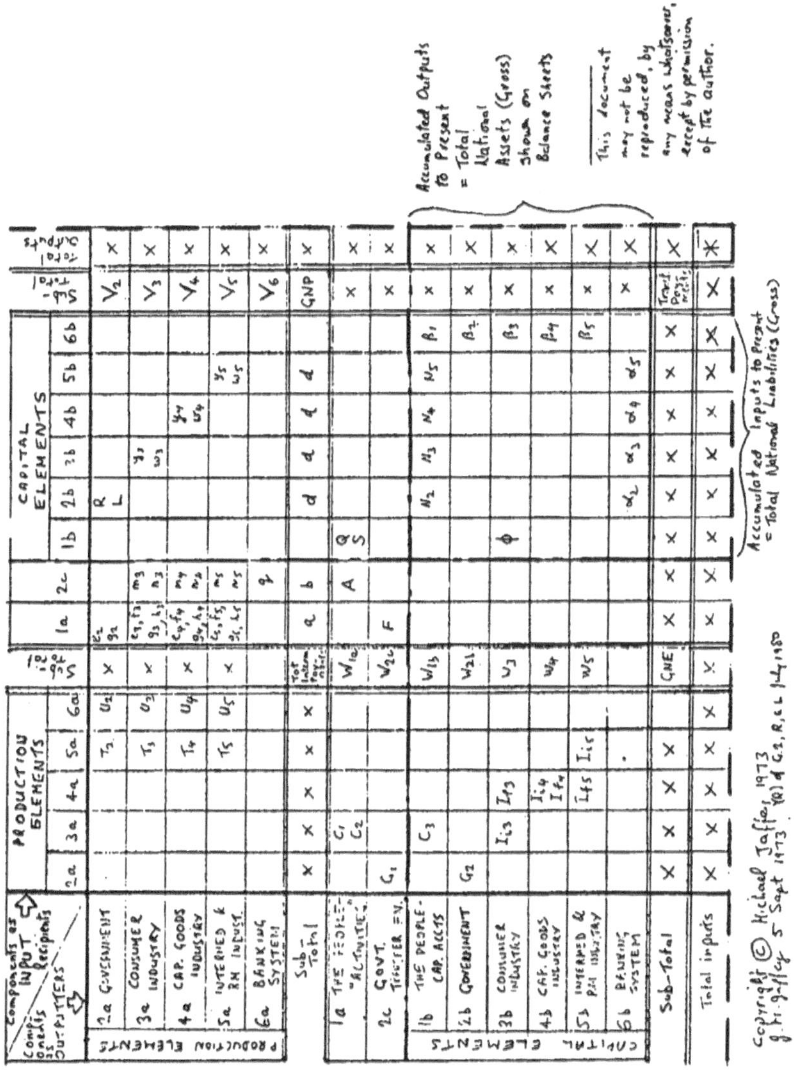

Figure 4.5: The Materials Sector

<u>Annual Operating Statement</u>

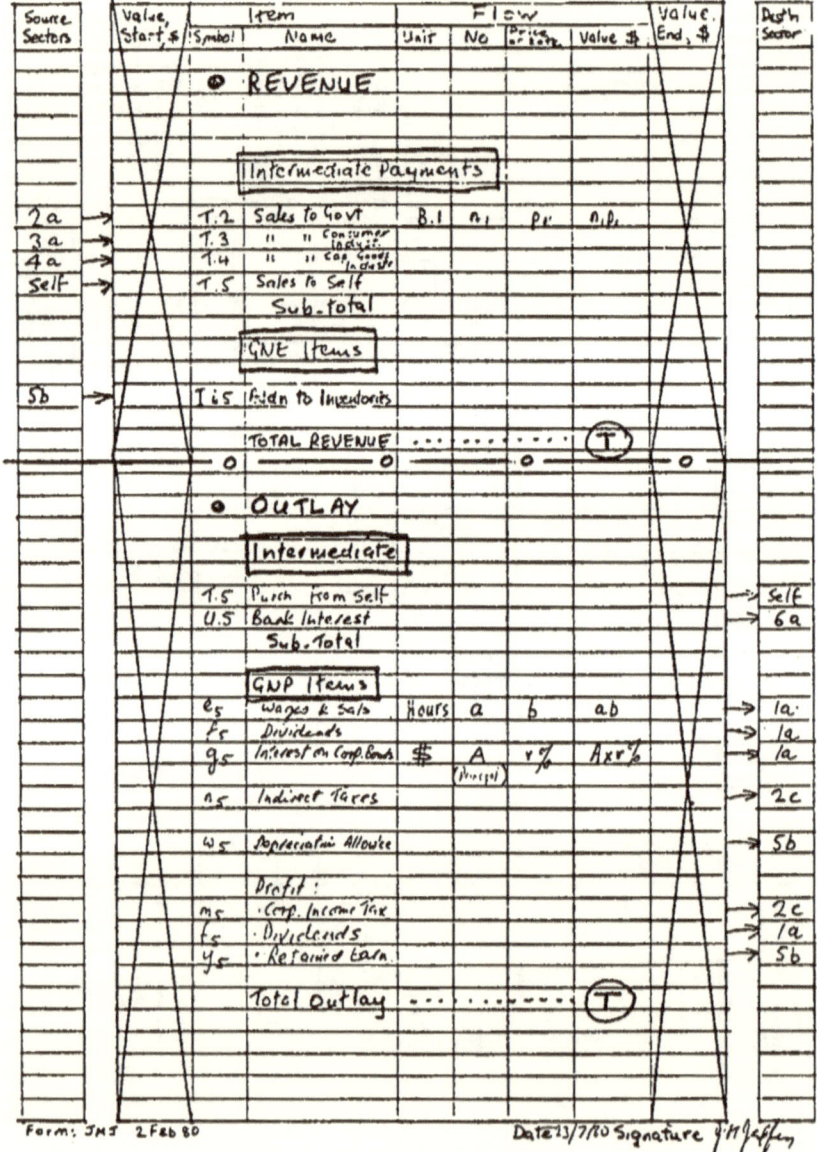

Figure 4.6: The Materials Sector

Annual Balance Sheet

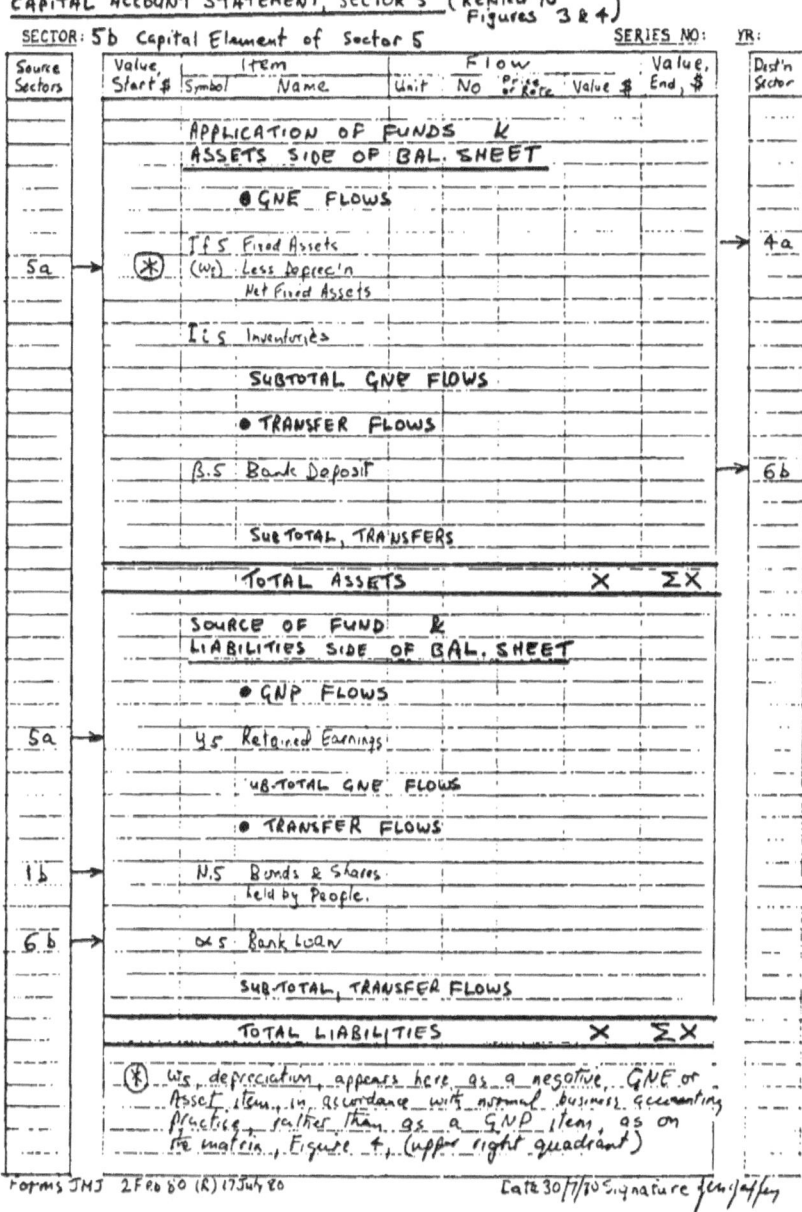

CHAPTER 13

Reforming Democracy

Three great reforms have been discussed, banishing boom and bust, transforming the broadcasting system, and replacing the income tax by a more rational means of extracting public funds out of the economy. Also we have laid out the giant programme that will vastly reduce our carbon emissions. With these we shall have taken a giant step towards reversing decline and placing the people in charge – people will realize that now their own well-being, the well-being of their society, comes first, and that our great corporations are there to serve us, and only us, and not left to their own devices to survive and make profits by any means they can think of, even if so doing destroys the environment and makes us all – well not quite all, not the one percent – miserable.

Radically transforming the broadcasting system will help to level the playing field of public opinion and start reducing the power of the business corporations, putting all the people back to work and banishing boom and bust will vastly increase the people's faith in their society, and transforming the public finance system will allow rational, democratic, decisions on the amount of government spending needed to meet the great challenges of our times and to engage in the Battle of the Climate.

But it is not enough merely to talk about great reforms. It will be a prime role of government now to launch, to set in motion these reforms, and drive the mega-projects of the great Battle of the Climate. But government will not of its own accord initiate the process, it must be prodded to take the lead. Our form of government is, and must remain, democracy, but democracy can have failings. Our quest for a New Enlightenment, a rebirth, of the West may appear laughable at the moment, the West is moving in the opposite direction. We may now be at a time when our democracy's shortcomings are a grave threat to the survival of civilization. Yes, democracy at least helps ensure that the squeaky wheel gets grease, but that may be a far cry from intelligent, far-seeing government: In the Chamberlain years, democracy in Britain practised appeasement in the face of the Nazi threat. Now there is little doubt that democracy in a large part of the Western world is burying its head in the sand in the face of the climate threat. In the view of the respected scientist and environmentalist, James Lovelock – he pleaded with his fellow greens to shed their anti-nuclear obsession, only nuclear power can save the climate – 'one of the main obstructions to meaningful action is "modern democracy . . . even the best democracies agree that when a major war approaches, democracy must be put on hold for the time being. I have a feeling that climate change may be an issue as severe as war. It may be necessary to put democracy on the hold for a while' [99].

A most alarming picture of the present American condition is laid out by Chris Hedges in his 'Empire of Illusion', already quoted in Chapter 9. 'Our nation has been hijacked by oligarchs, corporations, and a narrow selfish, political and economic elite, a small and privileged group that governs, and often steals, on behalf of moneyed interests'. Horror stories of dysfunctional government are now flowing daily from the United States. Yes, there is indeed universal suffrage there, but money from the very rich, from business corporations, and the so-called Super-Pacs (Political Action Committees), is used for torrents of highly partisan television 'political commercials' and 'attack ads', which influence the views of the electorate. It is not too much of an exaggeration to say that the US Congress is a bought entity, far from the kind of democratic assembly or parliament that can make intelligent choices for the benefit of the people, all the people.

Already discussed in Chapter 5 are serious failings that in some nations, and most particularly in the United States, have corrupted the quality of democratic institutions, to the extent that the US has become more of a plutocracy than it is a democracy. And already mentioned has been the EU Brussels bureaucracy which interferes with, and even overrides, the powers of the democratically elected EU member state governments. Francis Fukuyama[100] writes thus of 'political decay': 'Political systems develop, often slowly and painfully over time . . . But political decay occurs when political systems fail to adjust to changing circumstances . . . . Human beings are rule-following animals by nature; they are born to conform to the social norms they see around them, and they entrench those rules with often transcendent meaning and value'. That is much the same as I wrote in Chapter 4 on 'the inertia of the giant supertanker, Society . . . . it is difficult to deflect the giant vessel from its present course. Each individual person, ourselves, is programmed to play his present part, both at work and play, that he has been taught to do since infancy, over his lifetime he has acquired deeply ingrained habits, skills, routines, way of life'.

Yes indeed, a woeful situation. Who is going to mend these appalling departures from good government in the service of the people? Ultimately government itself of course, only they, short of revolution, can institute major reform, but often government will only do so if driven by popular outrage, the formation of reform movements, and with the help of a free press. But we must have a clear idea of precisely what good democratic government entails. If ever there was a time when such clarification was necessary it is now. There is now a 'contest between those who think that twenty-first century government can be effective and those who don't . . . Some of the most outspoken U. S. capitalists have begun to fight . . calls to raise taxes on those at the very top, with the argument that money is best left in the bank accounts of the super-rich because they are more effective at using it than the state is'[101]. That of course is self-interested twaddle, a symptom of that part of the American Dream which is now a nightmare, but even so it is essential to define just what is the role of the state in a well-governed, and decent, society.

Chapter 5's statement of the Social Contract defines five main estates of the realm in a democracy: the people, their elected government, the government departments, the business corporations, and the media. Of these five, three are involved in democratic government: 'The people elect their government to assist them govern the state. The government departments provide the publicly funded services and regulatory bodies'. This gives us a framework for improving our democratic institutions.

The election by the people
of their government

First is how popular opinion is formed. For the people to choose wisely the politicians and policies they will vote for, they must be well informed without biased or distorted information provided by special interests. This requires that they have good media of mass communication, both broadcast and print. And the electoral process must be good, both as to the funding of election campaigns, and then in the way these funds are used, how the issues are presented and debated.

First how public opinion is formed: At the risk of thoroughly irritating the reader by perpetually nagging on this matter, one can never emphasise too often the importance of ridding ourselves totally of the broadcasting perversion. This blot on our society must go, no longer will wealthy private interests and their political 'super-pacs' be able to flood the airwaves with 'political commercials' and 'attack ads'. It is illuminating to read the Charter of the British Broadcasting Corporation, which is perhaps the world prototype of the public service broadcaster. The Charter specifies that the mission of the Corporation is to 'inform, educate and entertain' and that it exists to serve the public's interest and promote its public purposes: sustaining citizenship and civil society, promoting education and learning, stimulating creativity and cultural excellence, representing the UK, its nations, regions and communities, bringing the UK to the world and the world to the U K[102]. Not a word on promoting consumer goods. That sort of aim is most certainly not what drives American broadcasters, ABC, CBS, NBC, CNN, Fox, and their ilk, that is not what they are paid to do: They who pay the piper call the tune.

Three alternative ways of transforming the broadcasting system were discussed in Chapter 9: by exhortation, bringing about a revulsion of public opinion; by using the free market, but requiring the recipients of advertising-broadcasting to pay for it; and by edict, by legislating a five-year conversion programme of the broadcasting system, on the grounds that advertising-broadcasting is seriously injurious to the health of democracy. Those alternatives have appeared in my past papers on the matter, but now, in these dire times, only the third alternative will do. Legislation is called for among the nations which will lead the New Enlightenment.

The other medium of mass communication, the press, newspapers, and magazines, probably need little change (perhaps the dreadful English tabloids excepted). The great newspapers remain crucially important as a source not only of news, but of commentary and the opinions of society's major commentators, experts, and savants, and leading political figures of the day. One may wonder however whether the institution of the 'editorial article' is justified – just who are the people who write them? Among the major newspapers, some are said to be conservative, others liberal, or 'left of centre' – how much does that give a slant to their news, and to their editorial opinions? For myself, I am far more interested in what their well-known columnists have to say, such figures as Paul Krugman and Thomas Friedman in the New York Times, Martin Wolf, Gavyn Davies in the Financial Times, Chrystia Freeland (Editor of Thomson, Reuters Digital), Jeffrey Simpson and Doug Saunders in the Globe and Mail. And also distinguished contributors in their pages, for example Nouriel Roubini and Timothy Garton-Ashe. All these people have important things to say regarding the health of our society.

The Electoral process

To improve democracy we need also to reform how political campaigns and the electoral process are paid for. We must replace funding by wealthy individuals, business corporations and special interests, by generous public funding, after all it is extremely important, how society arrives at what people and policies are needed to improve the people's lives and protect their future. In the recent 2012 American presidential election, already by the beginning of

June, a group of about 30 billionaires had spent more on the polls than the rest of America combined'[103]. That money bought blitzes of 'attack ads' on America's shameful broadcasting system.

It is not only in the United States that money may buy power. Headline news from Britain tells us of the resignation of the governing Conservative party's treasurer when the news broke that 'he had promised (to a group of reporters posing as rich would-be donors) private meetings with the prime minister in exchange for donations of 250,000 pounds'[104]. And at the same time a parliamentary enquiry is revealing the astonishing extent to which the British government had a cosy relationship with Rupert Murdoch's News Corporation. But in all this we must also never forget the importance of a free press – it is newspaper headlines which are revealing these unsavoury events to the public, and the present British government is now very low in the opinion polls.

For genuine democracy huge donations by rich individuals and powerful interests must be abolished. In its place should be the generous provision of public funds, and a low limit on how much individual members of the public can contribute.

And how should campaign money once raised be used? Most certainly not on political commercials and attack ads, rather through published party programmes, speeches and electioneering by the candidates, and many well organized debates among them, which are aired on television and reported on in the print press.

Consider how election campaigns might be conducted in a nation that is determined to have truly democratic elections, and also has a genuinely public-serving broadcasting system. Generous broadcasting time, indeed a special channel might be provided, both for candidates at the local level, and for national party leaders, to appear on television and argue their views on needed public policy changes. They would be helped by neutral, well-informed, moderators who raise questions on such important matters as have been discussed here, on total reform of the taxation and broadcasting systems, global warming, corporate social responsibility, foreign policy and the war on terror. Protagonists would appear and argue in person. The point is that through public funding, and the removal of advertising, there could now be a level playing field for democratic debate, and one which has the Social Contract in mind. Just consider how a televised US debate might be conducted between the Republican and Democratic candidates in an American presidential election:

Moderator: 'It is a well known fact that the United States alone among the advanced nations does not have universal health care, even though our country, in common with these other nations, have universal education for our young. Moreover our health care system is far more expensive than that of other nations, but still leaves nearly 50 million people uncovered and many inadequately covered. The largest cause of personal bankruptcy in the United States is high medical expenses. Further, presumably, in large degree, as a result of shortcomings in our health care system, the United States has the lowest life expectancy among the advanced nations. My question to you is: Is this is a satisfactory state of affairs, and if not, what we should do about it?

It would be fascinating to discover how the two candidates would respond. And as important would be to see democracy really working, going directly to the people, by-passing the health care lobby, and the forces maintaining the patently undemocratic status quo.

Of course, not only should broadcasting be used to extend full democracy to the public, generous broadcasting time should also be provided for business executives and industry trade associations to put their views forward on public policy, and regulations as it affects them. These too, perhaps for each industry group, would be discussed with the help of a moderator. Sound governance of a nation requires an input in elections on industries' needs and difficulties with current regulations and the suggested changes required. But now, instead of this, business corporations use television only to desecrate the airwaves their dreadful sales promotion 'messages'.

The form of democratic government

Then there is the form of democratic government. Most democratic nations are parliamentary democracies, in which the leader of the party which wins a majority in a general election forms the government. He and the governing cabinet he selects are all members of parliament. As a result of its parliamentary majority, the government can, in principle, initiate whatever new laws and measures it sees fit. These measures will become law, except in the rare event that the government falls as a result of a vote of no confidence in parliament – which can occur only if members of the ruling party 'cross the floor' to join the opposition. Any such action is very difficult in the United States with it's separation of powers between the President, the two Houses of Congress, and the Supreme Court. The President, and the two Houses are elected in separate elections, and may be of different parties, as is now the case, a Democratic President, and a Republican-dominated House of Representatives. At present government 'gridlock' is widely viewed as strangling government in the United States. Major action to launch a New Enlightenment in the United States would be far more difficult than in, say, the UK, France, Germany, and Canada.

The United States' separation of powers may have seemed a reasonable arrangement at the time of the Revolution, to guard against a home grown version of British tyranny, but is it not time to consider some alternative arrangement? This obviously would take an enormous effort, to bring structural change in the United States' institutions of government. And the separation of powers involves more than Congress thwarting the President, it also presents the spectacle of the Supreme Court declaring unconstitutional what good sense, and what the other, the democratically elected, arms of government deem to be important legislation to serve the people: Does it make any sense for lawyers to rule out legislation by interpreting words in a constitution written to serve the hugely different society of two and a quarter centuries ago? Surely elements of grand farce are now (writing in April 2012) playing out, lawyers arguing whether the people of the United States can decide to have universal health care just as they have universal schools for educating their children.

But perhaps we should realize that the United States is not a nation like the other Western nations,. It is a giant of many conflicting parts. The historian and journalist Colin Woodard, in his 'American Nations', presents a history of the nine rival regional nations constituting the United States, differing hugely in their origins and beliefs. The nations are Yankeedom, New Netherlands, Midlands, Tidewater, Deep South, Greater Appalachia, El Norte (Mexican), Far West, the West Coast, and New France (southern Louisiana) Woodard wonders whether the US political map will survive this century. He concludes 'Other democratic sovereign democratic states . . . can fall back on unifying elements we lack: common ethnicity, a shared religion, or near-universal consensus on many fundamental political issues. The United States needs its central government to function cleanly, openly, and efficiently, because it is one of the few things binding us together'. And quite patently the central government is not now functionally well.

Woodard may be only half, even a quarter, right about the huge conflict among America's nations, but when this factor is added to gross breech of the Social Contract, business corporations, and plutocrats, not the people, in charge, there is little hope that America is ready to lead the way in the New Enlightenment.

The Brussels weirdness

And if American society is broken, what about society in Europe?. Democracy there often seems successful at the national level, but very much less so at the level of 'Europe'. Grand farce is now playing out there with a bureaucracy in Brussels enjoying a moment of power – a huge smirk on the face of Jose Manuel Barroso, President of the EU Commission, as fellow technocrats take up the reins of government in Greece and Italy. But has Brussels the real power, with the German chancellor and the French president calling the shots within the Eurozone, and David Cameron outside saying things that seriously annoy Germany and France? Britain wants to take power back from Brussels, and Chancellor Merkel wants to add power to the centre, through a fiscally united 'more perfect union', a United States of Europe.

The present weirdness of the EU is highlighted by looking at the composition of the G20 group of nations, the world's twenty largest economies. Who are they? They include the original G7 advanced nations, the US, Canada, Japan, and in Europe, Germany, the United

Kingdom, France, and Italy, and the newcomers, emerging giant developing nations, of which there are twelve. That gives a total of nineteen nations. Where then is the missing nation? It is an entity called 'Europe', aka the Brussels bureaucracy. The 19 are represented by their heads of government – their prime ministers. presidents, chancellor, or king (Saudi Arabia), but the 'European Union' is represented by two individuals, the EU Council President, Herman van Rompuy, and the Commission President, Jose Manuel Barroso, ambiguous forms of civil servant. The Commission is viewed[105] as its most powerful part, and determines EU legislation. The President of the EU Council (van Rompuy) 'has no formal legislative power but is charged with defining the general direction and priorities of the Union'. What is one to make of all this – is it in the realm of Gulliver's Laputo? A French president, Clemenceau, said war was too serious a matter to be left to the generals, and now it seems that Europe's mess is too serious to be left to its political leaders. How to mend the Brussels mess is the subject of Chapter 14.

Lobbying

Lobbying is influence exerted on democratic government outside the elected government. Lobbyists are paid advocates of special interests who have direct contact with elected officials. One hears very much now of the huge influence of lobbies in the United States, for example, business lobbyists said to have much influence on regulations and laws, the Israel lobby and the Gun lobby. The world was struck at the lame response of both the President and the Republican contender in the approaching election following the recent hideous gun slaughter in Colorado, such is their craven fear of the gun lobby, the National Rifle Association. And, writing in January 2013, the same can be said following the horrific killing of 20 little children in Connecticut. Equally extraordinary is the hammerlock the billionaire casino owner, Sheldon Adelson, had on the Republican contender, to whom he promised one hundred million dollars in campaign funds, in pursuit of Adelson's efforts on behalf of the Israeli government's aim of preventing a two state solution. It was reported three months before the presidential election that '26 billionaires have given $61 million . . . Those 26 billionaires have a net worth . . . equal to 40 percent of all American households . . . How could it possibly be good for a functioning democracy if a bit more than two dozen people have a voice equal or greater than 50 million'[106]?

The role and size of government

Here we are referring to the government departments, the establishment of civil servants, what is called the public sector as compared with the private sector. There are many who contend that government is too big, notably Tea Party Republicans, for them government must be shrunk. We need therefore to be clear on what government does, and what we mean by government spending and size of government.

Government spending has two major categories, current spending and capital spending. Consider first current spending. It is of three totally different types, government services, grants to not-for-profit independent organizations, and transfers of money to households[107].

Government services are performed by the government's own work force, by the public servants we deal with when paying our income tax, by customs and immigration officials, by the police force and judiciary, the people operating national parks and maintaining highways, the military forces, and so on. And the public is also served by independent not-for-profit organizations which receive grants from government. Their object, like that of government departments, is service to the public, rather than profitability in the free market. These organizations are variously named, Crown Corporations in Canada, Quangos (Quasi-Autonomous Non-Government Organizations) in Britain, and more generally NGOs, without the 'quasi-autonomous'. They include public broadcasters, museums and arts centres, and many others, which it is deemed are best performed outside the business sector.

We might add that the resources used for delivering government services are not entirely those of the government, government departments buy their necessary materials and services, their water, electricity, oil and gas, from the business sector.

The third category of current government spending is transfers to households, the 'social safety net', such as old age security. welfare, unemployment, and health benefits.

To summarize, there are three categories of current government spending, government services, grants to NGOs, and transfers to households, and in addition there is capital spending. So when we talk of shrinking government we should specify what aspect of government, government services, grants to NGOs, or transfers to households we must shrink. So the question of the proper size of government is in fact several questions: What services should be provided by government (rather than by the private sector), what services are best rendered by NGOs, and how big should the 'social safety net' be? The amount of government capital spending will scarcely affect the size of government at all, if the government contracts the work out to construction companies, which is what should usually happen.

We are now ready to discuss that highly contentious matter, the government budget deficit: If the amount of all government's current spending, of the three categories, exceeds tax revenue, then the resulting deficit must be paid for by government borrowing. A well run government will not in the long run incur such a deficit, and have recourse to borrowing to cover it.

Finally we need to say some words on that entirely different category of government spending, additions to the nation's public infrastructure, highways, harbours, airports, dams, parks, and so on, that are vital for a nation's well-being, and of course the public buildings in which the government services are housed *(maintaining* the infrastructure, as opposed to creating it, is an item of current government spending, just as maintenance of its facilities is an operating cost of business). Government capital investment is paid for out of its depreciation allowance (money accumulated over the years to replace worn out facilities), and by borrowing, that is by issuing government bonds. As already discussed in Chapter 7 and 8, in the long run this is the only legitimate government borrowing. The public debt should reflect the size of the public infrastructure, plus only temporary amounts as a result of budget deficits, and it can only become very high if there has been a long history of government deficits. The debt will grow as the infrastructure grows but will tend to remain a constant percent of GDP which is also growing. The national debt for a well- governed nation will be between, say, 30% and 50% of GDP. A country without a public debt (therefore no government bonds!) would be an amazing nation which pays for all its infrastructure, its public works, out of its tax revenue, that is, it pays now for the future services the facilities will provide over thirty year lifetimes.

As was discussed in Chapter 8, there is a strange language misuse in the European Union, where the deficit is defined to include its borrowing to pay for infrastructure. That is no deficit, as already indicated, that is legitimate government spending – that is what government bonds are really for, not for covering the huge government current deficits that now plague the Western world.

If we define the total size of government as its total spending in the three current categories, then the size of government is only slightly affected by the capital expenditure category: it will need only a small staff to plan and supervise its capital spending – it lets contracts to companies which do the actual construction work. Sometimes, though, a government will use its own construction force to do work. One can think of circumstances when the management of capital spending adds significantly to the size of government, and that would be if government played a major role, using its own forces, in the Great Battle of the Climate.

Government spending
in Canada's national accounts

The various categories of government spending are depicted in Figure 1.1 in Chapter 10, which shows Canada's national accounts for 2005. The size of government, the amount of government spending at all levels, federal, provincial, and municipal, was $396.5 billions, 29 percent of GDP. Of this, nearly two thirds, 19 percent of GDP, was spent on services provided by the government itself, and the remaining 10 percent of GDP consisted of transfer payments to households, much of which would then be spent on consumer goods provided by the private sector. (These accounts have not distinguished payments to NGOs which are probably included in transfer payments). We also see that rather than running a deficit in 2005, Canadian government had a surplus, $12.3 billion, nearly one percent of GDP. And we can also see that this surplus, augmented by a $ 31.7 billion bond issue, and the year's depreciation allowance [108] – money set aside for replacing worn out facilities – of $44 billion, was sufficient not only to pay for government capital expenditure of $37.1 billion, but also to pay down the public debt by $50.9 billion, a whopping 3.7 percent of GDP. That is the opposite of what is now happening in the Western world.

That was in 2005 in Canada. In 2010, when the world was in depression, Canada's government spending was much higher, 39.7 percent of GDP, while that of the United States' was 38.9 percent, Australia's 34.3 percent, and Switzerland's 32.0 percent. These were the advanced nations with the lowest government spending. At the other end of the spectrum were France at 52.8 percent and Sweden and Denmark with almost as much. The UK was at 47.3 percent and Germany at 43.7 percent. No doubt added unemployment and welfare benefits were a major reason for this situation but there must be other factors. Denmark has low unemployment, only 4.2%, yet its government spending is 52% of GDP, while the United States, whose government spending is only 39% of GDP, has unemployment of 8.6%. One reason for this must surely be that the US has a far less generous safety net to help its disadvantaged, and another might be that in Denmark the government performs functions that in the US are performed by the business sector. 'Privatisation' is the term used when a nation's government decides to transfer some of its activities to the private sector. The 'Iron Lady', Mrs. Thatcher, is remembered for her privatisation policy[109]. An interesting question is how Switzerland manages with such low government spending. Denmark, like Switzerland has low unemployment, a low budget deficit, low public debt, and a large international balance of payments surplus (that is, it sells more to other countries than it buys from them). But Denmark, unlike Switzerland has very high government spending. I have lacked the opportunity to investigate more closely this and other seeming oddities.

It would surely be helpful if published statistics on government spending instead of presenting a single percent of GDP, reported the three very different categories, services provided by the government (19% of GDP for Canada in 2005), government transfer payments to households[110] (10% of GDP), and grants to NGOs. The term 'size of government' might then refer only to government services. The transfer item would then be a measure of something else, the generosity of the public, through their government, in putting money in the hands of the unemployed, the sick, and other disadvantaged people. By making these distinctions in our government spending statistics we would have far greater clarity than we now have in talking of the iniquities of 'big government'.

Does US government really need shrinking?

A huge issue in the election campaign that has resulted in the re-election of Barack Obama was size of government. In the Republicans' view, American government has become too large, it must be shrunk, the sickness of European 'socialism' counteracted. A quick look at World Bank statistics reveals the size of government (as just defined, that is, services performed by government, and excluding 'social safety net' transfers), for all the world's nations. Here are the figures for several advanced nations, for the year 2008, (for Japan and the US, 2007): Switzerland 10.8% of GDP, Japan 14.0%, US 16.2%, Germany 18.1%, Canada 19.3%, Italy 20.2%, UK 21.9%, France 23.2%, Netherlands 25.1%, Sweden 26.4%. The US figure is one of the lowest. And as so many commentators point out, the US has in addition a much poorer safety net than European nations. One could say of the US opponents of 'big government' that they 'protest too much'. Mind you, relatively small though US government is, perhaps it is very inefficient? In the US, do only deadbeats enter government – do the most efficient and effective aspire to work in business corporations? One does hear a great deal on overly detailed, badly drafted government regulations in the United States. (Unfortunately I have not had an opportunity to discover just how that extremely successful nation, Switzerland, manages so well with such 'small government' – presumably a great deal is successfully privatised).

A Long Term Planning Agency

Even if we make the reforms discussed above on how elections are conducted, and we elect individuals who reflect what the people want, or think they want, rather than individuals slanted towards business corporations and special interests, there will remain a less than ideal apparatus for wise public policy formulation. Parliaments suffer from 'short-term-ism', and can be deeply ignorant of terrible challenges and dangers ahead. Perhaps nations could set up new central long-term planning agencies charged with accumulating a balanced view of these future problems and what should be done about them. And they might reflect on the 'woes' that were the subject of Part One. The agency would be in constant communication with all elements of society and the public, with the several existing independent 'think tanks', and with the equivalent central agencies of other countries.

Perhaps the long term planning agency could become a formal part of the democratic government process – the people, parliament, the prime minister and cabinet, and the long term policy body. Of course, no institution, made of always fallible human beings, can be perfect, but there can be little doubt that there is a vital need to balance the short-termism of a Parliament or a House of Representatives. This new long term policy body may be particularly called for now with the climate threat hanging over mankind.

In Chapter 7 I wrote of the absurdity of boom and bust, and of unemployment when there was so much to be done. One task of this planning agency might be to perfect Keynesian principles, and develop long term plans for the economy, using all the available tools, including the national input-output model already referred in Chapter 11, and ideas of the sort put forward in Chapter 12 on the 'new economics', Yes, the social, economic, political, environmental system, full of wayward human beings, is hugely complex, but applying genuine scientific principles and the incredible power of computers, one can have little doubt that society will soon learn to manage the economy so that there is never involuntary unemployment.

Getting our production system to produce what people really want or need

One of our woes discussed in Part One was that though we have doubled our production, a large portion of the public is no better off – indeed poverty or near- poverty is at an extremely high level in the United States. Part of the reason for this I suggested was that a 'major part of people's income has been spent on often inessential consumer goods that fast become obsolete, at the expense of the basic necessities of life'. The reform of broadcasting so that it no longer serves as a sales promotion service for business will help, as will also the reduction of the huge income inequality between the rich and the poor, made possible by generous transfer payments, which will be facilitated by implementing the new 'return to society'. But I suggest we need more than this.

The principle that must always govern when we prescribe for society is the Social Contract – perhaps the reader is irritated by my continual reference to the Contract, but it is unavoidable. When we consider the value of any consumer good or service offered for sale, we need to find a way to ask whether it will improve the quality of life, and not just the goals of business corporations. Of course I'm not proposing a nanny state, individual people must be free to buy whatever they want. But there are surely steps that can be taken by society to minimize the degree to which new products of low, or even negative, utility are foisted on the public by corporations to expand their sales and profit. Replacing people by machines may seem modern and progressive, but they may not always be so, sometimes it just makes our daily lives less convenient and more uncomfortable, as well as depriving workers unnecessarily of their jobs.

Consider 'do-it-yourself' versus 'do-it-for-you', or if you like 'self-serve' versus 'being served'. In earlier times the rich made sure their lives were extremely comfortable and had servants galore to save them from chores. Even in quite recent times, without domestic servants, the principle of service applied. In filling stations an attendant filled your tank with gasoline, you did not have to get out of your car on a cold and blustery day, learn how to operate the pump, and how to pay. You just said 'fill it up please', and handed your credit card to the attendant. Of course the cost of this service was included in the price you paid for your gasoline, but for many people that was fine, one has so many other chores and problems to worry about. Now such personal service filling stations are rare, and one must get out of one's car and grapple with a machine, and then with a new payment gadget into which you push your credit card. Some other such woes, 'countless irritations, exasperating useless production' were discussed in Chapter 2, inconvenient machines you have to learn how to use to buy parking time, and the replacement by machines of the man in the booth at parking lots. No thought or action was required on your part except to hand him some money. Can anything be more obviously convenient and effortless than a simple old fashioned parking meter next to your car into which you slipped a couple of coins, no effort, no problem. Just the other day I was seriously annoyed by the new parking machine: I was already late for an appointment, and not only did I have to have to go through the usual sequence of actions, I had to wait for some other person to grapple with the machine – there is only this single machine serving a long line of cars. Consider, this is truly outrageous, the convenience of ourselves, the public, is low on the priorities of the companies which make and purvey these machines.

Another irritation is the dreadful, badly designed, telephone answering systems that nearly drive us round the bend. Also vexing are frequent new models of electronic equipment that we never asked for, must spend time reading badly written manuals to learn how to use – certainly there are many useful innovations, but must they be rammed down our throats without a by your leave? One annoying problem I have recently had is that many internet web sites became too big for my screen and I could only see a part of it at a time. The only solution was to buy a new wider screen. All these examples of undue mechanisation, or of the people be damned, are part of the reasons why though our economy is continually becoming more productive, that is, capable of producing more, this is not reflected by a matching increase in people's affluence or comfort. Perhaps one possibility would be laws requiring corporations to continue servicing existing models of consumer goods when they launch new models for the geeks and enthusiasts who love that sort of thing.

Another little annoyance, which is also a waste of scarce resources, and increases the burden of waste disposal, is unnecessary packaging of consumer goods. Sometimes one dances in rage while wrestling with the tough plastic enclosing a product, with no instructions given to tell one how to proceed.

None of this is to denigrate the vast advances in technology that are fast being made, especially in information technology. But what we must do is make sure that these huge advances are used only to improve mankind's lot. We can undoubtedly do better here – we are in danger of being bounced into a nasty future world we did not choose, in contravention of the Social Contract. Indeed that is already beginning to happen. A friend who gives lectures at a university tells me that it is forbidden to tell students to switch off their smart phones, which receive constant calls, and a columnist in the Globe and Mail, under the title 'A new culture of compulsion' writes that in cafes where people used to go to chat with friends, they now 'go on clicking on their BlackBerries. In restaurants two couples out of every three put their cell phones on the table before sitting down . . . How can all these BlackBerry types have so many friends on a full-time basis, ready to chat endlessly at any hour of the day? Don't these people have work?'. . . . This need to tweet all the time and everywhere has become a compulsion . . . What it reveals is a pathological incapacity to be alone with our thoughts for more than a few minutes . . . In a recent letter to La Presse (a Montreal newspaper), a desperate teacher pleaded for a ban on cell phones in the schools'.

But of course, this is nonsense, the Social Contract is being totally ignored. Of course a sane, well-governed, country can bring an end to the invasion of our lives by a gadget that somehow has been promoted to the level of personal compulsion. Chris Hedges, whom I quoted earlier on how the corporations have brought about in America an 'empire of illusion', in his latest book, 'The Death of the Liberal Class' describes how what was once society's bulwark against such perversions has now capitulated and now cravenly abets the abuse of the large majority. By the 'Liberal Class' Hedges is referring to what began with Hobbes, Locke, Spinoza, then the Scottish moral philosophers, the French *philosophes*, and the early architects of democracy, then in the nineteenth century John Stuart Mill. 'The liberal era, which flourished in the later part of the nineteenth century and the early years of the twentieth, was characterised by the growth of mass movements and social reforms that addressed working conditions in factories, the organizing of labour movements, women's rights, universal education, housing for the poor, public health campaigns, and socialism'. But now this class has been co-opted. Hedges describes their abject surrender, they are now (quoting C. Wright Mills) 'a decayed and frightened liberalism'.

Of course one cannot stop the advance of technology, and no one can deny how much it has contributed to making life better – but it can also make life worse at the interface between corporations and the person, whom the whole apparatus of society, including the corporations, is supposed to serve. Perhaps one function of the new long term planning agency might be to keep an eye on new developments, help to prevent the drive of clever new products, instead of helping mankind, instead enslaving them and bouncing them into a nasty future world. To this end, the agency would include not only technologically informed individuals, but also people versed in the humanities, historians, archeologists, social sciences, and the like. They would evaluate, and advise the public, parliament, and the government, to permit regulation in the area of new products promoted by corporations. There will be an outcry, no doubt, against such interference in the free market and modernity, but this has to be set against the alternative, already discussed, of mankind being bounced, undemocratically, into a nasty future world. One thing that can be confidently affirmed is that it is total nonsense that smart phones must not be switched off in school or university classes.

Ending Obscene Inequality

Just as I was putting this work to bed, and about to try to arrange its publication, I suddenly realized I should say something more on one of the most discussed questions of our times, the increase in income inequality, especially in the United States, but also, in some other Western countries. Any non-American observing the just- fought US presidential campaign must have been surprised how Republicans shied away from talking about inequality – it is all right talking of alleviation of poverty, but in no way must it be linked to the huge incomes of the 'one percent' – I recall being nonplussed at angry Republicans reacting with charges of 'class warfare' if the question of raising the taxes of the super-rich was raised. There is also a strong right wing view that their hard-earned tax dollars unjustly finance redistributive social safety net benefits, often to the indolent and undeserving. The American situation is extreme, but it exists in other countries too, the feeling that one is parting with a chunk of one's income each time one fills out one's income tax return. Chapter 10 was on how we can rid ourselves of the income tax through a totally new public finance system, the 'Return to Society'. As a result it will be determined by debate in parliament what proportion of GDP is to be allocated to personal use and what proportion for public purposes, including what is allocated to the social safety net. It will no longer be a question of each member of the public been asked to part with some of their hard-earned money to give to welfare bums and the great unwashed. Instead the matter can be settled by sensible discussion in parliament on what is a suitable share of a nation's total economic output should be allocated to each category of public spending, including for helping society's unfortunates. That is a thoroughly decent thing to do: Faith, hope, and charity, and of these the greatest is charity. Of course no perfect way is possible for wayward human beings, but surely a more reasonable way can be devised than can now be squeezed out of the income tax. By my proposed method, each citizen will no longer feel he's parting with some of his income – what you are paid at your job you keep.

There are of course two sides to the problem of inequality, not only excessively low incomes at the bottom, but also grossly large incomes at the top. What can we do about them?. As was discussed in Chapter 10, the so-called progressive income tax we now have does little to solve that problem. Interestingly Sweden, the world's most equal nation by its ratio of the disposible income of its top ten percent of earners to bottom ten percent of earners, nonetheless has more billionaires for its size of population than most other nations, nearly as many as the United States. So presumably it is not worried about that tiny group of super-rich. Perhaps we too need not worry about this tiny proportion of the population – provided we make the institutional reforms that have been proposed here, as well as put in place laws and regulations that prevent them from doing harm – for example, the way billionaires financed 'attack ads' and 'political commercials' in the US presidential campaign, using the perverted broadcasting system. Perhaps as a result of the reforms discussed in these pages our society will throw up less obscenely rich people.

CHAPTER 14

The Future of Europe

Europe is in crisis, the nations of the original Age of Enlightenment are at odds with each other. Our goal of a new Enlightenment will be difficult, one might say impossible, without a reinvigorated, and in some sense, united Europe. The great heritage, the values, the attributes, of these nations of the Enlightenment, of the rule of law and accountable government and of the Social Contract, must be revived and extended – but in some form of collectivity among sovereign governments – a sort of permanent alliance based on common principles and beliefs.

Chapter 19 below discusses the 'initial core group of nations' that will initiate the New Enlightenment, and it will be observed that six of the seven nations are European – the other is Japan. So what needs to be done to arrive at a new European treaty links closely with what is required of the larger Enlightenment effort which embraces not only Europe but also the United States, Canada, Australia, and New Zealand, and possibly, within a wider notion of 'the West', such nations as Brazil, Argentina, Chile, and Mexico. The larger renaissance also involves a reinvigorated West that leads the entire world in waging the Great Battle of the Climate.

The European Union has two serious problems, the immediate difficulties of the Eurozone common currency, and the Union's dysfunctional, undemocratic, Brussels arrangement trying to be the government of a united Europe that does not exist. We shall take each of these problems in turn.

Of the EU's present twenty-seven member nations, seventeen are Eurozone members sharing the common currency. Britain is the only large EU nation outside the Eurozone. The Euro may be nearing terminal collapse, something which was entirely predictable, yoking diverse, both culturally and linguistically, sovereign, nations in a single currency. In a 1997 paper[111] at the time of the introduction of the euro, I wrote: 'Maastricht may serve as a cruel yoke for some nations, turning them into depressed areas. Generally parts of countries with single national currencies are relatively depressed, and must be subsidized by other parts. Once proud European nations are in danger of becoming the depressed regions of a united Europe'. Canada for example makes money transfers that are straight grants. These so-called 'equalization payments' are routinely transferred by the federal government, from the 'have' provinces to the 'have not provinces'. The aim is to help guarantee 'reasonably comparable' levels of health care, education, and welfare in the provinces. The total amount that will be available is contributed by every province in Canada, and the money raised is then redistributed to those provinces whose per capita GDP is less than the Canadian average. In 2010, Alberta had the highest GDP per capita, Prince Edward Island the lowest, less than half Alberta's. PEI received a transfer payment of $2350 per capita, about seven percent of its total personal income per person, quite generous.

Canada has one great advantage in pursuing unity and equalization that Europe hasn't, a common language and culture, apart from the single exception of Quebec. One consequence is the movement of labour from have-not provinces to have provinces like Ontario and Alberta. Though there is some such migration among Eurozone nations there will obviously be less than occurs within unilingual, unicultural federations such as Canada and the United States. Greece and Italy are hugely different nations from those of Northern Europe. One prominent economist, Nouriel Roubini (Dr Doom as he is called because he correctly warned of the present economic debacle), argues against the continued existence of the Euro, in the same terms I have written about Canada's equalization payments. 'Italy has done something similar for decades, with its northern regions subsidizing the poorer Mezzogiorno. But such permanent fiscal transfers are impossible in the Eurozone, where Germans are Germans, and Greeks are Greeks'. Roubini continues: 'the monetary union's slow-developing train wreck will accelerate the peripheral nations default and exit. The present chaos in Greece and Italy may be the first step in the process. Unless the Eurozone moves towards greater economic, fiscal, and political integration . . . recessionary deflation will certainly lead to a disorderly break-up[112]. Roubini's view is shared by the prominent economics commentator, Martin Wolf [113]: 'The Eurozone as designed has failed . . . . It has only two options: to go forward to a closer union or backwards towards at least partial dissolution'. The politicians were the driving force in the adoption of the euro. Helmut Kohl was explicit: a common currency symbolizes the nation state – the United States of Europe. The euro was a political project, and though it appears that some economists warned of its inherent dangers, Martin Wolf was one such, I do not recall that their views received much public attention at the time.

The successor to the Euro

So what must Europe do about the Euro in this context? It is interesting to speculate about what a Chinese-type Brussels would do in the present circumstances. China now proudly talks of its 5000 years of existence, but it only started becoming what it is now about 2200 years ago[114], when the 'victory of the so-called First Emperor, Qin Shishuangdi . . . at the end of the Warring States period', brought into existence the heartland of modern China, but still a small fraction of China's present territory. The country further doubled its size in the following 400 year Han dynasty, and then over the next millennium China extended itself militarily, incorporating many different peoples, to its present huge size. Despite their diverse origins and original languages nearly all Chinese now view themselves as the same Han people, although they may not understand each others' speech, they share the same language in its written form. And of course this China has a common currency.

What is especially fascinating from the point of view of this work is the abiding absence of notions of democracy and free speech, not only in the past, but now. The following is from an interview with a self-designated Chinese Orwell[115]: For the public there is no 'information about the Tiananmen Square crackdown of 1989, and only Communist Party – approved material on the mass murder and indoctrination of the Cultural Revolution'. Most young Chinese know nothing of the Tiananmen Square massacre, 'an entire year can indeed disappear from history'. But these young uninformed Chinese are affluent, are acquiring Western gadgets and lifestyles, and deem themselves happy. But from our Enlightenment perspective, there is a huge absence in their lives – the truth.

Unless Europe adopts some degree of the 'chinafication', the forced merging of diverse nations, the Euro probably must be abandoned (even the centralised fiscal oversight now being enacted is unlikely to help because it tackles the wrong problem, budget deficits instead of inter-nation trade deficits). Europe would then return to drachmas, francs and deutschmarks, and find another way of achieving a new European Enlightenment entity, the trustee and guardian of the great heritage from Greece and Rome. This is not to say that some degree of currency commonality might not be retained, but that would be only a minor, symbolic, element in the Europe of the New Renaissance, a commonality of governance principles would be far more important. One currency possibility to replace the symbolism of the Euro might be to have German, French, Portuguese, Spanish, and so on, currencies which will be named, respectively, the euro-d, the euro-f, the euro-p, the euro-s, etc. (just joking? – maybe).

So much for the currency, now to the common governance principles that must be adopted by nations to qualify them for membership of the new Europe, in place of the present cumbersome, opaque, undemocratic arrangement. This might be achieved on the basis of a new treaty among sovereign equals, which would replace the present Lisbon and Maastricht treaties. Its signatory nations would be required under the agreement to observe a set of institutional forms and principles of the sort that have been discussed in the preceding chapters.

The form of the new European Treaty

In brief outline this includes first a reaffirmation of the Social Contract as defined in Chapter 5, which puts the people and their governing institutions firmly in the saddle, and harnesses the business corporations and the financial system to serve the people, and only the people. The treaty then lays out a programme of institutional reform which member states will be obliged to undertake, whose five major parts are.

1. Economic Management

    a. Restarting each economy and permanently maintaining full employment.

    b. Adopting new definitions of public debt and deficit. The budget deficit will be defined as the amount by which government current spending (on both government services, and transfers such as welfare, health, and unemployment benefits, and subsidies) falls short of government revenue. In other words, the Maastricht 3% deficit will be banished. Good government will require maintaining over the long run a zero deficit or a small surplus. The present public debt will be divided into two parts, the 'infrastructure debt', bond issues to pay for capital investment in new government facilities; and 'accumulated overspending debt', borrowing because the government has been 'living beyond its means'. In the long run the latter should be zero.

    c. Currency reform. This will involve dismantling the Eurozone, and the return of individual national currencies, which might either return to their original names, deutschmark, franc, lira. etc, or, for European symbolism, might be called euro-d, euro-f, euro-l, and so on. Nations now outside the Eurozone, Britain, Sweden, Denmark and some others, would then choose whether to retain their present currency name or not. The notion of a two-speed Europe, northern and southern, each sharing its own common currency is conceivable, but might be just as defective as the present system, and in any case might seem odious as implying 'those undisciplined southern loafers'.

2. Apply the principle that all services in the economy exist to serve only their paymasters. A genuine service for the public must be paid for by the public, either directly out of personal expenditure, or collectively out of taxes. If instead a service, purportedly serving the public, is paid for by business corporations, then it exists to serve them, for sales promotion or public relations purposes. Where such bogus people-serving services now exist, they must, over a reasonable period of time be converted into genuine services for the public. The most important present instance of such 'bogus' services are the misappropriated broadcasting systems paid for by business corporations. The degree of this misappropriation varies widely in the EU, being much less prevalent in the Scandinavian nations. Correcting this terrible anomaly must have the highest priority for members of the new European Alliance. These nations will resolve over a period of five years to transform their broadcasting systems, so that they become entirely normal services for the public, like all their other services for people, paid for by the people themselves.

On the one hand will be the public broadcaster, of the BBC type, and on the other, perhaps the major part, will be broadcasting directly paid for by individuals out of personal expenditure. The only way in which advertising may use the airwaves is in solely advertising channels, broadcasting of what in the United States are called 'infomercials'. If some members of the public wish to spend their time listening to companies promoting their wares, they should be free to do so.

Other bogus services for people too must be reformed in like manner, which means the phasing out of 'corporate social responsibility' and sports marketing. Such services as Facebook, now totally funded by advertising should be changed so that like newspapers they are partly paid for directly by consumers. On Facebook as with newspapers, and unlike the 'American broadcasting model', one may totally ignore the advertising, there is no interruption of service.

3. Over a period of five years each nation will replace its present taxation system by a new 'Return to Society'. By this means it will be decided annually, in each nation's parliament, what share of the nation's spending will be private and what is public. This will also be an annual vote on the 'role and size of government'.

4. Each nation must aim, by some means of regulation, to ensure that all new consumer services are in accord with the Social Contract, that is that they do not make people's lives more difficult and less pleasant. Automation and mechanization are to be lauded where they increase productivity, and the economy's output, but never at the expense of placing an added, involuntary, 'self-serve' burden on people's lives.

5. Each nation must launch its mega projects of the Great Battle of the Climate, and to reshape society, according to the guidelines as laid out by the European Alliance Secretariat.

The new supra-national body

What might the new alliance or confederation of European nations be called? Perhaps something like AEN (Alliance of European Nations), or the ETO (European Treaty Organization). It will be an association of sovereign European states, to be served by a successor supra-national body that will replace the present, undemocratic, over-sized Brussels tangle. Its role will be coordination, assistance, and monitoring, with regard to the member nations' activities under the new European Treaty. It may also set common standards where this facilitates inter-nation trade among member nations, but only as agreed by member state governments. The question also arises of a common external face to the rest of the world, for example military forces, and foreign policy. All such questions must be agreed on at quarterly assemblies of the heads of government of the signatory nations (or rarely, at especial emergency sessions).

The supra-national body will be headed by a Secretary General agreed on by the signatory nations' governments. He will deliver monthly progress reports to these governments.

CHAPTER 15

The Blind Men and the Elephant

Different writers' explanations of our society's decline call to mind the Indian fable of the blind men describing the elephant: each has touched a different part, one the trunk, another a leg. Society is very large, and incredibly complex, and the different theories of societal decline differ greatly. But each may be partly right.

Just when I thought this book was complete and ready for publication, three new books came to my attention, which I read, and as a consequence, added the present chapter. As with the blind men, each writer's account of our society's fall differed greatly, not only from each other's but also from my own account. This did not necessarily mean that any version was wrong, rather that perhaps each was partly right and that together they constituted a comprehensive explanation of our society's difficulties. The three books are respectively:

- Niall Ferguson's 'The Great Degeneration: How Institutions Decay and Economies Die;

- Chrystia Freeland's 'Plutocrats: The Rise of the New Global Super-Rich and the Fall of Everyone Else'; and

- Thomas Edsall's 'The Age of Austerity: How Scarcity Will Remake American Politics.

I find all three books exceptionally interesting, and for the most part find little to disagree with. But that in no way invalidates the argument of this book. None of these writers has noticed that 'elephant in the room', the giant sociological obscenity which no one sees, regarding which I wrote in Chapter 9: The day must soon come when people will suddenly realize that what is now coming over the airwaves is an obscenity, a crime against humanity, and feel such deep revulsion, that they will fast replace it by broadcasting to serve them, and them only. It will at last dawn on them that what is now broadcast over the airwaves is paid for by business as a virtually round-the-clock sales promotion service, to get them to rush to buy whatever they choose to produce. They will realize that instead their broadcasting must become like all their other services, their education, their health care, their entertainment, everything else they need and buy'. And this same sociological obscenity contributed to the shear nastiness of the US presidential election campaign in the form of oxymoronic 'political commercials', and 'attack ads', many of which were paid for by a number of billionaires in an incredible bout of plutocracy.

As each book is quite complex, the 'Indian fable' difficulty also applies to trying to state briefly its argument. The following, I think, is the gist of Ferguson's case. He uses Adam Smith's notion of the 'stationary state', the 'condition of a formerly wealthy country that has ceased to grow. It's two major characteristics are (1): though a rich country, the wages of the majority are miserably low, and (2): a corrupt and monopolistic elite is able to exploit the system of law and administration to their own advantage. In Smith's day it was China, now 'this is the case in important parts of the Western world today'.

The fall of the West, in Ferguson's view, is due to institutional degeneration. The four pillars of western society are representative democratic government, the free market, the rule of law, and civil society, that is, the realm of voluntary organizations. 'Together, they are the key components of our civilization'. Here are a few ways, in Ferguson's view, these institutions have degenerated. In the realm of democratic government, modern nations have developed institutions undreamt of a hundred years ago' to regulate economic and social life and redistribute income. 'The welfare state seems to create an ever-increasing number of dependent drones whom the worker bees have to support. And it seeks to finance itself by accumulating claims on the future, in the form of public debt' and 'public debt – stated and implicit – has become a way for the older generation to live at the expense of the unborn'. Ferguson is referring not only to the high official public debt in the form of bonds that was discussed in Chapter 8, but also to the 'far bigger unfunded liabilities of welfare schemes like – to give the American programmes – medicare, medicaid, and social security'.

I have difficulty understanding this reference to large unfunded liabilities. This has already been discussed in Chapter 8, on the unfunded future liabilities of British government retirees. It is true that these liabilities are increasing in size, people are not only living longer, but are having smaller families so there will be fewer people to support them in their old age, but that surely is a problem for future generations to solve. Each generation must look after its sick, its disadvantaged, its unemployed, and its retirees. For example, it has been suggested that the age of retirement be raised because of increasing life expectancy. And there is an important other factor to be considered, as a result of continual productivity increase, our society is becoming increasingly richer, and could easily afford to support its sick and retired, were it not for the institutional faults that are the subject of the present work.

This matter of huge unfunded liabilities bequeathed to future generations is enjoying a great vogue these days. It is the subject of a new book by Kotlikoff and Burns, entitled 'The Clash of Generations'. I believe it is a highly over-done fear, readily nullified if we make the necessary institutional reforms.

And what about worker bees having to support drones? If a nation provides generous income for the part of its labour force that is unemployed, sick, or needing support because of disabilities physical or mental – the village idiot for example, does that mean an appreciable part of the population, the more feckless lot, the skivers, will take advantage? Perhaps, but how much does it matter? Does it have an appreciable effect on the economy – will it seriously reduce GDP, will it rob the good workers of an appreciable part of their income in supporting loafers and deadbeats? I haven't yet had the opportunity to make a statistical appraisal. One might look at Sweden, which redistributes income greatly. Is that nation failing to prosper? One does hear complaints of excessive bureaucracy, the Swedish writer, Henning Mankel is disillusioned on this score. Set against this however is what Ed Broadbent, former leader of Canada's social democrats (the National Democratic Party)' tells us in an article on growing inequality. 'A recent study showed that if Americans want to experience the American Dream of upward mobility, they should pack up and move to Sweden. They would have to leave the most unequal democracy and move to the most equal'. Even so, the whole question of excessive government bureaucracy should certainly be studied carefully.

Ferguson has much of interest to say on rule by lawyers replacing the rule of law, 'lawyers, who can be revolutionary in a dynamic state become parasites in a stationary state'. Also he is concerned about the large decline in membership in voluntary organizations and charities, of people getting together to solve problems, instead of relying on government bureaucracies: 'civil society withers into a mere no man's land between corporate interests and big government'. Reading Ferguson made me think of two events, one fictional, the other real. In the mid-nineteenth century, in Jules Verne's *Round the World in Eighty Days*, the hero, Phileas Fogg, is a member of the Reform Club who sets out to circumnavigate the world on a bet with his fellow members, beginning and ending in the club. Another geographic feat, one that actually happened, also in mid nineteenth century, is the subject of Alan Moorehead's *The White Nile*: 'No unexplored region in our times, neither the heights of the Himalayas, the Antarctic wastes, nor even the hidden side of the moon, has excited quite the same fascination as the mystery of the sources of the Nile . . . Every expedition that was sent up the river from Egypt returned defeated. By the middle of the nineteenth century . . . this matter had become the greatest geographical secret after the discovery of America' And then in mid-century, the Royal Geographical Society organised an expedition led by Burton and Speke, as a result of which the Nile's source was discovered in what

Speke named 'Lake Victoria' in the middle of the 'Dark Continent'. And how dark it was.

In these two cases it was 'civil society', not government, which took the initiative. And the great actions that are the subject of this book will also be driven by civil society, whose actions, laid out below in Part Three, will lead eventually to government involvement. When one comes to think of it, it has usually been civil society which has driven governments eventually to take action. So it was in the great reforms of the nineteenth and early twentieth centuries, the abolition of slavery, child labour, and universal suffrage – the heroic suffragette movement.

Ferguson also convincingly writes of the failings of the American regulatory process – over- complex regulation instead of clear, simple rules, which if broken will put the offender, including rich and powerful bankers, in gaol.

Even so, I don't see that the matters which Ferguson discusses in any way invalidate the case I am making here, of vital institutional changes that need to be made, of business corporations exceeding their proper role, taking the broadcasting system away from the corporations and placing it at the service of the public, and replacing the income tax by the Return to Society.

Chrystia Freeland's 'Plutocrats' is not only about an increasingly wide gap between rich and poor, and of obscenely high incomes of the frequently not particularly worthy, it is also about a dizzyingly changing world brought about by clever young Mark Zuckerberg types manipulating incredibly fast changing technology in a totally free market. I felt increasingly as I read it, I am in a foreign country, I don't know what's going on. But it is also a world not under any overall management and good governance to make sure of compliance with the Social Contract, that the well-being and comfort of humanity is always served, that the human race is not being bounced into some nasty Brave New World – Aldous Huxley, where are you when we need you? Cynthia Freeland's book left me feeling uneasy. Vanity of vanity, all is vanity.

What can we do? We must put the people in control, so that they can steer the world in accordance with the Social Contract. People first, Mark Zuckerberg second. Freeland also argues as does Ferguson that a self-serving 'renting-seeking' elite at the top has kicked away the ladder so that others can't come up. 'By early in the 14th century Venice had become the richest city in Europe, it was an imperial power', had sovereignty over a wide area. Venice was invigorated by new blood rising to the top. But then in 1315 at the peak of their power came the *Serrata*, or closure –oligarchs cut off new entrants, and that was the beginning of the end for Venetian prosperity. Venice entered what Ferguson calls the 'stationary state'.

Thomas Edsall's 'Age of Austerity', like the others is a fascinating read, and most informative. The United States is in a terrible state, its parts in mortal combat with each other. Edsall's book buttresses what Woodard tells us in 'American Nations', that was discussed in Chapter 13. Woodard writes that all that holds these American nations together is the Federal Government, and that is made difficult if the Federal Government is dysfunctional, in gridlock, which in large measure it at present is. This is how Edsall puts the matter in 'The Age of Austerity': 'The broad compromise of long standing between one political party promoting a social safety net and the other party asserting that hard-earned tax dollars unjustly finance those benefits is no longer sustainable. That compromise . . . required a growing economy to fund an array of programs while keeping taxes relatively low in order to moderate hostilities. . . . Now we have entered a period of austerity markedly different from anything we have seen before. The two major political parties are enmeshed in a death struggle to protect the benefits that flow to their respective constituencies . . . A brutish future stands before us. Edsall's book is an eye-opener for the non American reader. The US has woes one could not decently wish on one's worst enemy.

One aspect of the age of austerity is unemployment. 'U.S.-based multinational firms are steadily cutting employment in America while they hire more and more overseas. U.S. multinational corporations cut domestic employment by 2.9 million during the

2000s while adding 2.4 million workers overseas, according to the Department of Commerce'. And while serious poverty has increased, corporate profits are high. Reading this immediately reminds us of what John Stone said in Chapter 5 on the Social Contract: *'Companies are designed to multiply capital . . . . To that end they will do anything to survive and prosper. . . . . They are obliged to do all those things, if they can increase their profits. . . . . A company is a moral imbecile. It has no sense of right or wrong. . . Any restraints have to come from the outside, from laws and customs that forbid them from doing certain things of which we disapprove.* What the U.S. Federal Government could do to reduce this unemployment would be to enact regulation that prevented American companies from building their facilities in cheap labour countries, reducing the extent of 'globalization'. It has always been argued by the Great and the Good that free trade is a benign thing, everybody prospers. Well, this isn't really 'free trade' spontaneously occurring among nations, if it simply means building your factories in other countries to use their cheap labour.

So these three writers say most interesting things about the state of the West, but in no way is what they write in opposition to what I have argued in this book, re-affirming the Social Contract that places the people in the driver's seat. And I believe all three writers have one deeply serious omission – they are not alone, most of the world is failing in this: There is a giant elephant in the room that no one sees: the world, human civilization on this planet, is under grave climate threat, unless very soon collective action is taken calamity lies ahead.

CHAPTER 16

Reversing Decadence and Decline

I shall repeat a question I asked earlier, are we really in decline, or is our society merely enduring one of its low spells? After all the Great Depression of the 1930s was brutal, yet we recovered eventually – though this needed the help of a dreadful world war. After the war we experienced strong economic growth and great optimism was in the air. Many people even thought our society was wondrous, and some thought that the American Dream was the model of what the good, progressive society should be. But the theme of this work is that all was not well with the American dream, and the heartland of that dream is now fearfully unhappy and wracked in confusion and vitriolic contention. The most constant themes of our commentators and savants now is that the West is in a sorry state and in decline, and that power and influence are moving to the emerging giants, China, India, Russia, and Brazil.

The argument of this work is that the West, or large parts of it, are in their present dire state only because they have been contravening the Social Contract that exists between the people, and the state: The State's institutions exist for one purpose only, to serve us, the people, but we have governed badly and abdicated our responsibility in a huge tilt to the business corporations. The latter have thereby acquired much of the broadcasting system, and used it to serve their own growth and profit goals, and are also performing other functions that are rightly the people's prerogative. The consequence has been that the people are ill-served, there are forces for decadence and decline, and society is not rising to the terrible challenges of our times. Making matters worse is that the economists, the doctors of the economy, have shown that they would be better designated the *witchdoctors* of the economy, with their weird potions and mathematical models and wild predictions. As a result we have deep, unrelenting, recession, the Eurozone common currency may be in terminal difficulties, and we have woes, many of which have been described in these pages, and which passed unnoticed among the economists.

So one might say that ours is a society already much degraded. But if we act intelligently, we can propel ourselves out of this nadir and resume our upward climb and, this time a *genuine* upward climb, not the flawed, sick, climb of the last half century. In launching the New Enlightenment we shall be bottoming out from the nadir. Thoughts of decadence and decline will start to disappear. The people's state of mind will improve. An uplifting of people's hopes will commence with the Clarion Call which will be the first item of our Action Plan, the subject of Part Four of this work. Here are some words from the Call:

> *First we must understand the root causes of our difficulties. We have been transgressing the great Social Contract that exists between ourselves, the people, and the state: The state's institutions exist for one purpose only, to serve us, the people. But we . . . have governed badly and abdicated our responsibility in a huge tilt to the business corporations . . we have left them to produce whatever they can persuade people to buy that will give them profits, even at the cost of the environment and the health of society. But now we must harness them to make their profits working for us, the people. . . . but first we must stop the present recession in its tracks – it is nonsense that part of our economy be shut down when there is so much to be done.*

And that will quickly happen. People will start to be put to work, and for those still waiting for work, ample incomes will be provided. Jobs will be provided for all within the next two or three years. People's spirits will immediately be raised. Now there is very little confidence in our political leaders, that they know what to do. But that will fast change, people will believe, here at last are leaders who know what they are talking about.

And the fast appearance of new jobs will result in a mood shift in the population. And then, when in sequence huge measures are proclaimed, the New Enlightenment, will be underway. The airwaves will no longer be spouting the irritating claims of the adman. Trust will build in our major institutions, and then the move away from the income tax to the Return to Society will give the people further hope in the future.

Taking over the airwaves to serve the people and society will signal the start of the long climb back from degradation and decline. And this, along with the transformation of our public finance system, will make adequate funds available for society's purposes, to engage successfully in the Battle of the Climate, and confront the world's other burgeoning difficulties.

Ferguson's Remedy

In Chapter 15 I discussed Niall Ferguson's broad view of societies, and why they rise or decline. If one knows what causes their decline, then, quite logically, to recover, what a society must do is quite clear, it must remove those causes. This, Ferguson's writes, means that it must reform its governing institutions, which allowed the present degraded situation to come about, and thus far, I am in full agreement: the present work is all about correcting our institutions of governance. . . .'Europeans and Americans alike are frittering away the institutional inheritance of centuries. To arrest the degeneration of the West . . . will take heroic leadership and radical reform[116]'. With much of that one cannot argue, debt levels are too high, civil society (that is, the role of voluntary and non-government organizations) has declined, and, at least, in the United States, lawyers play too great a role. I find convincing Ferguson's view of over-complex regulation, too bureaucratically detailed in some areas, but also lacking teeth in other areas, and, as I have referred to above, US business has successfully prevented financial and emission-cutting regulation.

While I fully agree with Ferguson that our civilization is in a sorry state, and that radical reform is required, I differ with him on some of the underlying causes. I must, like a broken record, repeat. 'But what about the broadcasting perversion and the dysfunctional taxation system'? What about business corporations run amok in contravention of the Social Contract? And I don't quite understand his argument that we are sinning by bequeathing huge liabilities on our descendants: Ferguson uses as his example the huge unfunded liabilities of the United States Medicare, Medicaid and Social Security programmes. But, as I've discussed in Chapter 15, surely each generation simply makes payments to its own aged, its sick, its poor, and others in trouble. If, because of increasing life expectancy, and low present birth rates, there will be a lot of these unfortunates to be supported in the future by a smaller working age population, that surely is a problem for the future generation to worry about and to solve. Besides, our societies are supposed to be getting richer all the time because of ever-advancing technology – and the only reason they haven't been is because of the grave institutional faults which are the subject of this book, If we are getting continually richer we should be able to become more generous to our society's casualties and *miserables,* the wretched, the poor – they're always with us.

Niall Ferguson himself is an exceptionally hard worker, with a prodigious output of most engaging and challenging works. I'm sure that he believes that Western society has become effete, and suspects coddling by an over-large social safety net has contributed to this, and that we need to see more hard work and self reliance as the cure. What I believe is that the me-me self-regarding compulsive shopping society bred by the perverted broadcasting system is more at fault. On one matter I strongly agree with Ferguson is the 'politically correct' view that Western imperialism and colonialism have inflected only pain and misery on the rest of the world. On balance, this is absurd – I could write much on this but this is not the time and place. As I noted in Chapter 15, the central African Dark Continent was very dark in the mid-nineteenth century, before European intervention kick-started it into the modern world. There were many Mugabes, and Idi Amins, and nothing to counter the darkness they presided over.

The very long run

But we must not only talk of the here and now. We must place our whole question of a 'new enlightenment' in a far broader context or run the risk of being absurd, fiddling while far larger considerations need our urgent attention. Is humanity itself, ourselves and our forebears a mere tiny, inconsequential, footnote in the life of the universe? The eminent scientist, Martin Rees, tells us[117] that according to prevailing scientific theory, the universe came into being about 13.5 billion years ago following the Big Bang, and our own earth was formed about 4.5 billion years ago, and will live another six billion years, until the sun swells up into a red giant and vaporises everything remaining on our planet's surface'. In the world's 4.5 billion years existence to date, humans, ourselves, *homo sapiens,* have existed only forty thousand years, one hundred thousandth of the world's history, and what we call civilization, which emerged only five thousand years ago in Mesopotamia, and on the Nile and the Indus, has existed for only *one millionth's* of the earth's existence, a mere eye blink in celestial time. And this eye blink is – to mix metaphors – hanging on a thread, human society may commit suicide in the present century, as a result of misusing technology: 'Within fifty years, little more than one hundred millionth of Earth's age, the amount of carbon dioxide in the atmosphere, which for most of earth's history had been slowly falling, began to rise anomalously fast'[118]. We are transferring carbon from the earth and dumping it in the atmosphere at an accelerating pace, its atmospheric concentration increased by nearly twenty-five percent in the last fifty years. The danger exists of runaway global warming, especially when methane from the melting tundra is released, as a result of which civilized life on the planet may be extinguished.

Compounding this danger, other hideous threats confront us, either through human error, or through the actions of mad, fanatical terrorists. Human society may have only a fifty percent chance of surviving this century[119]. This fifty percent includes the danger of runaway global warming. This danger is explained by the eminent scientist-environmentalist James Lovelock, in his 'Farewell to Gaia'. If we avert that danger by the measures that were discussed in Chapter 11, our survival odds might improve to, say 75%, but that also is unacceptable danger. So as we devote ourselves to launching a rebirth of our ill-governed society, we must have these hideous terror and error threats in mind, it would be absurd making a huge effort to save tomorrow, if tomorrow may not come – instead eat, drink, and be merry, *apres moi le calamité*.

But no, that will not do, we must not give up on the New Enlightenment, so this means our grand action plan, the battle order, must include action to make sure tomorrow *does* come. What can we do? We must make sure that a hugely competent organization, linked to the highest level of government, be made responsible for averting error and terror. We know what a few demented crazies can do, that has was demonstrated in New York on 9/11, and lately by the hideous atrocity in Norway. We must not shy away from opening some major questions. For example, huge resources, major military forces, are now deeply engaged in Afghanistan, whose aim is to neutralize the world terror threat, Islamic martyrs seeking paradise. But surely it is time to ask whether the multi-billion dollar resources, spent on this military endeavour could not be more successfully spent in guarding against terror attacks within our own countries – let Al Qaeda do what it will, it cannot penetrate our borders. Perhaps at the same time might we not 'quarantine', physically isolate, the terror regions, Pakistan's North West Frontier and Afghanistan? And has enough effort yet been made to demonize world-wide the jihadis, the crazed killers, to brand them, in every nook and cranny of the world's surface, for what they are, not human beings, but monsters, the enemies of mankind? Has any truly unequivocal declaration yet been made in the United Nations, matched by similar declarations by every single national government in the world? Have the world's religious leaders, including mullahs, made unequivocal declarations, pronounced fatwas against the suicide bombers?

Our aim must be to do whatever it takes to reduce the chance of apocalyptical catastrophe as a result of terror and error and of runaway global warming from a 50% probability to a tiny fraction thereof. We must ensure that human existence is not a tiny, inconsequential, blip in the Earth's 10.5 billion life time. And if we succeed, the consequences could be extraordinary. As Martin Rees writes, 'Science is advancing faster than ever, and on a broader front: bio-, cyber-, and nanotechnology all offer exhilarating prospects; so does the exploration of space'. Instead of vanishing without a trace, human life could be extended throughout the galaxy.

The long run effects of technology

But now back to the matter at hand, the New Enlightenment. We need here to say a few words on technology, which is at the root of change, starting with the first stone tools used by hominids about three million years ago. But it is only in recent times, following the industrial revolution and burgeoning human population that dangerous change has occurred threatening the future of humanity. Humans with their bare hands, or with primitive weapons, can do little damage, but with technology they can make life hugely better, or they can create hell on earth. The prime question now is, do we drive changing technology or does changing technology drive us?. Technology is now exploding with new inventions, new gadgets appear every day. Free enterprise, business corporations, make them, promote them, every young person buys them, they're today's rage. There is virtually no social control, the people decide nothing, the Social Contract is breached. Woes arising from this were the subject of Chapter 2, 'countless irritations, exasperating useless production', 'nirvana of gadgetry'. Yet from all this brilliant technological innovation, were we the people fully in control, we could bring immeasurable blessings to mankind.

Here is a way of looking at the matter. What is called the 'rate of technological progress' is about 2% annually. This means that with the help of new machines and technological knowhow a nation can produce on average 2% more goods and services annually, per person. Thus if a country's population is increasing annually by one percent, and its rate of technological progress is two percent, then that country's 'economic growth rate' is three[120] percent – its GDP is increasing at 3% in real terms, that is, in constant dollars (this of course assumes no change in employment rate – if there is an increase in unemployment, the economic growth rate will be below 3%).

But does this 2% increase in output per person mean that material well-being will improve at the same rate? No, it is most unlikely to do so. The economy's output is expended, on the one hand, on goods and services for the people – both personal and public consumption – and on the other hand for such public purposes as justice and law and order, national defence and environmental protection. Goods and services for the people might be placed in four categories. The first is basic necessities, including food, shelter, clothes, health care, and transportation both to place of work and for shopping for necessities. The second category, only a little less necessary if people are not to be bored, are sports, entertainment, news, and travel services and facilities. The third category might be broadly designated as cultural and intellectual pursuits and facilities, literature, learning, music, art, theatre, including what have been the glories of civilization through recorded history. And there is a fourth category that is of growing importance, in the sense that it occupies an increasing role in our lives, what many people do and talk about, and what, for want of a better word, I'll call gadgetry, including the items I discussed in Chapter 2, some of which I designated 'countless irritations, exasperating useless production'. The gadgets themselves may not be noxious or useless, many are marvellous and potentially very useful, and could enhance the human experience, but at present our society's governance shortcomings foster their use mainly to further business corporations' marketing aims, rather than to benefit people and society. But they could, if society were better governed.

There is another factor that reduces the rate at which our real affluence increases. That is speeded up obsolescence. 'New models' appear frequently, which there is advertising pressure to acquire. But how new are they sometimes – just a slightly different appearance or shape? Has anything radically better in car design appeared in recent years? Some changes I find worse, and I curse them. Raising or lowering windows by pressing a button with far less accuracy than the old handle. And what happened to those splendid little triangular 'no draft' windows which used to direct fresh air onto your face on a hot day? (I suppose car manufacturers wanted to encourage us buy their air conditioners). And separate chrome car bumpers front and back, the absence of which now means that you get dents on your car body itself, and need expensive body and paint work. There is indeed always method in the business corporations' madness. And all these things in their small way are contraventions of the Social Contract.

Now let us step back and consider the very long run implications of 2% annual productivity increase. It means that in fifty years, production increases 27o%. So if the 'basket' of goods and services produced is unchanging, exactly the same things produced, no improvements or new products, then 2.7 times as many of everything will be produced. For example if the poorest segment of the population was undernourished. receiving only say ten dollars worth of food each day, now, fifty years later, they will be amply fed, receiving 27 dollars worth of food daily – indeed they may have bulging stomachs. But in fact not the same basket of goods is on offer, fifty years later, there are design improvements – or changes – of existing products, and there are totally new products, many of which sales promotion tells people they *must* have, they come to acquire the status of necessities. This must be much of the reason that so many people remain, or think they are, still poor, and public infrastructure crumbles, for example in the United States, people are buying so many of the new products that they become deficient in the basic necessities. And of course there is another reason some people stay poor, and that is mal-distribution of income, growing inequality between rich and poor.

Now, if we consider the very long run, and once good societal governance has been established, so that production is no longer in totally uncontrolled fashion merely devoted to ephemeral new products that supersede other products, with ever quickening obsolescence and shortening lifetimes, we can expect that the eventual consequence of annual 2% productivity increase will be greatly shortened working time, people needing to put in only twenty, eventually even less, hours per week. The world will be highly automated, perhaps fairly long hours will still be required for top managers, scientists, technological experts, and so on, but very much less required for the great majority of humanity.

We very much need some serious reflection at this point. If one is thinking of going to the trouble of embarking, with considerable hard thought and effort on a New Enlightenment, shouldn't one hesitate a moment? Is it all worth the effort – *plus ca change plus c'est la meme chose?* What makes for human happiness? Vanity of vanity, all is vanity. Just give us enough to eat and other necessities, give us law and order and security against wars and mad tyrants.

John Maynard Keynes was the father of macro-economics. Just to read his essay 'Economic Possibilities for our Grandchildren' explains why he was a giant among pygmies in the world of economics. And he would have disowned the handiwork of his modern progeny, the 'dynamic stochastic general equilibrium modelling', discussed earlier, which helped to blind the world to the impending economic crisis. The purpose of his essay was to 'take wings into the future', and much of what he says reflects what I have just written, vanity of vanity, *plus ca change.* Here, briefly, is Keynes' explanation of the past and the future: Since about 2000 B.C. to the beginning of the eighteenth century' only 300 years ago, 'there was no very great change in the standard of life of the average man living in the civilized centres of the earth . . . Language, fire, the same domestic animals that we have today, wheat, barley, the vine, the olive, the plough, the wheel, the oar, the sail, leather, linen and cloth, bricks and pots, gold and silver, copper, tin and lead – and iron was added to the list before 1000 BC, – banking, statecraft, mathematics, astronomy and religion', all had all been there and before about 1700 A.D, and there had been little change in living standards. It was only after that, that rapid change in human life commenced, and that was due to two reasons, 'the beginning of the great age of science and technical invention' along with the accumulation of capital equipment. And fast technologically-driven change continues and will lead to a huge problem: 'Three hour shifts or a fifteen hour week may put off the problem'. And what is the problem? 'If, instead of looking into the future,. We look into the past, we find that the economic problem, the struggle for subsistence, always has been hitherto the primary, most pressing problem of the human race – not only of the human race, but of the whole biological kingdom from the beginnings of life in its most primitive forms'. But the future will be entirely different from the present and will have many new problems to solve that we can leave to those who follow us. Here our concern is to stop our society's present rot, and reestablish the primacy of the Social Contract.

Part Three

Grand Strategy

Let us restate our aim. It is to reverse the decline of the West, which means that we must mend its faulty institutions that have been dragging it down. Inseparable from this goal is taking action to avert global climate catastrophe – it is pointless to strive to revive our sick civilization, if the coming state of the planet will be inhospitable for any form of civilised life. There is also a link that binds together the twin goals: the same institutional shortcomings that are driving down the West are also responsible for its carbon emissions – had these governance faults not been there we would not now be transferring billions of tons of CO2 annually into our atmosphere. And it is those same faults that are now hindering our efforts, late in the day, to bring global warming under control and mitigate its effects. A precondition for averting climate calamity is institutional reform – never mind 'enlightenment'.

While on the one hand rescuing the West involves only action in Western nations, on the other hand, saving the world's climate must involve all the world's nations. But there is also a world, a universal, component of a re-enlightenment in the West: it is also a question of saving civilization throughout the world – that is, of course, if we accept that the form of civilization, the heritage from Greece and Rome, through to the Enlightenment, is the highest form yet developed on the planet. That, of course, as Bertrand Russell explained, is a value judgment, and will only be valid to the extent that worldwide this value judgement is accepted.

One last point must be made before we discuss our strategy for what we might call 'The Great War of Civilization': It is the matter of timing. On the climate front we must act immediately, no delay there can be countenanced. On the other goal we can proceed at a more leisurely pace – but be comforted by the knowledge that the institutional reforms necessary to meet our climate goals will also improve our Western civilization – we shall, to a degree, be killing two birds with one stone.

In Part Two, our diagnosis, we prescribed the set of actions necessary to achieve our goals, but merely talking about them remains a far cry from actually 'taking arms against a sea of troubles and by opposing end them'. How do we get from a small nucleus of ideas in a handful of minds, to a great engine of change which will move the world in new directions?

Clearly this small number of minds must convince other minds of the correctness of their views until eventually the aggregation of convinced people constitutes a force sufficient to lead to action. Movements have played a large part in bringing about the world's major reforms, for example, in Britain, the anti-slavery movement, and the movements to end child labour and bring universal suffrage, first to men, and finally to women through the suffragettes – they chained themselves to lampposts and went on hunger strikes.

But now a new factor is added: These past movements grew and brought change over decades, but now we need a sequence, ideas, a movement, political action, that is exceedingly quick, a couple of years. We must consider how on earth this can be done. One clear advantage we now have is readily accessible and transmittable data through computers, the internet, Google, Facebook, Twitter, and a multitude of electronic gadgetry. Perhaps an intelligent approach will include enlisting as allies our intelligent young who like to be able to tell their elders and betters what to do, and have less of a vested interest in the old order. What is the best strategy to follow is the subject of the following three chapters.

CHAPTER 17

Driving Action within Each Nation and World Wide

The Copenhagen climate conference, and its successors in Cancun and Durban, were lessons on how not to approach a global problem, by seeking agreement at a conference of all the world's nations. This is not the way, with 200 diverse nations, the advanced, the giant emerging, and those still in an early stage of development; some convinced, others sceptical, some democratic, some autocratic, some corrupt, some gangster led.

What is now needed without delay is a 'Core Group' of able, dedicated, nations to drive the Great Battle of Civilization, not only to save the world's climate, but to start the mending and reinvigoration of ailing Western society. If the European Union is transformed into the entirely new model proposed in Chapter 14, it will constitute a forceful ally of the Core Group.

To build the core group, probably a start would a be made with a small initiating group of highly convinced, influential, able, nations, which would work quickly both to start mending themselves and by their example, and by diplomatic endeavour and other forms of pressure, build up the core group until it includes many important nations and has become a major force to be reckoned with, eventually the bandwagon that every one wants to jump on. But how do we get there? 'Troublesome Young Men' is the title of a recent book about a group of men, some remarkable[121], who battled hard against the appeasers, Chamberlain's Tory establishment, to bring Churchill to power. But the establishment hung on until after dire events were well under way, and only then did the troublesome men's efforts at last bear fruit and put Churchill in the driver's seat.

And that was in wartime, bombs were falling. Now, in peacetime, with no bombs falling and in the face of sceptics and deniers, and powerful vested interests, the challenge facing our band of the troublesome is even greater – here, in Canada where I live, the perils are not even on the radar, scarcely a single word on climate change. We need, at least in a number of key nations, a determined band of troublesome men and women to initiate a changed course, to wrench our nations out of their present doom-laden course and address now two great challenges, the immediate imperative of saving the climate, and the less immediate but also vital task of reversing our society's degradation and decline – indeed this might amount to just one great challenge – a mended society would in short order address the climate problem.

For the battle of the climate, it is difficult to see this action occurring outside the Western world. For all the talk of rising China, the West alone is where this action must be driven. Certainly China is rising fast, its population is twice that of the West narrowly defined (considerably less with a broader definition of the West to include Japan, South Korea, and Latin America). But in economic power China's GDP is still only about a third of the West's narrowly defined. And what of India? India too is rising fast but is scarcely a natural ally of China, from which it differs in so many ways, culturally, racially, historically, and in its political organization – India probably differs no less from China than it does from the West.

Besides, our aim here is a renaissance of the West, a recovery from a needless decline from a priceless heritage, our civilization which progressed from ancient Greece, through Rome, mediaeval Europe, the Enlightenment, the American and French Revolutions, and the British Industrial Revolution, to make what we in the West like to believe is the model which eventually all the world will adopt, though that will here be treated as a moot point. China may choose to continue with its own Confucius-based tradition of benevolent authoritarian government – though that clearly needs mending. Here we are unconcerned with these other civilizations, whether the Chinese and other rising giants will remain content with the state of their societies, here the matter at hand is to pull our Western civilization back from degradation and decline.

As already observed, the two great challenges, the climate and our ailing society, are strongly linked. Here we describe how a single Western mission focussing simultaneously on both goals might play out. The West will drive the whole world's battle of the climate. At the same time it will mend itself, in its New Enlightenment.

It is well that we should understand just how determined and forceful our effort will have to be, first at the level of the small initial driving core of troublesome men and women, and then in the initial driving core of nations. It is exceedingly difficult to change the great ship of society's course, and most particularly democratic society. The approach offered here will have to be very determined indeed.

Assembling the initial core nations

How are we to assemble an initial driving 'core group' of able, dedicated, nations' to drive the Great Battle of Civilization? One way would be for a small number of exceptional individuals, having put together a plan, to call a meeting of several hundred prominent, capable, people, many of whom are distinguished scientists (in physics, chemistry, the earth sciences, and the information and computer sciences), engineers, and macro-economists. Among the group too should be other prominent and able people, not neglecting historians, philosophers, and retired statesmen. Probably the deliberations of this group should be held in secret, to avoid distraction and media distortion.

The next step would be to try and convince the head of government of one of the expected future initial core nations, and then the latter would arrange a meeting of the government heads of several, say seven, suitable nations to form the initial driving core. Clearly the head of government first approached – the prime minister, president, or chancellor – would have to be an exceptional individual, of the sort that one might have difficulty finding. If so, the only practicable alternative is instead to form, at great speed, a movement – past great movements have required many years, but now the movement for the Battle of the Climate must be built at lightening speed. The originating handful of members will recruit other prominent and able individuals. As already observed, one important group to target would be the young, many young idealist students would undoubtedly be extremely happy to tell their elders of the establishment, how terribly, wickedly, wrong they are. Here they would have a more useful target than the World Economic Forum in Davos, or the G8 Conference. One can envision a new Occupy group, but this time one with coherent, convincing, aims, clever young people, who have not yet been drawn into and acquired vested interests in the existing order, and can further the cause with huge fervour.

Of great value, right from the start, in expanding the movement, would be an eloquent statement or manifesto, perhaps the 'Clarion Call for the Enlightenment, presented in Part Four, and accompanying it the two sets of graphs and diagrams presented in Chapter 11, demonstrating that global warming is fast happening and that our carbon emissions are the main cause. Accompanying this will be an explanation, so far strangely lacking, of the only possible, and obvious, way of mitigating climate change: quite simply, total electrification of the economy, largely on the basis of nuclear power, as well as moving extremely fast to a new lifestyle based on transformed transportation and communication systems and redesigned cities. That this is the only way forward will be backed up by statements, or perhaps a joint statement of major national scientific academies such as the U.S. National Academy of Sciences and the Royal Society.

CHAPTER 18

The Facts and Statistics

In the last chapter we talked about process, about an initial driving core of nations which would snowball and carry the drive forward. And in Part Two, our diagnosis, we broadly laid out what must be done, but actual action can come about only if there is a carefully laid out strategy and battle plan, and for that we need facts and statistics. An array of data has been assembled for a set of 41 nations which include all the world's full democracies, and all others, worldwide, each of which emits over 1% of the world's carbon dioxide emissions. Together the set produces 84 % of the world's economic output[122], and 86% of all its carbon dioxide emissions. For planning the conversion of our economy so that it no longer uses fossil fuels, the data and the engineering knowhow are readily available, but for the other challenge, improving our Western civilization, we are entering contentious territory, value judgments are involved: Here we have tried to measure how well each nation's governance is ensuring its compliance with the Social Contract, that it serve its people.

The statistics are set out in two tables. For each nation, Table 1 shows measures of society quality and Table 2 gives carbon dioxide emissions, as well as data useful for planning its emission reduction programme. In both tables the nations are listed in descending order of their ratings according to the Democracy Index published annually by *The Economist's* Intelligence Unit[123]. The least democratic nation appearing in the table is Saudi Arabia which is only 18.4% democratic and produces 1.37% of the world's emissions, and the most democratic nation is Norway, 98% democratic - according to *The Economist*, almost perfectly democratic! (even if *The Economist* is exaggerating, Norway must be fearsomely democratic).

Quality of Society

To answer this contentious and complex question conclusively requires more exhaustive research than my resources have allowed, but what appears in Table 1 is surely sufficient for arriving at tentative conclusions. It shows for each nation its rating according to measures published periodically by three organizations[124], respectively the Democracy Index, the Failed State Index, and the Corruption Perceptions Index. In addition it shows GDP per capita, degree of income inequality (the Gini coefficient – the higher the Gini, the greater the income inequality), and two measures of the extent of advertising-funded broadcasting – the extent to which each nation is free of the 'broadcasting perversion'. Each of these is discussed in turn.

The Democracy Index (DI)[125] For each nation, five factors are measured, respectively electoral process and pluralism; functioning of government; political participation; political culture; and civil liberties. Nations are rated from 0 to 100% – a totally authoritarian nation would have a rating of 0%, and a perfect democracy would be rated 100%. It will be no surprise that North Korea is the most authoritarian, it is only 10.8% democratic, and that seems borne out by the ludicrous spectacle, following the death of Kin Jong Il, of thousands of people in paroxysms of grief, all desperately weeping in unison – they daren't do otherwise. North Korea does not appear in the table, its only merit perhaps being that it produces few emissions.

The DI places the nations in four categories, full democracies, with scores of over 80%; flawed democracies with scores from 60 to 80%, hybrid regimes 40 to 60%, and authoritarian regimes less than 40%. Only 12.3 % of the world's population now lives in full democracies, and 36.5% in authoritarian countries.

The Failed State Index (FSI)[126] (In the table I've inverted it to become a 'Stability Index'). It will be no surprise that the world's most failed state (least stable) is Somalia which is 95.3% failed, and that many other nations are only a little better. And, again no surprise, at the other end of the spectrum, the least failed state is Norway (the index-makers' favourite) which is only a little failed, 15.6% (in the table 84.4% stable), with the other Scandinavian and some other smaller Western nations close behind. A totally stable country, scarcely human, with rock-like stability, would score 100%.

The Corruption Perceptions Index (CPI)[127] which rates countries according 'the degree to which corruption (electoral fraud, nepotism, and bribery) is perceived to exist among public officials and politicians' – 'perceived' because corruption is not documented, but it comes to be well known, and much talked about, for example, in China the public takes it for granted that when a dam fails or a great many houses fall down in an earthquake, that the responsible officials were bribed to relax design or construction standards[128].

Denmark, New Zealand, and Singapore are jointly rated the world's least corrupt nations, 93% corruption-free, with the other Scandinavians, and Canada, the Netherlands, Switzerland and Australia only a little behind. And the most corrupt are Somalia, Burma, Afghanistan and Iraq, all less than 15% *in*corrupt (they are 85% corrupt).

In addition to these indexes I also examined the United Nations' 'Human Development Index' but decided to omit it as unreliable, scarcely credible. It is described as a measure of four factors, life expectancy, literacy, education, and living standards, and places the world's nations in four groups, each of about 42 nations. At the top are the 'developed countries', with scores of 80 and above. Below that are the three other groups in descending order of development. Though as one might expect, the western nations are all in the top group, so are some dubious others, and there are other oddities in the ratings which suggest that the HDI cannot be taken seriously. Is the United Kingdom really the least developed of the Western countries? And are the United Arab Emirates, Qatar, Bahrain, and Barbados really among

Table 1: Quality of Society – page 1

		Demo-cracy Index %	Stability Index %	Corruption Perceptions Index %*	TV & Radio Broadcasting as a % of all Advertising	Advertising as a % of GDP	GDP per person ($ thousands)	Income Inequality (Gini Coefficient)
Category 1: Full Democracies (Democracy Index above 80%)								
Western	Norway	98.0	84.4	86	16	1.4	55.5	25
European	Iceland	96.5	75.1	85	--	--	38.8	28
Nations	Denmark	95.2	80.9	93	17	1.5	37.1	29
(including	Sweden	95.0	82.5	92	15	1.5	39.1	23
Czech	Finland	91.9	83.9	92	20	1.6	35.3	27
Republic)	Switzerland	90.9	81.8	87	11	1.8	42.9	34
	Netherlands	89.9	76.7	88	21	1.6	40.8	31
	Luxembourg	88.8	77.2	85	--	--	82.9	26
	Ireland	87.9	81.3	80	30	1.6	41.7	29
	Austria	84.9	77.3	79	32	1.4	40.3	26
	Germany	83.8	70.5	79	23	1.7	35.6	27
	Malta	82.8	59.8	56	--	--	25.0	--
	Czech Republic	81.9	65.4	46	--	--	25.5	--
	U.K.	81.6	71.7	76	35	2.2	35.8	34
	Spain	81.6	63.7	61	43	1.4	33.7	32
	Belgium	80.5	73.3	71	35	1.2	37.8	28
	Portugal	80.2	72.4	60	53	1.3	23.0	39
	France	77.7	70.9	68	36	1.3	33.7	33
Other	New Zealand	92.6	80.0	93	48	2.4	27.3	36**
Western	Australia	92.2	77.2	87	43	2.2	42.0	31
Nations	Canada	90.8	76.7	89	43	1.4	40.1	32
	United States	81.8	70.5	71	47	2.4	48.1	45
Other	South Korea	81.1	65.5	54	--	--	30.1	31
Full	Uruguay	81.0	65.5	69	--	--	13.5	43
Demo-	Japan	80.8	73.9	78	46	1.5	33.8	38
cracies	Costa Rica	80.4	56.6	53	--	--	11.5	57
	Mauritius	80.4	63.0	54	--	--	13.4	--

Table 1: Quality of Society – page 2

	Demo-cracy Index %	Stability Index %	Corruption Perceptions Index %*	TV & Radio Broadcasting as a % of all Advertising	Advertising as a % of GDP	GDP per person ($ thousands)	Income Inequality (Gini Coefficient)
Category 2: Flawed Democracies (Index 60 -80%)							
	Greece	79.2	61.7	35	56	1.2	30.1	33
	Italy	78.3	45.1	39	54	0.9	30.5	32
	South Africa	77.9	43.4	45	--	--	10.7	65
	India	72.8	34.0	33	--	--	3.5	37
	Brazil	71.2	43.8	37	--	--	11.1	54
	Poland	70.5	59.1	53	--	--	18.6	34
	Mexico	69.3	36.5	31	--	--	14.8	52
	Indonesia	65.3	30.7	28	--	--	4.3	37
	Ukraine	63.0	42.0	24	--	--	6.6	28
Category 3: Hybrid Regimes (Index 40 - 60%)							
	Turkey	57.3	35.7	44	--	--	13.3	40
	Russia	42.6	34.1	21	--	--	15.8	42
Category 4: Authoritarian Regimes (Index below 40%)							
	China	31.4	30.8	35	--	--	7.6	42
	Iran	19.4	23.1	22	--	--	12.6	45
	Saudi Arabia	18.4	35.3	47	--	--	22.1	--

* 100% = Absolutely free of corruption;   0% = Totally corrupt

-- = Not available

** = 1997

This table includes all fully democratic nations, and all nations with CO_2 emissions exceeding 1% of the world total.

this group of most developed nations, only slightly less developed than the UK, and more developed than Chile, Argentina, Brazil, and Russia, shown by the HDI as developing countries? The UN makes some strange judgments. Libya had been a member of the UN Human Rights Council (along with other such undemocratic and corrupt nations as Bahrain, Jordan, Qatar, Saudi Arabia, China, and Russia) but was ejected only when the United Nations censured it in the strongest terms and the coalition forces intervened militarily.

How much are the DI, the SI, and the CPI to be relied on?

Notable is the extent to which the three indexes are in agreement in rating the Scandinavian nations, New Zealand, Australia, Canada, the Netherlands, and Switzerland the highest. Also, with few exceptions, other West European nations and the United States rate high, though the US, Britain, France and Germany, have notably lower scores – do the smaller nations try harder – they can't be powerful so perhaps they can shine by being good? That the Democracy Index is over-generous in classifying the Czech Republic, Spain, Portugal, and South Korea as full, rather than flawed, democracies is suggested by their lower CPI and SI ratings. As for Italy, these two indexes indicate a very high degree of corruption and instability in that marvellous nation of the original Renaissance, and of the Roman Empire, and this seems borne out by the ludicrous *affaire Berlusconi*. To have as prime minister someone who owns a vast share of his nation's media certainly contravenes the Social Contract.

The present turmoil in the Middle East gives us an opportunity to test the SI. Yemen is rated 83% failed, Syria 73%, Egypt 69%, Jordan 64%, Libya 58%, Tunisia 56%, Bahrain 49%, all failures waiting to happen. (And indeed, in August 2012, now happening, in Syria with terrible savagery). According to the other indexes, they are all also very undemocratic and corrupt. Libya's democracy score at 19% is one of the world's lowest, which accords with the late Muammar Gaddafi's megalomaniacal ravings. The indexes indicate a link between lack of democracy, instability, and corruption. China is rated only 31% democratic, 31% stable, and 35% incorrupt. Understandably the Chinese rulers are nervous, they have been blocking electronic media bringing in the bad tidings from the Middle East. Autocracies clearly are more unstable than democracies, their peoples after stifling their discontentment and angry feelings for so long may eventually explode in rage. It is very notable on our television screens the faces of the Middle Eastern protesters contorted with rage[129]. In autocratic cultures there may be a strong link between the patriarchal relationship within families and the hierarchy of power in the state. This notion of hierarchy is also found in Confucianism though there is at least a claim of benignity. Most highly authoritarian regimes are also highly corrupt, for example China, Iran, and Egypt.

The three indexes broadly agree that the regimes which now most enshrine human rights, civil liberties, freedom of speech, the rule of law, and democratic government, are, apart from Japan and possibly South Korea, and several Latin American nations, Chile, Uruguay and Costa Rica, all Western nations. And perhaps not only Latin American nations but also Japan and South Korea might be included in a broadened definition of the West. The Latin Americans are all former colonies of Spain or Portugal, and speak Spanish or Portuguese, while Japan and South Korea have to a degree modelled themselves on the Western Democracies, and have comparable scores in all the indexes. Apart from these fairly 'Western' countries, elsewhere, in Eastern Europe and the Balkans, in the Middle East, Asia, Latin America, and Sub-Saharan Africa, what may be called the 'western attributes' are lacking, in major cases, severely so.

What is missing from
the Democracy Index

Missing from the DI are what are some essential requirements of democracy. It lacks several factors much evident in the present United States Presidential campaign, how election campaigns are financed, how this money is employed, and the power of lobbies financed by corporations and special interests. As already discussed, lobbying groups have a huge influence on public policy, it is said now of the US that what business wants, business gets[130]. And lately, overshadowing all, have been the grotesque 'SuperPACs' (Political Action Committees).

The DI also falls seriously short by omitting some important dimensions of Social Contract compliance, whether each of the estates of the realm is performing only its proper function, in particular, whether the business corporations usurp what are functions of the people. The index fails to indicate who is the paymaster of each nation's broadcasting system, whether it is paid for by, and therefore serves, the people and society, or whether it is paid for by business corporations and special interests to serve their sales and profit goals.

One cannot restate what I wrote in Chapter 9 often enough. Business corporations do not spend huge sums of money with the aim of letting the public have ideas and attitudes unsupportive of their marketing goals. How can this nagging backdrop to modern life not help mould people's knowledge, opinions, attitudes and values, hence public policy? Not only does the DI fail to consider the broadcasting perversion, it also leaves out other similar contraventions of the Social Contract, for example 'corporate social responsibility', which implies that business corporations know, and should decide, what charitable good works and symphony orchestras should be supported by the people, and make donations on their behalf.

For measuring the extent of the broadcasting perversion in Table 1, I have had difficulty finding statistics. Ideally Table 1 would show for, each country, the percent of broadcasting that is directly paid for by people, the rest being paid for by advertisers. Regrettably the best I have been able to find is what share of each nation's advertising is through radio and television. I've also been able to find what percent total advertising constitutes of GDP. Clearly if a large share of all advertising is on radio and television, and total advertising constitutes a large share of GDP, then we can assume that the public are subjected to a great many television and radio commercials.

As can be seen from Table 1, in Greece, Italy, and Portugal, about 55% of all advertising is on radio and TV, and in the US and New Zealand about 47%. In contrast, only 11% of Switzerland's advertising is in the broadcasting system, and in the Scandinavian counties between 15 and 20%. The US and New Zealand are also the nations with the most advertising of all kinds. 2.6 times as much as in Italy. According to one source three fifths of the world's advertising ($300 billion out of $500 billion) is American[131].

So Americans and New Zealanders are exposed to a lot of broadcast advertising, in these two nations broadcast ads amount to 1.3 percent of GDP – this might sound like only a little, but from my Canadian experience – the Canadian figure is only 0.6 percent of GDP – it means that it is difficult to avoid a continual barrage of radio and TV advertising, if one is not careful to avoid homes, restaurants, barber shops, and so on, where TV or radio are ever- present. In contrast, in Switzerland, Sweden, Norway and Denmark the GDP shares ranges from only 0.2% to 0.25%. I will comment on these very large differences among nations later. It is perhaps not by coincidence that Oliver Bennett in his 'Cultural Pessimism finds Western degradation very advanced in the US and New Zealand[132].

I suspect that the absence of good statistics on how nations' broadcasting systems are funded is probably due to the extent to which the world regards advertising-funding as the norm, and other broadcasting as the freak – well of course, silly, broadcasting always has advertising! In the US the public broadcasting system, PBS, used to be called 'National Educational Television' perhaps to explain its oddity – it's not normal broadcasting, its special programming for educating children. Though part of its funding comes from government, it is also heavily reliant on donations from business corporations – (this is obviously a form of Corporation Social Responsibility – these corporations showing what good upright citizens they are), as well as donations from the public, solicited in frequent campaigns by groups of earnest public- spirited volunteers appealing for help from 'viewers like you'. And how it needs help. Republicans in the House of Representatives have been reported as seeking to cut the government subsidy to public broadcasting, despite the fact that it is now only one tenth of the BBC's public funding, or allowing for Britain's far smaller GDP, one 70th of the BBC's funding. Here is a case of American exceptionalism, a nation which sees nothing odd about having broadcasting for the public that is merely one of its business corporations' advertising media.

Another requirement of a good society is that it be a good provider of goods and services for its people, and the only indicator for this in the table is its GDP per capita. This for a variety of reasons is an imperfect measure, that fails to indicate whether there is gross income inequality, and for example, that 50 million Americans lack heath care, and that the major source of personal bankruptcy in the US is medical expenses. In contrast there is no such thing as poverty in Sweden, or lack of health care, although Table 1 shows that the average American income is 23% greater. Nor does GDP per capita disclose whether some of the consumer goods provided are of little genuine utility, acquired as a result of intense sales promotion. And of course, high average per capita income does not mean there are no poor, and, as the table shows, the US, with a Gini coefficient of 45, has the most unequal income distribution of the advanced nations. In Western Europe Britain is the large country which is most unequal with a Gini of 34, and Japan also has a high Gini value of 38. In contrast the value for Sweden is 23, and, interestingly Europe's largest economy, Germany has a Gini of only 27. Another measure of inequality is the ratio between the incomes of the top 10% and the bottom 10%. These show low values of about 6 for Sweden, Norway, and Finland, and an even lower value for Japan of 4.5. This low value for Japan is at odds with its high Gini value, second only to that of the United States among the advanced nations. This needs further study: is it possible to have a low top 10%/bottom 10%, but to have high inequality among the remaining 80%? The most unequal Western Nation, the United States has a ratio of 15.0, and at 13.6 the UK is also very unequal. But before being too hard on the West for its inequality we should look at the others: Brazil and Argentina with ratios of about 36, Venezuela 50, but that is low compared with Namibia's 129. And for these countries the incomes of the lowest are extremely low.

There are other measures of the good society missing in Table 1, for example what share of people's lives is spent in traffic gridlock for want of good urban transport, the blight of landscapes and city approaches by billboards, ugly urban sprawl, the absence of urban parks, and badly planned cities.

The big and the bad carbon emitters

We have just discussed the controversial, values-governed, part of the New Enlightenment, what constitutes a good society, now we enter what should be the uncontentious, measurable, science and engineering governed part, which nations are the big, and which are the bad, emitters of carbon dioxide. Table 2 shows, for the set of nations listed in Table 1, data necessary for waging the Battle of the Climate. It includes all the world's biggest emitters, each of which emits one or more percent of the world's total annual emissions. Of the 22 such nations, the fully democratic group includes nine, in the order of the amount they emit, the US, Japan, Germany, Canada, the UK, South Korea, Australia, France, and Spain. The 13 nations outside the fully democratic group range from China, which already in 2007 was emitting 22.3% of the planet's carbon dioxide emissions, to Turkey, which emitted slightly less than 1%. In addition to the thirty-eight nations in the table, there are 177 other nations, some tiny, for example Andorra and Bermuda, or very under-developed, for example, Somalia (the world's most failed state whose only merit may be that it isn't a bad polluter) each of which emits less than one hundredth of 1% of the world's emissions. Together all these 177 nations emit only about 15% of all emissions.

Just because a nation is a *big* emitter, does not necessarily mean that it is a particularly *bad* emitter, it may merely mean that it is a big nation. The table gives us some idea of which nations are the worst, most culpable, emitters, by telling us each nation's 'carbon intensity', a term I have applied to its emissions / GDP ratio, expressed in the table as tons of CO_2 emitted per million dollars of GDP. The biggest emitter, China, emits 649 tons per million dollars of GDP, and that means that given its GDP of 10.1 trillion dollars, it puts 6.5 billion tons of CO_2 into the atmosphere each year (these emission data are for 2007). The fully democratic West European nations on average have a carbon intensity of about 240 tons per $ million of GDP, about one third

Table 2: Data for the Battle of the Climate – page 1

		Percent of World's			Population Density (people per square mile)	CO2 Emissions Intensity (tons per $ million of GDP)
Group	Nations	CO2 Emissions	GDP	Population		

Category 1: Full Democracies (Democracy Index above 80%)

Group	Nations	CO2 Emissions	GDP	Population	Pop. Density	CO2 Intensity
Western	Norway	0.15	0.35	0.07	37	168
European	Iceland	0.01	0.02	0.005	8	195
Nations	Denmark	0.17	0.27	0.08	330	246
(including	Sweden	0.17	0.48	0.13	52	140
Czech	Finland	0.22	0.25	0.08	40	347
Republic)	Switzerland	0.14	0.44	0.11	476	117
	Netherlands	0.59	0.91	0.25	1154	256
	Luxembourg	0.04	0.05	0.007	487	268
	Ireland	0.15	0.23	0.06	153	255
	Austria	0.23	0.45	0.12	253	208
	Germany	2.69	3.96	1.23	597	269
	Malta	0.01	0.01	0.006	3308	267
	Czech Republic	0.43	0.35	0.15	336	480*
	U.K.	1.84	2.95	0.91	650	247
	Spain	1.23	1.84	0.60	207	260
	Belgium	0.35	0.53	0.16	883	262
	Portugal	0.20	0.33	0.16	360	236
	France	1.27	2.90	0.95	261	173
		9.89	16.32	5.07		
Other	New Zealand	0.11	0.16	0.06	40	273
Western	Australia	1.28	1.19	0.31	7	424*
Nations	Canada	1.90	1.80	0.50	9	419*
	United States	19.91	19.76	4.53	82	399*
		23.2	22.91	5.4		
Other	South Korea	1.72	1.96	0.72	1255	345
Full	Uruguay	0.02	0.07	0.05	51	129
Demo-	Japan	4.28	5.82	1.90	87	291
cracies	Costa Rica	0.03	0.07	0.06	213	159
	Mauritius	0.01	0.02	0.02	677	228
		6.06	7.94	2.75		
Total Full Democracies		39.15	47.17	13.22		

* Culpably high emitters' (intensity 400 and over)

Table 2: Data for the Battle of the Climate – page 2

		Percent of World's			Population Density (people per square mile)	CO2 Emissions Intensity (tons per $ million of GDP)
Group	Nations	CO2 Emissions	GDP	Population		

Category 2: Flawed Democracies (Index 60 -80%)

	Greece	0.33	0.44	0.16	210	304
	Italy	1.56	2.39	0.87	499	258
	South Africa	1.48	0.71	0.73	103	827*
	India	5.50	5.41	17.12	904	403*
	Brazil	1.26	2.95	2.92	60	169
	Poland	1.08	0.97	0.57	318	442*
	Mexico	1.61	2.09	1.63	144	289
	Indonesia	1.35	1.39	3.54	321	387
	Ukraine	1.08	0.41	0.69	197	1049*
		15.25	16.76	28.24		

Category 3: Hybrid Regimes (Index 40 - 60%)

	Turkey	0.98	1.29	10.7	237	302
	Russia	5.24	2.86	20.9	21	692*
		6.22	4.15	3.2		

Category 4: Authoritarian Regimes (Index below 40%)

	China	22.30	13.63	19.83	357	649*
	Iran	1.69	1.12	0.98	105	597*
	Saudi Arabia	1.37	0.84	0.42	34	649*
		25.36	15.59	21.2		

Other		13.9	16.1	34.1		
World		100%	100%	100%	100%	100%

Emissions of culpably high emitted (*)
= 63.26% of world total

the Chinese amount. The Czech Republic, which is the only former Communist bloc full democracy, is twice as carbon-intensive, at 480 tons per $ million of GDP. We might say that China and the Czech Republic have very 'dirty' economies, in contrast to Switzerland with the cleanest economy, with a carbon intensity of only 117. The large Asian full democracy, Japan, has an intensity only a little higher than the West European average.

Apart from New Zealand, the western nations outside Europe, the US, Canada, and Australia also have dirty economies, with intensities of about 400 or more, two thirds higher than the Western European average. Outside the full democracies we find eight dirty economies, some extremely dirty, ranging from Ukraine, an astonishing 1049, through South Africa 827, Russia 692, China and Saudi Arabia 649, Iran 597, Poland 442, and India 403. It is surely no coincidence that dirty economies abound in the former Soviet Union, the Czech Republic, Poland, Ukraine, and Russia, their dirtiness no doubt a result of their former communist economy without the efficiency resulting from the spur of competition of a market economy. China's dirtiness at 649 is a large contributor to global emissions. One recalls the highly polluted Beijing air which was a source of worry before the Beijing Olympics. If China's carbon intensity were halved to 325, still far above the Western European average, world emissions would be reduced by 11%. China's position in the world's great Battle of the Climate is very clear.

But caution is necessary: As already discussed, China's huge pollution cloud of sulphates is helping delay the onset of calamitous global warming, and the speed at which China cleans its dirty skies must be coordinated with the progress of the world's carbon emission-cutting mega-projects. Otherwise the world's danger is increased of calamitous runaway global warming.

We need to look at the factors that determine a nation's carbon intensity as shown in Table 2. Here are six main factors: First is whether fossil fuels have a large share in its energy mix, and also what kind of fossil fuel – coal produces much more carbon dioxide than does natural gas. Some countries use more 'clean energy', in particular hydro-electric power (if they are lucky enough to have the necessary topography, rivers and rainfall), and nuclear power. What many environmentalists call 'green' energy, solar and wind, nowhere yet makes a large contribution, and indeed as already discussed, wind power is a false hope, a delusion – and also an example of how nations can be wilfully blind. One might add that failures of societal governance are the biggest causes of societies' problems, whether degradation and decline, economic depression and unemployment, or failure to carry out the obvious ways of curbing greenhouse gas emissions.

The second factor determining nations' carbon intensity is the kind of economy they have. Nations with large resource extraction, metallurgical, construction, and heavy industry components will be more energy intensive than those more dependent on light manufacturing and large service sectors. The third factor is their land areas. Huge countries like the US, Canada, Australia, Russia, Brazil, and China will have commensurately extensive transportation systems, which are highly energy intensive. The fourth factor is whether nations are large users of public transport, fast inter-urban trains and good urban transportation systems, or rely more on personal automobile and air transportation – one immediately thinks of the United States, an automobile society supported by far lower gasoline prices than other countries – that is, they tax gasoline less, and of course that has helped the Detroit manufacturers of gas guzzlers.

The fifth factor is economic efficiency. Competition in the free market raises energy efficiency – the less energy (indeed the less of all its purchased inputs) any business corporation uses, the lower its costs, the greater its profits. As already observed, this inducement was lacking in the former members of the Soviet bloc. Finally, the sixth factor is whether a nation has an energy policy that encourages, or obliges, the use of less fossil fuels through energy efficiency and by substituting other energy forms, and to make its economy less energy-intensive by using different forms of transportation and other changes in life style.

Culpable dirtyness

It is useful to introduce the concept of 'culpable dirtyness': Of the six factors only two are non-culpable, the second factor, the kind of economy, and the third factor, the nation's land area, perhaps best expressed as population density per square mile. The world economy needs highly carbon intensive resource extraction industry for its raw materials, and the nations which are the source of these resources will accordingly seem dirtier but may not necessarily be culpably so. Similarly population density. Russia, with its huge area has a density of only 21.3 people per square mile and Canada, also huge, has an even lower density of 8.6. These lower densities mean larger transportation systems and these are energy intensive. Of course, large parts of Russia and Canada are scarcely inhabited at all, but even so this low density must account at least a little for their high dirtiness scores. Tiny Netherlands, however with the extremely high population density of 1156 people per square mile, needs much smaller, and, because of its flat terrain, less costly, transportation services, and might, on this account, be expected to have a lower carbon intensity than its 256, higher than the West European average (but we cannot rush to judge, this higher carbon intensity may be due to its industry mix, which I have not had an opportunity to study). Switzerland appears on this account exemplary, which despite a lower population density than the Netherlands, and its mountainous terrain affecting its transportation systems, still has the very low carbon intensity of 117, the lowest among all the world's advanced countries. A large factor in Switzerland's low carbon intensity is the fact that its electricity supply is 95% 'clean', partly hydro-electric, made possible by its mountainous terrain, and partly nuclear. Another large factor in Switzerland's low carbon intensity, one supposes, is its well-known industry mix with large tourism and banking industries. And visitors to Switzerland are familiar with its excellent electric trains. How do China and the US show up? They are both huge with roughly the same areas, China's population density is much the higher, respectively 360 people per square mile versus 82. Despite this China's economy is much the dirtier, no doubt for a variety of reasons, especially its large proportion of culpably high emitting industry, with a lack of strict anti-pollution regulation.

Nuclear power generation statistics

Missing from the table are statistics on nuclear power, which will be a major weapon in the Battle of the Climate. At present (as of early 2012), in the world, there are about 440 nuclear power plants in operation, with an output of 375 gigawatts (GW). In addition only 63 GW of new capacity is under construction, which is an indication of how pathetically the world is yet engaging in the battle of the Climate. Of this existing capacity, 58% is in the West, narrowly defined, or 75% including Japan and South Korea. Though China at present has only 2% of the world's nuclear capacity, of the 63 GW under construction, China accounts for 43%, and Asia as a whole 66%. The West on the other hand is building only 7%. The West at present talks, but not much of nuclear power, but rather of windmills, the new symbol of the great and the good: – and the East acts. The Chinese leaders can decree if they wish a sudden huge programme of nuclear station and high speed train construction, just as they, unfettered by economists' defective notions, were able to switch to infrastructure construction when their exports declined in the present world recession.

The present 375 GW of nuclear generation capacity constitutes 15% of the world's total electric power capacity. Of the remainder, 17% is hydroelectric and 2% 'green' – wind, solar, geothermal, and tidal – while the rest, 66%, is fossil fuel fired, producing, in advanced nations, about 30 percent of their carbon emissions. There is little more potential for hydro-electric generation in the world, most rivers with hydro-electric possibilities have already been exploited, and as already noted wind turbines are a false hope, and there is little sign of the other green possibilities making big headway. So that means that the 66% of our generating capacity that must be replaced must be mainly nuclear – and there is no rhyme nor reason, apart from societal inertia, and poor governance, why this cannot be fast done. That is clear from several nations' electric power systems which already have a high nuclear component, France 79%, Belgium 56%, Sweden 45%, Switzerland 40%, South Korea 38%, Japan 28%, Germany 27%, UK 21%, and the US 19%.

But this 66% of present electricity generation capacity that must be replaced is only a small part of the nuclear power generation capacity that the world will need. The present electricity generating system serves only the part of the economy which now runs on electricity. Yet to be converted to electricity is most building heating, most transportation equipment (automobiles and road transport, buses, many trains), and many industrial processes. If we assume that the economy is now only one third electric, that means we must enlarge the electric power system by a factor of three. But we shall still be falling short, because that deals only with the present economy, in 2011. In another 40 years, the world economy growing at say 3% or even more annually, as the BRICs (Brazil, Russia, India, China), relentlessly grow, the world's electricity system will be over three times as large. Nuclear generation now supplies 15% of our present supply. If all additional capacity over the next 40 years is nuclear, then present nuclear capacity must be increased by a factor of 27 (by a factor of 3 to make the present electric power system fossil fuel-free, a further factor of 3 to make the economy all electric, and another factor of 3 for economic growth. And if we can find green solutions (solar, wind, tidal, etc) to supply a quarter of this then we shall need to multiply our nuclear plant by a factor of only 20. If over the next forty years we can convert to a new, low energy intensity economy, which we, like Switzerland should, that needs half as much energy per unit of GDP, we need multiply our present nuclear capacity by a factor of only 10. Better still, if we reduce our energy intensity by a factor of three we need to multiply our nuclear capacity by only 7. The world must no longer dally. The above, starkly, are the figures we shall have to contend with in the Battle of the Climate.

CHAPTER 19

The Initial Driving Core

Chapter 17 argued that action on the climate could not come from conferences of all the world's nation, but required a core of able, determined nations to drive the whole process. Chapter 18 then presented statistics necessary for determining membership of the core, and for deciding their strategy.

The process is started by a small initial driving core of highly committed, highly competent, nations. Table 3 rearranges the nations listed in Table 2, selecting seven nations to constitute the initial core. This initial group has three small nations, Sweden, Switzerland, and the Netherlands, and four 'heavy hitters', Germany, the UK, France, and from outside Europe, Japan.

The UK, France, and Germany together account for 60% of Western Europe's economic output. The inclusion of France in the core is important because alone among the world's nations its electricity generation is already nearly 80% nuclear, and it has the TGV (Trains Grand Vitesse) network of very fast electric trains, and probably as a result, it has much the lowest carbon intensity of all the large nations. In addition, the three smaller core nations, few will disagree, are highly able and effective. Switzerland has demonstrated that it is brilliant at reducing its emissions, and Sweden too is a very low emitter. The Netherlands however is not, its carbon intensity is at the level of the UK's and Germany's, and earns its place in the driving core by being very well governed, and capable of adopting sound policies. Some further words are called for on Switzerland. It is one of the world's most environmentally conscious nations – elsewhere the

Greens have been strongly anti-nuclear, and are responsible for the burgeoning wind turbines destroying landscapes. (Swiss sentiment has just changed post-Fukushima, but can that view long prevail in the face of the reality of climate change?). And Switzerland is also one of the top re-cyclers of wastes, recycling is enforced by law. Its dense electric train network is much used, with 47 train journeys per person per year. It is not difficult to see why Switzerland has the world's lowest carbon intensity among advanced nations. Such is the drive of the Swiss to save the environment that they have a policy to reduce their *total* energy use by 50% by 2050, which presumably means that they aim to convert to the low energy life style discussed in Chapter 11. Such changes much reduce the size of the effort needed to reduce carbon emissions. It would indeed have been remiss to have omitted Switzerland from the initial driving core, as I nearly did, only very recently becoming aware of its impressive environmental record.

It will also be observed that the seven nations of the initial driving core are also democratic, and European, apart from Japan, and the three smaller nations are rated by the indexes as among the world's most 'enlightened', exhibiting best the western attributes. Further, Western European democracies have so far been at the forefront of the world's efforts on the climate front. The United States is not a signatory of the Kyoto Accord, and the Republican contenders for the presidency in the last election denied that the climate threat exists. While our proposed 'new Europe' that was the subject of Chapter 14, will continue its efforts on the climate front, that will not be its first preoccupation, and that is why there is a need for a separate organization, the driving core for the great battle of the climate.

There are good reasons for also including Japan in the initial core. Apart from its high ratings by the democracy, stability, and corruption indexes, it has one of the world's largest economies, it is extremely competent technologically, and can carry out vast projects. Japan already has, after the US and France, the world's third largest nuclear capacity, as well as high speed trains. Another good reason may be provided by the earthquake-induced nuclear calamity – Japan's exceptional qualities may now be demonstrated in the speed of its recovery from the worst disaster to hit Japan since Hiroshima and Nagasaki. Japan may succeed

Table 3: The Initial Driving Core

% of World's

CO2 emissions	GDP	Nations of the World	Governance Index % (2)	Broadcasting Index % (3)	Emissions Intensity (4)
		1.Good Governance, Index >65%			
		(a) Initial Driving Core			
0.17	0.48	Sweden	90	85	140
0.14	0.44	Switzerland	87	89	117
0.59	0.91	Netherlands	85	79	280
2.69	3.96	Germany	78	77	269
4.28	5.82	Japan	78	54	291
1.84	2.95	UK	76	65	247
1.27	2.90	France	72	64	173
11.1	7.1				2.48
		(b) High Emission Intensity			
19.91	19.76	USA	74	53	399*
3.18	2.99	Canada, Australia	86	57	422*
2.95	3.80	(c) South Korea and Spain	69	NA	308
1.67	2.72	(d) Small European nations	71-90	47-84[1]	244
38.7	46.7	Total, Good Gov. Nations			
		2. Intermediate Governance 64-35			
5.50	5.41	India	47	NA	403*
3.64	2.09	Poland, South Africa, Ukraine	61 to 43	NA	691*
6.76	10.11	Italy, Brazil, Turkey, Mexico, Indonesia, Greece	41-59	Italy 46	265
15.9	17.6				
		3. Authoritarian with high emission. Gov. Index <35			
22.30	13.63	China	32.5	NA	649*
5.24	2.86	Russia	32.6	NA	692*
1.37	0.84	Saudi Arabia	33.6	NA	649*
1.69	1.12	Iran	21.5	NA	597*
30.6	18.5				
14.8	17.2	4. Other World Nations, small on underdeveloped	NA	NA	360
100%	100%				

(1) Scandinavian Nations >80, Portugal 47
(2) Governance Index = average of democracy, stability and corruption indexes
(3) Broadcasting Index: % of all advertising not on TV & Radio, ie. Print media, billboards, mail, neon, etc. (When index = 100% there is no broadcasting advertising)
(4) *CO2 emissions intensity 400 & over.

as it did when suddenly in 1868 its driving elite decided that its previous 250 year self-imposed isolation from the outside world must end, and it must transform itself from a feudal state into a modern industrial nation. 'Japanese modernity is an extraordinary achievement: the only non-Western country to industrialize in the nineteenth century, by far the most advanced country in East Asia, the world's second largest economy' (until recently overtaken by China), 'an enviably high standard of living, arguably the best transportation system in the world'[133]. Also Japan likes to think of itself as Western rather than Asian, but at the same time it has succeeded in remaining highly distinctive, both culturally and socially'[134]. How the Japanese rallied and were supportive of the disaster victims was most impressive, there was no looting, in strong contrast to what happens in other countries when calamity strikes, when louts take the opportunity to help themselves[135]. Japan also carries a useful lesson in human decency for many Western nations, as noted earlier, it has the world's least income inequality between the very rich and the very poor, only the Scandinavian nations come close in this measure.

The addition of Japan to the otherwise European initial core will also extend the idea of the New Enlightenment beyond being a too narrowly Western project, underlining what we in the West at least like to think is the universal nature of the Social Contract and the western attributes. And here is a little geopolitical thinking, a Japan that sees itself as Western rather than part of the hegemonic Asia block that some people fear may come into being.

Finally a few words on Canada: I am Canadian, and would have liked it to be in the initial driving core. Canada is a highly competent nation, there is no more worthy people. Moreover Canadians like to think of their country as being more progressive than the United States, which hasn't universal health care. Most Canadians would be thrilled to have been chosen for the initial core – the saviours of civilization.

Unfortunately that is not yet to be. Canada's efforts in the Battle of the Climate have been most half-hearted, and now is it is hugely wrapped up in the exploitation of the oil sands, regarding which the prominent NASA scientist, James Hansen, has protested that it would mean 'game over' for the environment.[136] But Hansen may be unduly pessimistic, that is, if governments change direction and adopt the kind of huge emission reduction programme discussed in Chapter 11. If they do, then the oil sands producers will go bankrupt, they will have no buyers for their product.

Also making Canada unsuitable for the initial core is the continued contamination of its so-called public broadcaster with advertising interruptions, the very symbol of North American consumption nirvana. But I am most hopeful that Canada will quickly change direction and enter the core. I must report one encouraging sign: here in Ottawa, bicycles have become the 'in thing' among the young, bicycle lanes have been marked out, narrowing car-driving space on some city thoroughfares.

So now we have in the initial driving core seven highly capable and well-governed nations, which, though producing only 11% of the world's emissions and 17% of its economic output, 'punches above its weight', a group whose voice will be heeded. There is also another factor which should give this group added influence. While the world continues to dither and flounder, in addressing global warming, as well as the economic meltdown and high unemployment, the core will be acting determinedly, making root and branch changes. The core will have a strong appearance of forcefulness, of knowing what it is doing, and many other nations will quickly seek to join them.

The United States and the initial core

But should not the US to be in this initial group? Arguably not. In this huge diverse nation there have been, and continue to be, large forces that have worked to block action on global warming, and deny any human agency in its existence. Also rendering the US an unsuitable member in the initial core is its division of powers and a Congress often serving special interests and blocking legislation. Just how unfocussed is the United States on the Battle of the Climate is that it has not even made a start to raise the price of its gasoline to European levels. The US has continued to maintain its extremely low gasoline prices, to fuel its gas guzzlers, no matter what the world's needs have been. The United States requires a short, sharp shock.

But it is of course vital that the US soon join the core, and most probably if the initial core acts determinedly and immediately to launch its great projects, the United States will soon follow suit. There are many enlightened forces in this great nation who would wish to be on the right side of history. The launching of the New Enlightenment driven by the determined initial driving core will hasten the rise of these strong American forces of enlightenment. One can confidently say that once the initial core's giant projects are underway, and with great publicity, the rest of Western Europe, plus Canada, Australia and New Zealand, and perhaps South Korea and Taiwan will seek to leap on board, raising the core's share of global GDP to 27%. And assuming that the US too will early join the core, it will now include all the full democracies and account for 47% of the world's economic output as well as 39% of its carbon emissions. This core will now be the band wagon, onto which most of the rest of the world will want to jump. And the core will enact policies that will make it difficult not to jump.

China and the core

And of course China must soon be induced into the core, its emissions still growing fast, from an economy that uses 45% of the world's coal, the dirtiest of all fuels. Its electricity generation is 75% coal fuelled. China insists on its fast economic growth rate, so what must it do? This has already been stated in Chapter 11. At racing speed it must take both, parallel, tracks, electrification based on nuclear power, and at the same time fast moving to the low energy world of the future, based on transformed transportation and communication systems and urban redesign. And its new affluent must stop ordering gas guzzling Cadillacs from General Motors.

Yes, but how to oblige China to do all this? There are two ways, a sort of carrot and stick. The carrot is expressed praise, and it is sincere praise, for China's ability to get things done – it may not be a democracy that consults the people, but it can make sharp policy changes, and it is highly competent and showed at Copenhagen that it understood the concept of carbon-intensity reduction. Not only that, China already has the world's largest programme of nuclear station construction, and is building fast electric trains.

So expressed admiration (the carrot) may encourage China to intensify its nuclear and fast train efforts, but what stick? This is where the other half of the New Enlightenment comes to our assistance: As a result of its governance reforms, especially its replacement of the income tax by the Return to Society, and its adoption of the New Economics that banishes boom and bust, and ensures that the unemployed will always have adequate income, the core nations can practice a degree of economic autarchy, becoming less vulnerable to international trade retaliation. Thus the core nations are in a position to place high tariffs on global warming laggards, on those nations which are failing to cut their emissions. Of course this must be done carefully to avoid retaliatory withholding of particular vital raw material imports. The main point is that with the New Economics, even if economic activity temporarily falls, the unemployed people can continue to be sure of decent income. And it is important also to remind China how dirty its economy is, 649 in the table, nearly three times the West European value. The dirtyness is culpable: China must be induced to start using a good part of its phenomenal economic growth rate on cleaning up its economy, not on buying Cadillacs. It may well be that not only China, but also the United States, must be subjected to the policy of the stick: If urgent appeals from the core to the US to change course are ignored, then a trade tariff will be placed on it. Until the US sets in motion the needed mega-projects of nuclear generation and electrification of its economy, and radical transformation of its transport system, a tariff will be placed on US exports, rising progressively at the rate of, say, 25% each year. Sorry, United States old chap, nothing personal, the world's climate must be saved.

The League of the Social Contract

Perhaps the core group might be given another name. One theme runs through all I have written, the transgression of the Social Contract which requires that public policy should have only one ultimate goal, the service of the people. Nothing perhaps could better remind the members of the core group of this than calling it the 'League of the Social Contract'.

As the core grows, there will be some difference between the wish of a nation to join the group and its fitness to belong. The members of the Group should have the ultimate say on who may join. And what of the United Nations? Only a small proportion of its members exhibit the Western attributes which it is our present purpose to bolster. The UN may be the place of record of the stand of each of the world's governments on major issues, but it is also an organization which could be comfortable with a Gaddafi on its Human Rights Council.

Part Four

The Action Plan

In Part One we discussed a set of phenomena that our society exhibits, what most people see as, at worst, necessary evils, part of the human condition, but what are in truth symptoms of a society gravely ill. Part Two then offered a diagnosis of the sickness, and prescribed a remedy, the governance institutions that must be reformed and the grand projects we must embark on, for the symptoms to disappear, and for our civilization to resume its upward trajectory. Next, in Part Three, we developed our strategy, how we can make the needed changes come about.

All that is no more than thinking, nothing has changed on the ground, but at least we can now hope. All that remains now is a little further thought, laying out the battle plan, exactly what must be done, by whom, when. From that point on the only thinking that will be required will be by our appointed peace time generals, to direct action, to change things on the ground. And then in some years time it will be found that our battle plan is no longer a plan, it is a historical record of what was actually done. Well of course not exactly, but we may at least have done enough to stave off disaster, and rescue our civilization.

The following 'action plan' unfolds exceedingly fast, it leaves only two years to bring together the initial driving core of nations, fully committed to a plan of action, so that in the third year the great programme of the New Enlightenment can get underway, other nations fast attaching themselves to the core. This will be 'the first day of the future', the great re-balancing will begin towards full compliance with the Social Contract, and to convert our society not only to one that emits little carbon, but is also highly civilised. Two years is optimistic. If the core nations can manage to get started in three years, that will still be laudable action. Even if we fall short and serious climate change occurs, nonetheless we shall still have a much more civilised, humanity-serving, if somewhat warmer, world for those who follow us.

The First Year: Action by the Small Group of Determined Individuals

First the seeds of change are sown. A small group of highly competent and dedicated individuals, the 'initiating group' is brought together from one or more of the nations which will likely comprise the initial driving core nations. Their first task will be to put together a Manifesto for the Future, that will be the basis for action. This Manifesto will comprise on the one hand the Clarion Call that will be delivered to the public on Launch Day, and on the other hand, a set of exhibits that will show that the Clarion Call is not just fine words, but is a statement of what will be the new reality that will be brought into being. The exhibits will include:

The diagrams that clearly, and unequivocally, demonstrate global warming and human agency (Figures 2.1 and 2.2 in Chapter 11).

Outline of the great programmes soon to be launched:

- to restart the economy, and end unemployment.

- to transform the broadcasting system, to serve the people and society.

- to replace the income tax by the Return to Society.

- to wage the Great Battle of the Climate.

- to transform the transportation system to provide the public with fast access to both work and play, and remove the curse of traffic gridlock.

Next, with the help of the Clarion Call and exhibits, the initiating group will enroll to the cause several hundreds of eminent, influential, individuals, including not only those with technical expertise for the major reforms ahead, scientists, engineers, macro-economists, and public policy planners, but also eminent historians, philosophers, biologists, medical scientists, literary figures, and the like. At this stage governments, the political process, and the media are not engaged, so as not to hamper progress by partisan and wild claims and pronouncements.

The Second Year: Engaging the Initial Driving Core Governments

This will be a crucial year. The initiating group of eminent individuals will approach directly one or more suitable heads of government, likely members of the initial driving core. By the end of the second year the all-important group of seven nations will have been formed, their heads of government and their cabinets totally committed to the Great Battle of Civilization. They will have met with the leading members of their opposition parties, so that the programme can in year three be launched on a non-partisan basis.

In this year, the starting group of several hundred eminent individuals will not be idle. They will explore in detail the kinds of ideas discussed in the preceding chapters, in particular on ending the Great Recession, on the reform of broadcasting, and on replacing the income tax by the Return to Society. Also, approaches will be made to one or more national science academies, for example the Royal Society in Britain, and the French and German academies. These bodies will be asked to lay out before the public a statement on the set of projects required of the world's nations, to limit calamitous climate change. Such a set of actions was the subject of Chapter 11 above. Also set in motion will be the use of the national income input-output models to arrive at, by simulation, for each nation, an optimum programme of emission reduction projects. The programme will have two parallel parts: the electrification of society on the basis of new generating stations, (most of which will be nuclear); and the re-making of society, both to make the economy far less energy-intensive, and to improve the quality of life. This will be achieved through new transportation and communications systems and urban redesign using the concept of the 'three-dimensional elevator', and by replacing much travel, in particular commuting and business travel, by virtual travel, and virtual conferencing.

The academies might also consider sponsoring a multi-disciplinary study group to explore the questions raised in Chapter 12 on 'The New Science of Economics'.

The Third Year: Launch of the Great Transformation

This is what will happen. This will be year one of society's new trajectory. Each nation of the initial driving core will be galvanised by a clarion call to action. The call will be given on a non-partisan basis by the by head of each government, in the presence of the leaders of the opposition parties. Required is a ringing declaration along the following lines:

THE CLARION CALL

'We have grim woes, accelerating warming threatening our habitat, Mother-Earth, at the same time as deep depression grips our economies. To add further to our woes, our quality of life is falling, and warnings are being sounded of decadence and decline.

There are grave institutional faults in our society that not only have made it possible for these terrible things to come about, but also obstruct our efforts to get our society out of its mess. But by determined action, and plain commonsense, there is still time for us to avert climate calamity, while ending the absurdity of unemployment when there is so much to be done. At the same time we shall be starting the great turnabout to build a society and economy more comfortable for human beings.

First we must understand the root causes of our difficulties. We have been transgressing the great Social Contract that exists between ourselves, the people, and the state: The state's institutions exist for one purpose only, to serve us, the people. But we, through our elected representatives, have governed badly and abdicated our responsibility in a huge tilt to the business corporations.

Our business corporations are magnificent and inventive instruments of production, but we have left them to produce whatever they can persuade people to buy that will give them profits, and enable them to survive in the free market, even at the cost of the environment and the health of society. But now we must harness these brilliant machines to make their profits working for us, the people.

But first we must stop the present recession in its tracks – it is nonsense that part of our economy be shut down when there is so much to be done. We shall ensure that ample funds flow to all the unemployed while we set in motion the great projects that lie ahead. Indeed boom and bust, the cyclic succession of good times and bad times, is a nonsense, we can split the atom and reach the moon, but we can't keep our economy fully employed at all times – the times are too serious to be left to our economists' conflicting theories.

Next we must move to re-balance our society so that each sector plays only its proper part, with ourselves, the people, at the helm. Our first move will be to place all of society's main means of mass communication, television and radio broadcasting, at our service. At present these are mainly paid for by business as a virtually round-the-clock sales promotion service, to get people to rush to buy whatever they choose to produce, some of which is of little genuine utility.

Instead we must change broadcasting, to serve us, the people. There is only one way we can do this, we must pay for it directly ourselves, out of our own pockets, or collectively, out of taxes, which is what we do for all our other services, we pay for our education, our health care, our entertainment, everything else we want and buy.

We shall now have broadcasting that is not only better, truer, and unpunctuated by grotesque, irrelevant, advertising interruptions, but also broadcasting that does not pollute the public's thinking. And it will cost us less. We may <u>think</u> that present broadcasting is free, but we pay huge sums for it, which the corporations recoup by raising the price of the consumer *goods they sell us. We pay not only for the programmes – much of them trash to lure us to buy their stuff, but also for the costly commercials – they are far more expensive than the programmes they interrupt, and to pay for the advertising agencies who make them.*

Many of us, my fellow citizens, will, at the start, feel the change we are making a brutal jolt, but we will implement it gradually, and at the end we will say 'Thank God! How did we ever endure that rubbish!'. This great reform, long overdue, will also have symbolic power: It will signal the start of re-balancing our society in favour of ourselves, the people.

That is the first great reform that we shall launch. The other, in parallel, will be the abolition of that old bugbear, the income tax, to be replaced by a far better way of raising our public funds, of which there is now a great need, to meet our challenges. The present income tax is thought to tax the rich at a higher rate than the poor, but that is nonsense, as the present great and growing income inequality shows. We will over the next five years replace the income tax by a new 'Return to Society' to be paid by all economic endeavour.

The Return to Society will be determined democratically in Parliament, for example 35% of GDP will go to society to be used for public purposes and 65% to labour and capital for private spending – and in dangerous times when society and the planet are threatened it may be necessary to raise Society's share.

There is also one other reform that we must immediately enact: It might simply be called 'correcting a book keeping error' but it causes a huge amount of public grief. The public debt must immediately be divided into two public debts, good public debt and bad public debt. Good public debt is the sum of government bonds that have been issued to pay for a nation's capital spending, for creating the nation's public infrastructure. That is really what government bonds are for, just as business corporations issue bonds (and shares) to pay for their capital assets, their plant and equipment. If this good debt is large, all that means is that the nation has a large public infrastructure. In contrast, 'bad public debt', is government borrowing because it is 'living above its means', its revenue from taxes is not enough to cover the cost of the current government services it provides, and the unemployment, healthcare and welfare transfers it makes to household . Business corporations go bankrupt if their operating costs exceed their revenue, but governments instead may borrow their way out of trouble – and that in the long run is very bad – the equivalent of individuals running up huge credit card debt. This distinction between good and bad public debt is vital – a government may otherwise unnecessarily cut government spending, throwing people out of work, when all it has been doing is adding to the vital public infrastructure.

And now to the great projects ahead. What must be done to save the climate is obvious, but our minds have been addled these many years, not least by our corrupt broadcasting system: There is a simple logic: What causes most of our greenhouse gases? Burning fossil fuels. So we must quickly stop most of that, which is possible only by totally electrifying the economy. This will require building many new generating stations, and most of these can only be nuclear, there is no other way – wind and solar power can make only a minor contribution, and capturing and storing the emissions is proposed only by a desperate fossil fuel industry trying to save itself. At the same time we must convert everything to run on electricity – aircraft and ocean transport alone cannot be electrified.

We shall also set in motion a second set of great projects. We must convert our society and way of life to use far less energy, on the basis of new transportation and communication systems and redesigned cities. All this can be done – and <u>must</u> be done – we cannot just sit aside and watch while calamity threatens our planet. Besides this will be a blessing in disguise – we shall be building a much more comfortable society and way of life for human beings'!

LET THE ACTION BEGIN

In the initial core nations a start will be made immediately to end the great recession by putting the unemployed to work, while ensuring that those still temporarily unemployed, receive generous government support. Pending the start of the large scale projects for the Great Battle, governments can have little difficulty finding work that must be done, for example improving existing infrastructure, roads, parks, and in a general urban beautification programme. Most of this work will be performed by the private sector on contract to the government. All work on adding to the public infrastructure will be paid for by borrowing, additions to the public debt. That is without any doubt the legitimate role of public debt. Transfers to the unemployed can also, in the short term, be paid for by borrowing – the increased public debt can be paid down once the economy has been fully restarted – or perhaps better by printing money and sending it directly to the unemployed, who will spend it on life's necessities. Aggregate demand in the economy will build up, there will be confidence in the air, Keynes' multiplier will come into effect, and recession and unemployment will become a thing of the past.

The governments will immediately set in train certain elementary global warming measures, not only to show seriousness but also for appreciable emission cutting. They will (some governments may have already done so) progressively over a four year period, place high taxes on 'gas guzzlers', for example the annual vehicle tax on these will be $1000 or more, while small fuel efficient and electric cars will be totally exempted. At the same time, urban public transport will be expanded to the extent possible with available equipment. Train services between city centres will be extended with existing rolling stock, and the acquisition of fleets of high speed trains will be set in motion.

Programmes will be launched for the total transformation of national broadcasting systems. Over a five year period all television and radio broadcasting will be converted to a normal service for the public, free of advertising. There will be both a public broadcaster and many pay broadcasting stations to suit all tastes, points of view and needs.

Planning will commence for the replacement of the income tax by the Return to Society. Within three or four years the income tax will be merely a bad memory.

Planning will start on the great construction projects for the transformation of society, in accordance with the optimum programmes determined from the national income input-output studies.

And it will be announced to the world what great actions are afoot, and other nations will be pressed to join the core which soon will be the great bandwagon, onto which the world's nations will be anxious to jump.

Subsequent years

Already a beginning has been made in the Core Group of nations, in the third year of the Action Plan, on four major reforms of the New Enlightenment. These are: (1) Ending for ever the sad cycle of boom and bust; (2) Normalizing the broadcasting system, placing it at the service of the people and society; (3) Replacing the income tax by the Return to Society; and (4) Setting in motion the mega-projects of the Great Battle of the Climate and to transform our society. There remain a number of other reforms to be made that were discussed in Part Two, our diagnosis of society's problems. Among them will be the following:

- The establishment of national central planning bodies as part of the democratic government process, for continuous study of society's long term problems, perhaps in the spirit of this present work. One function of the central body will be steady management of the economy, without periodic recession and involuntary unemployment.

- The appointment of national 'Watchdog' agencies to ensure that each economy's production system functions in accordance with the Social Contract, that the 'tail does not wag the dog', that society is not bounced willy nilly into some future that, on mature, intelligent reflection, it would rather not go. Just because advancing science makes something possible, does not mean that that something should come about. This is obviously a difficult area which needs careful further study. One initial measure that would please many people, and would symbolize 'people before machines', would be quickly restoring individual parking meters, but of improved design to take not only coins but also credit cards.

- Another such initiative is ridding us of that pest, the terrible, frustrating, telephone answering systems. Leading the way will be government departments whose answering systems will be models of simplicity and brevity, and always with the option of speaking to a human operator.

- Machines and automation will of course continue to replace humans in the production process (leading eventually to shorter working hours), but inconvenient, time wasting, machines should not replace people at the human, consumption, interface, placing an unwarranted 'self serve' burden on the public who are forced to deal with machines instead of friendly, helpful humans. (I have left out of consideration here the possibility that speeded up evolution is fast selecting a form of human who is unhappy unless grappling with machines).

Afterword

Much has been written above on our society's woes and griefs, and how we are to be rid of them, but in fact this can all be boiled down to a handful of ideas, if we put just a few things into effect, our society will bottom out of its time of troubles and be on the rise once again. Within our sick society is a second Age of Enlightenment struggling to get out.

But we must act fast – recently terrible news has emerged, extensive bubbling of methane up in the Arctic, 25 times more potent a greenhouse gas than carbon dioxide – time is now of the essence. We need a great spur to action: 'Depend upon it, sir, when a man knows he is to be hanged in a fortnight, it concentrates his mind wonderfully'. Dr Johnson's words now translates into 'When the human race knows that, unless it acts immediately, civilization's future on this planet will be at grave risk, this will concentrate its mind wonderfully'. And at long last - if humanity is sane and deserves saving - it will act decisively. These are six actions all of which we, our society, must set in motion immediately.

1. We must reaffirm the Social Contract: the only justification of society is that it serve the people, and only the people, and their physical environment. There are five[137] subordinate 'estates' serving them, the government which helps the people to govern, the public service departments, the business corporations, the financial system, and the media. But several estates, most especially the business corporations and financial institutions, have exceeded their responsibilities, the tail has been wagging the dog, with hellish consequences.

2. We must immediately, in compliance with the Social Contract, start the transformation of the broadcasting system, so that it is no longer an advertising service for business corporations and special interests, but instead serves the people and society. This may seem trivial, but it is not: not only are programmes continually interrupted by annoying irrelevancies: society is bathed in an ambience of lies and deceit that distorts public opinion and is an obstacle to sound public policy.

3. We must immediately restart the economy, boom and bust is an absurdity that will no longer be tolerated. The economy will immediately be engaged in the pressing projects of the future, while those people still awaiting re-employment will be provided with adequate income. The pressing public projects will be funded by government borrowing - infrastructure debt is 'good debt', that is what government bonds are for. At the same time we must immediately subdivide the public debt into the 'good public debt' and the 'bad public debt'. The latter is that which has been incurred over the years because the government has been 'living beyond its means', borrowing to pay for current government services, and for health, welfare, and unemployment benefits.

4. We must plan and then get underway the mega-projects of the Great Battle of Civilization and of the Climate.

5. We must replace the dysfunctional income tax by a new Return to Society which will democratically allocate the national product between personal and public spending. Fast implementation of this reform will make much easier solution of our problems of high public deficit and debt.

6. And in Europe the Eurozone woes must be fast corrected, and probably not by political integration into a new United States of Europe, but through a totally new form of political organization, without the unnecessary straitjacket of a common currency. That is what is necessary for the heartland of the original Age of Enlightenment.

Those are the major actions that will start the healing of Western society's ills and make it healthy, and mankind's beacon on a hill once more. Many other changes will in due course come about once the Social Contract has been reaffirmed and adopted as society's governing principle. Irksome nonsense like 'corporate social responsibility' and 'sports-marketing' will be abolished. The business corporations will have only their proper, and vital, function, to act as society's brilliant, inventive, and ingenious producers of the goods and services which the people, and their government, buy from them. And they must no longer force unnecessary irritations on the public through excessive mechanization at the human interface, for example, badly designed telephone answering systems, that make us scream and waste our time.

It has been written that 'those who cannot learn from history are doomed to repeat it' and that has happened in Britain in the failed austerity policy of the present Conservative government, under the stewardship of its Chancellor of the Exchequer, George Osborne. In 1929 the British economy was in deep depression, and for the general election of that year, the leader of the Liberal Party, Lloyd George, made the nation the following 'Pledge':

> 'If the nation entrusts the Liberal Party at the next general election with the responsibilities of government, we are ready with schemes of work which we can put immediately into operation, work of a kind which is not merely useful in itself but essential to the well-being of the nation. The work put in hand will reduce the terrible figures of the workless in the course of a single year to normal proportions . . .'

This pledge was accompanied by a pamphlet that Maynard Keynes helped write, which contained the following passages:

> 'The Liberal Policy is one of plain common sense. The Conservative belief that there is some law of nature which prevents men from being employed, . . . that it is 'financially 'sound' to

301

maintain a tenth of the population in idleness for an indefinite period, is crazily improbable ... The objections that are raised ... are based on highly abstract theories, venerable, academic inventions...and on assumptions which are contrary to the facts.... There is work to do; there are men to do it. Why not bring them together? No, says Mr. Baldwin. There are mysterious, unintelligible reasons of high finance and economic theory why this is impossible. It would be most rash. It would probably ruin the country. Abra would rise, cadabra would fall. . . . And if everyone were to be employed, how can you be perfectly sure that they will still be employed three years hence? If we build houses to cover our heads, construct transport systems to carry our goods, drain our lands, protect our coasts, what will be left for our children to do? No, cries Mr. Baldwin . . . The more work we do now the less there will be to do hereafter. Unemployment is the lot of man. This generation must take its fair share of it without grousing.

Unfortunately the British electorate believed Mr. Baldwin who campaigned on the theme of 'Safety First', and returned him to power, and the nation was condemned to more years of depression. And now history is repeating itself under the present Conservative government, with George Osborne, talking in much the same vein as Mr. Baldwin. And the deficit after three years of determined austerity policy refuses to shrink, the economy refuses to grow, and there is now, at time of writing in January 2013, even talk of a triple-dip recession.

And now in Canada: It's economy is not in quite so fragile condition, but faster than I can write, gross breaches of the Social Contract occur here in Canada's capital city. They may seem trivial but they are not, this symbolizes a gross misappropriation of roles.

- Filling my tank at one of few remaining service stations offering human service while you remain in your car – a dear, cheerful, old fellow, who recognises each of his thousands of customers, he's as happy as a mudlark – but people like him are being put to pasture by machines no one ever asked for and are a pain in the neck for us, the customer, whom the economy is supposed to serve.

- The Masters golf tournament: It was terribly exciting this year, in extra time play-off. And who should be the beneficiaries of this great game? – well of course, the players, and ourselves the public who watch it on television. But sadly there is one other who trumps us, the business corporations: Here in Canada it was impossible to watch without advertising interruptions which intensified at the tournament's climax. And it was hideous trying to watch the London Olympics on North American television. Many stations offered non-stop coverage, but saw it as a magnificent advertising bonanza. In the United States there were complaints that people could not watch great events in real time, but hours later, so that broadcasters could profit from prime time advertising rates. In North America the broadcasting system serves the business corporations, not us, the people.

- In Ottawa is Canada's magnificent National Gallery. Before me is an attractive card 'cordially inviting' me to the opening of the Van Gogh exhibition. And who is the card from? It is from the Chairman of the Gallery's Board of Trustees, and the Director of the Gallery. And also one other: the President and CEO of *Sun Life Insurance Company*. Why is *he* there? Is not the purpose of a life insurance company simply to provide us, effectively and efficiently, with life insurance, not to help us, the people of Canada, to pay for our National Gallery? This is called 'corporate social responsibility', but supporting the arts is our responsibility, not theirs, and besides it is not they, but ourselves who really pay – though they didn't ask us if we mind – through an elevated price of our life insurance.

- 'Fat is the New Normal', so tells us the Globe and Mail. Two thirds of Canadian adults are overweight or obese, so are one third of children. And they are surprised to be told so – they think they are normal. And this creates a serious problem. So doctors have advised, instead of telling people to lose weight, that it 'should be made easier for them to get out and be physically active in their communities'. But never mentioned is the barrage of junk food commercials they are exposed to daily on TV – one doesn't question the sacred right of corporations to desecrate the airwaves.

Those four instances are where I live, in Canada. Meanwhile south of our border, there is a conjunction of events that portends ill for the heartland of the West's societal dysfunction:

- Television viewing has risen sharply to 5.3 hours daily – to 7.4 hours for 65 year olds and older. And not only that, advertising interruptions have increased to occupy a third of airtime. And that excludes extensive TV viewing through digital video recorder 'time switching', and online on computers. Two thirds of homes have three or more TV sets. And despite the advertising onslaught, consumers are not spending.

- In the presidential election campaign vast sums were spent on TV 'attack ads', but, we are told[138], 'the public's trust in public speech, whether by politicians or in the media, has disintegrated, and to such a degree that it has undermined the possibility of straightforward communication in the public sphere '. Well of course: no one believes the absurd TV sales promotion commercials, and no one believes political commercials either.

- 'Fossil Fuel Industry Ads dominate TV Campaign: As Mr. Obama seeks re-election . . some of the mightiest players in the oil, gas, and coal industries are financing an aggressive effort to defeat him. . .

- 'Life Span Shrinks for Least Educated Whites in the US' according to the New York Times[139]. And the lives of the women have fallen and are now the shortest among the advanced nations. So serious is the problem that the National Academy of the Sciences has carried out an investigation. One of the causes given was obesity. As a result of googling I learnt that 'America's kids are bombarded with TV commercials for unhealthy foods full of sugar, salt, and fat . . . kids 8 - 12 see 50 hours annually' So at last a finger was pointed at television. But, as in Canada, never is the colossal evil mentioned of a broadcasting system that serves not the people but business corporations. There's an elephant in the room. Somebody complains, 'it's a bit crowded in here, isn't it, I wonder why? No one notices the elephant – the TV sets belting out junk food ads.

Just recounted are instances of what is happening in the North American part of Western civilization – daily there are others, and it won't stop until people SCREAM

We must at last wake up and SCREAM, Up with this nonsense we shall no longer put! And perhaps a few determined individuals will get together to start the chain of events that will bring on the New Enlightenment.

APPENDIX 1

Macro-economic Model Simulation of the Great Economic Recovery

It is surely reasonable to believe that if economics were a genuine science, in the sense that physics, chemistry, and biology are real sciences, our nations would long ago have rid themselves of the curse of cyclic boom and bust. And our present prolonged recession is doubly absurd at a time when there is so much work to be done, huge projects to remake our society as a non-emitter of greenhouse gases and to provide a saner more pleasant life for our peoples. Some words on what the shape of such a new economics might be was the subject of Chapter 12. Here, in this Appendix, is a simulation of a process that lifts our economies out of recession, and puts our nations back to work. The simulation is in the form of a macro-economic model based on the standard system of national accounts used by all nations.

It also makes use of the unchallengeable (though challenged) Keynesian precept that what the economy's producers produce (both business corporations and government) must equal what the economy's buyers buy (households who buy consumer goods and government which spends on services, both business and government which invest in new public infrastructure, and other, importing, nations). Business corporations will not expand their output by hiring workers and adding to their plant unless there is a prospect of selling their product. Hence unemployment will remain if the public, and the government, don't want, or can't afford, to buy what business wants to produce.

The simulation covers a period of six years: and is represented by six flow charts, for each year of the recovery period. The basic structure of the economy is the same as that in Figures 1-1 and 1-2 in Chapter 10, which uses Canada's official national accounting statistics for 2005. For simplicity the economy has been shrunk to the round number size of one trillion dollars, and the various flows modified to suit my purposes – for example Canada had a budget surplus of 0.9% in 2005, but in the starting year, the model depicts a large deficit of 8 % of GDP. The following is the state of the economy at the end of each of the six years of the simulation.

- Year 0, the economy in deep recession with 9% unemployment, and a government current deficit of 8% of GDP – that is, what the government spends on services and transfers to households exceeds what it collects in taxes by this huge amount.

- Years 1 to 4: Recovery from the recession. In the fourth year unemployment has fallen to 3% of the labour force – this is what is widely regarded as full employment, for example, the United States, under its 'Full Employment and Balanced Employment Act' of 1978 requires the Federal Government to ensure that not more than 3% of people over the age of 20 are unemployed – famous last words! US unemployment is now stuck at 9 %.

- Year 5: The first year of 'fiscal re-balancing': the deficit is brought down to 6.1% of GDP from 8.9% in year 4. In the next two or three years the deficit can be stabilised at around zero percent of GDP.

The whole scenario accepts the fact, ignored only by those suffering from 'deficit phobia', that ridding a nation of its budget deficit is not, when the economy in recession, its first priority.

For simplicity, I have assumed that there is zero population growth and zero inflation, so that what the model depicts is real economic growth, and the economic growth rate is also the average rate of personal income increase. Two factors determine the annual economic growth rate, annual productivity increase, and annual increase in employment. Over the four years from year 0 to year 4 the average rate of economic growth is 4.40% per annum. Part of this is because employment increases over the four years by 97/91, or 1.61% annually, and the rest is due to an average annual productivity increase of 2.75%. This latter element has two parts, the rate of technological progress, a long term underlying factor, which is, say 2% annually, and the rest, 0.74%, through better utilization of labour – in the depths of the recession some workers still employed are not fully utilized, but retained either from employer loyalty or because of their skills which may not be easy to replace when needed in the future.

The Strategy of Recovery

The public policy decisions that the 5-year simulation reflects are as follows.

- Capital investment: This will rise rapidly from 20 percent of GDP to 27 percent in the fourth year. This will be a consequence of huge projects launched for the Battle of the Climate.

- Government Services will grow very little in absolute terms and will fall appreciably as a percent of GDP.

- Government unemployment and social welfare benefits will be at a generous level – the disadvantaged will be well cared for.

- Personal consumption will grow at a healthy rate as incomes increase from the depths of the recession.

The policy is Keynesian in that it restores full employment, but it also relies heavily on the business sector to carry out the huge construction programme, under strong inducements and incentives, if necessary the force of law, whatever it takes to oblige the business corporations to collaborate in the national plan. An example of the use of law would be to make fossil fuel fired stations illegal and perhaps also wind turbines, if unaccompanied by huge energy storage reservoirs. There is also a high rate of capital investment by the government itself, but the construction work is contracted out to business. Government as such grows only a little.

Simulation of Recovery from the
Great Recession: Year-Ø Unemployment: 9%
National Accounts ($ billions)

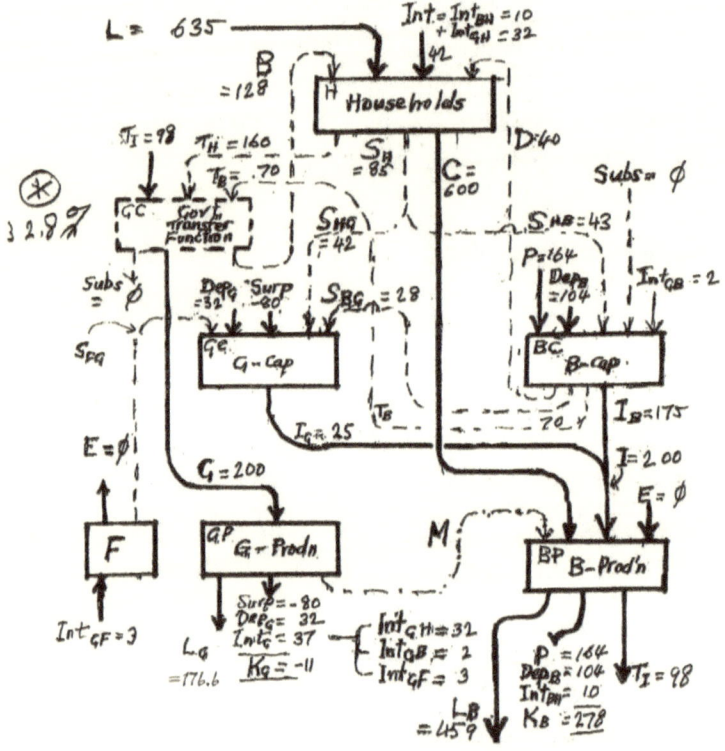

GDP Expenditure-Based			GDP Income-Based	
	$ billions	%	$ billions	%
C =	600	60	L = 635	635
G =	200	20	K = 267	26.7
I =	200	20	T_I = 98	9.8
E =	∅			
Y =	1000	100%	Y = 1000	100%

JHP 2011

Simulation of Recovery from the
Great Recession: Year-1 Unemployment: 7.5%
National Accounts ($ billions)

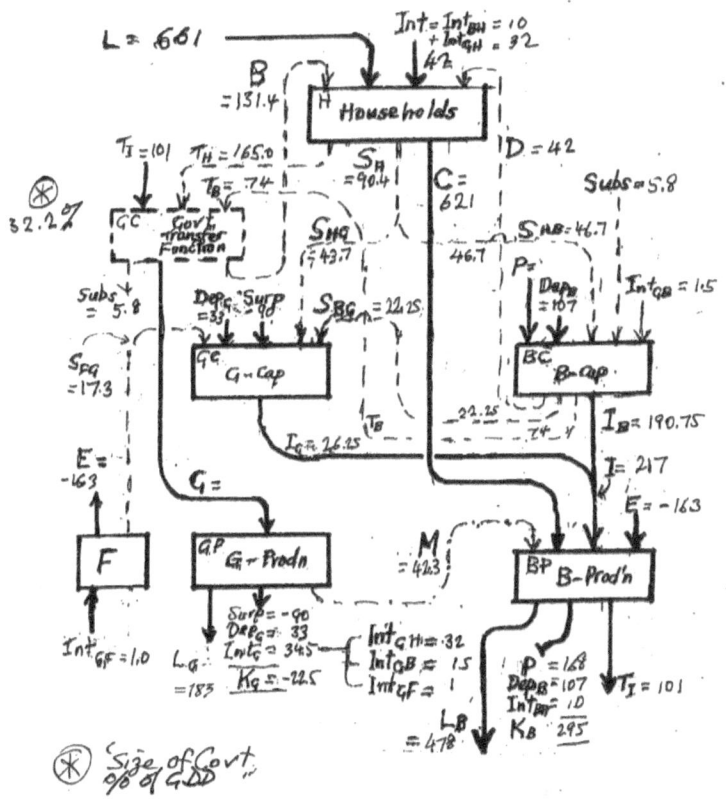

GDP Expenditure-Based			GDP Income-Based	
$billions	%		$billions	%
C = 621	60.6	L = 661		64.5
G = 202.8	19.8	K = 262.5		25.6
I = 217	21.2	T_I = 101		9.9
E = -16.3	-1.6			
Y = 1024.5	100%	Y = 1024.5		100%

JMf 2011

Simulation of Recovery from the
Great Recession: Year-2 Unemployment: 5.5%
National Accounts ($ billions)

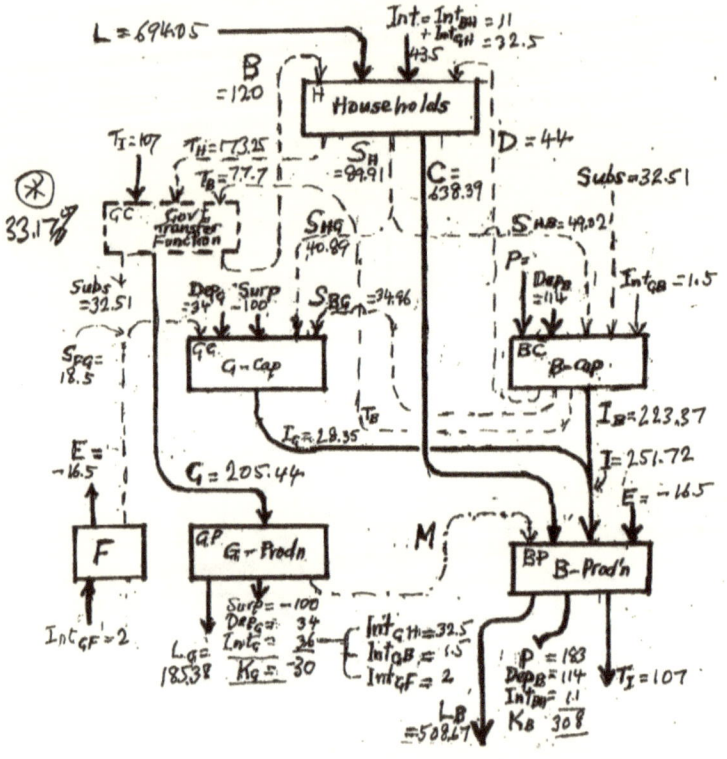

GDP Expenditure-Based		GDP Income-Based	
$ billions	%	$ billions	%
C = 638.39	59.2	L = 694.05	64.3
G = 205.44	19.0	K = 278.0	25.8
I = 251.72	23.3	T_I = 107.0	9.9
E = -16.5	-1.5		
Y = 1079.05	100%	Y = 1079.05	100%

J.M. 2011

Simulation of Recovery from the
Great Recession: Year-3 Unemployment: 4%
National Accounts ($ billions)

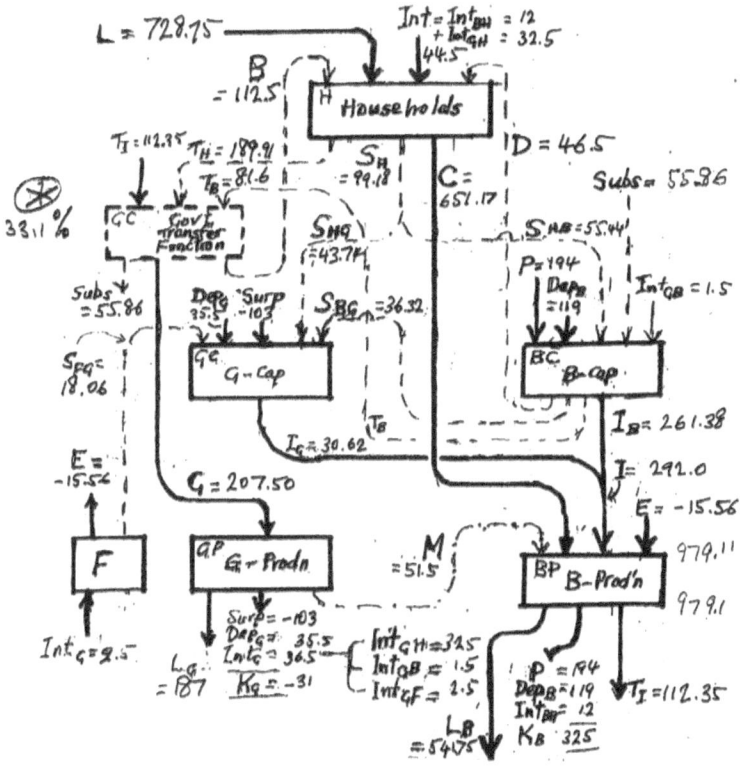

GDP Expenditure-Based		GDP Income-Based	
$ billions	%	$ billions	%
C = 651.16	57.4	L = 728.75	64.2
G = 207.50	18.3	K = 294.00	25.9
I = 292.00	25.7	T_I = 112.35	9.9
E = -15.56	-1.4		
Y = 1135.10	100%	Y = 1135.10	100%

JMf 2011

Simulation of Recovery from the
Great Recession: Year-4 Unemployment: 3%
National Accounts ($ billions)

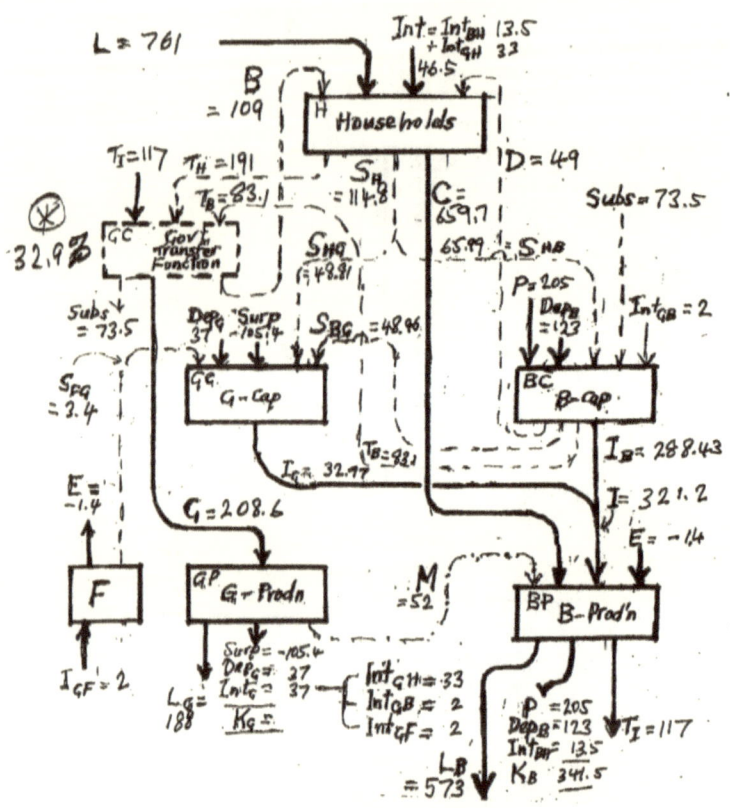

GDP Expenditure-Based		GDP Income-Based	
$ billions	%	$ billions	%
C = 659.7	55.5	L = 761	64.0
G = 208.6	17.6	K = 310	26.1
I = 321.2	27.0	T_I = 117	9.9
E = -1.4	-0.1		
Y = 1188.1	100%	Y = 1188.1	100%

JMP 2011

Simulation of Recovery from the
Great Recession: Year-5 Unemployment: 3%
National Accounts ($ billions)

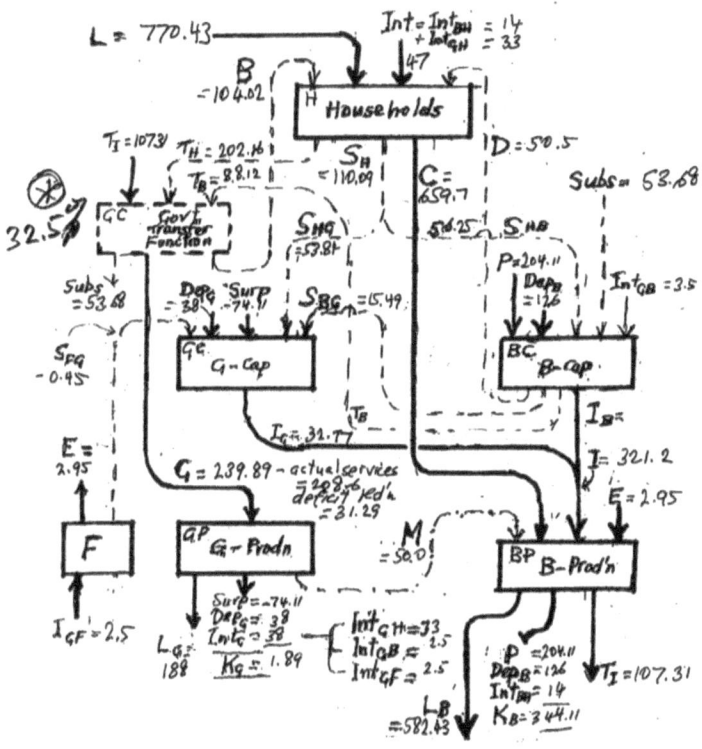

GDP Expenditure-Based			GDP Income-Based	
	$ billions	%	$ billions	%
C =	659.7	53.9	L = 770.43	62.9
G =	239.89	19.6	K = 346.00	28.3
I =	321.2	26.3	T_I = 107.31	8.8
E =	2.95	0.2		
Y =	1223.74	100%	Y = 1223.74	100%

JMF 2011

315

The programme is underpinned at the start by a public affirmation of the Social Contract, embodied in the Clarion Call. And in parallel with the construction programme, public policy will include a programme of broadcasting transformation so that within five years television and radio broadcasting will be fully a service for the people, no longer an advertising medium. And not only this, other policy measures will be instituted which ensure full compliance with the Social Contract. The business corporations, society's magnificent work horses will be placed fully at the service of the people, through such measures as ending 'corporate social responsibility' and preventing the bouncing of the public into a world that does not make their lives easier and more pleasant, but which serve primarily the corporations sales and profit goals.

The results of the simulation

The results of the five-year simulation are summarised in the following table. It shows the components of GDP for year 0, year 4, and year 5. For each year it also shows for each component the average growth rate during the four years of recovery, and the growth rate in year 5, the first year of government deficit reduction. As will be seen there are four categories of economic flow, respectively GDP expenditure-based, GDP income-based, intermediate purchases, and transfer payments. Each is discussed in turn.

GDP expenditure-based

This is expressed thus: $GDP = C + G + I + E$, where:

- C is personal spending on consumer goods and services .

- G - is services performed by government, justice, parks, the military, the diplomatic services, the road system, internal revenue, public broadcasting, museums, and whatever other services are provided by government rather than by the private sector.

TABULATION OF RESULTS

			Percent of GDP			Growth Rate	
			Year 0	Year 4	Year 5	Years 0 to 4 average	Year 5
GDP Expend- iture based	G	Personal Consumption	60	55.5	53.9	2.40	0
	G	Govt. Services	20	17.5	19.6	1.06	15.0
	I	Investment	20	27.1	26.3	12.57	0
	E	Exports less Imports	0	-0.1	0.2		
		GDP	100%	100%	100%	4.40	3.0

			Percent of GDP			Growth Rate	
GDP Income - based	L	Labour Income	63.5	64.1	63.0	4.63	1.20
	P.	Bus Open Profit	16.4	17.3	16.7	5.74	2.44
	Surp.	Govt. Open Surplus	-8.0	-8.9	-6.1	-7.14	+24.1
	K	Dep Depreciation	13.6	13.5	13.4		
	Int$_G$	Interest -Publ. Debt	3.7	3.1	3.1		
	Int$_B$	- Bus. Debt	1.0	1.1	1.1		
	T$_I$	Indirect Taxes	9.8	9.9	8.8		
		GDP	100%	100%	100%	4.40	3.00

	Year 0	Year 4	Year 5
Part of Govt. Services, G purchased from Business Sector (M)	3.5	4.4	4.6

			Year 0	Year 4	Year 5	0 to 4 avg	Year 5
Transfer	T$_A$	Income Tax, personal	16.0	16.1	16.5	4.53	6.00
Payment	T$_B$	Income Tax, Corp.	7.0	7.0	7.2	4.38	6.14
between	S$_G$	Purchases of Govt. Bonds, by persons, business, other countries	7.3	8.5	5.7		
Persons,							
Govt.	S$_{IB}$	Personal Purchases of business securities	2.8	4.1	2.9		
&							
Business	B	Unemployment & Welfare Benefits	12.8	9.2	6.8	-3.94	-7.4
	Subs	Govt. Subsidies	0	6.2	6.0		
	Divs	Dividends	4.0	4.1	4.5	5.20	3.06

317

- I - is capital expenditure by business corporations and government on capital facilities, buildings, structures, plant and equipment (I have searched the internet for the definition of T used in national accounting statistics, and find a surprising lack of clarity, whether or not I include government capital spending. It appears often to be treated as part of G, government spending, and this strange definition accounts for the peculiar Maastricht deficit (3% of GDP instead of 0%) that was discussed in Chapter 8. In contrast, as is clear from Figure 1 in Chapter 10, the Canadian GDP statistics define government investment correctly, as part of I, and not part of G.

- E - is net exports of goods and services – that is the extent to which exports exceed imports, referred to usually as the current account balance. For some nations E is negative, for example for the United States notoriously so, running large current account deficits, which it is enabled to do because the dollar is the international reserve currency.

GDP income-based

This is the other side of the ledger: To produce the GDP, business and government must make payments to the 'factors of production', primarily Labour (L) and Capital (K). The components of capital are profits, P, or in the case of government, surplus, (Surp) – in today's world notoriously negative. Another capital component is the depreciation allowance (Dep), money set aside to be used to replace worn-out or obsolete plant. The final capital item is interest payments (Int) to the buyers of government or business bonds.

The final component of income is the item T-I, indirect taxes. These are not treated like a factor of production in the national accounts, but in the revised form of public funding, the 'Return to Society', outlined in Chapter 10, it becomes a fully-fledged factor of production to stand alongside Labour and Capital.

Intermediate purchases

In these highly aggregated flow diagrams this appears as a single item, M, the purchase of materials and services by government from business corporations, but in the actual highly dis-aggregated real world, with hundreds of sectors, this constitutes a huge number of flows, in particular purchases of materials and services by companies from other companies. One example of these intermediate purchases that was discussed at length in Chapter 10 are those of the perverted broadcasting system from advertising agencies. This system is of course not a real service for people, included in C, consumption, it is an M item, a business service.

Transfer payments

These are the transfers of money between the main 'players', house-holders, government, and business. These transfers include:

- Income taxes T-H, personal income tax and T-B, corporation tax.

- Savings, S, what is not spent, and consists of the purchase of bonds and shares (and also in increased bank balances not dealt with in this simulation exercise, but which would be shown in a more advanced model). In this simulation there are four S items, respectively S–HG (household purchase of government bonds), S-HB (household purchase of corporation bonds and shares), S-BG (business purchase of government bonds), and S-FG (for-eign purchase of government bonds, of which perhaps the most discussed example is the trilliondollars of US treasury bills that have been purchased by China.

- Government transfers to persons, B (unemployment and welfare benefits).

- Government subsidies to business corporations, Subs, whose pur-pose is to encourage certain types of activity, for example the building of nuclear stations for the Battle of the Climate, to support fledgling industry, or to save failing corporations, thereby avoiding large unemployment.

What we learn from the simulation exercise

There is vigorous economic growth, at an average annual rate of 4.4% during the recovery period, 2.5% in year 1, 5.3% year 2, 5.2% year 3, and 4.7% in year 4. Following full restoration of employment in year 5, the growth rate falls to 3%, and in succeeding years should remain steady at an average of 2 %, the long run rate of technology advance (steady because in the New Enlightenment the business cycle will have been banished!).

In the recovery period, despite a huge annual increase in capital investment – at an annual rate of 13.3% in the business sector, and 7% in the public sector, personal consumption increases at the healthy rate of 2.4%, while government services grow only at a modest 1.06%. Bearing in mind that our hypothetical economy is of a fairly Keynesian bent, at the depth of the recession. benefits, B, constitutes a large, 12.8% of GDP, and at no point do we have a deeply deprived public, a condition now besetting the United States. Benefits' share of GDP falls gradually each year to 9.1% in year 4. Then in the first year of strenuous reduction of the budget deficit, B falls only slightly to 8.5 % of GDP.

And what of the great bogeyman, the deficit? The deficit rises in the four years from its atrocious 8 % of GDP, to as high as 12.5%, and in year 4 is still 8.9%. And the sky doesn't fall in, interest on the government debt, remains a modest 3 percent of GDP – and that's not all misery, the investors in bonds receive their risk-free income. Annual purchase of government bonds, by households, business corporations, and foreigners rises from 7.3% of GDP to 8.5% of GDP.

And then, deficit-phobics, rejoice: In year 5, the deficit falls to 6.1 percent, and government bond sales fall sharply from 8.5% of GDP to 5.6 percent. And one can be confident that if government stays with the same policy, the deficit will have disappeared three or four years hence. From that point on, government bond purchasing will continue at a lower level, for its only legitimate peace time purpose, paying for government capital investment and infrastructure building.

Labour income: During the four years of recovery, labour income increases at 4.6% annually, but as the number employed grows by 1.6% annually, wages and salaries grow at a not unsubstantial 3.0%. Though personal income tax increases by 4.6% to help pay for the huge projects of the climate, nevertheless, as already mentioned personal consumption still increases at a substantial rate. And indeed this rate is more substantial than the figures may suggest. In the four years total consumption increases by 10%, shared by the same-sized population. But because we have started re-balancing the economy in compliance with the Social Contract, we have started placing the broadcasting media at the service of the people – 'de-advertising' it – and have implemented several other measures to put the people in the driver's seat, we shall have removed what I might call the Galbraith effect – the way in the past a once-affluent society becomes less, not more, affluent over time.

Profits: And how does business fare in the recovery? They will have no reason to complain, profits grow at 5.75% annually, by 1.9% more than the rate at which the corporate income tax increases. Some readers of this work may have mistakenly thought that its stance is anti-business, anti-capitalism. No indeed, the position here is strongly capitalist – defined as for-profit corporations operating in a free market, but one that places capitalism at the service of the people. As I have repeatedly observed the business corporations until now have run amok, left to their own devices, but now they will be harnessed to the service of the people. (And here endeth the lesson, sorry dear reader!).

And now fiscal rebalancing – addressing the deficit. How is this achieved? Under this particular scenario, the year-5 diagram shows that it requires, perhaps temporarily, stabilizing the mega-project programme at its year 4 high level, and also maintaining consumption at its year 4 level. Both personal and corporate income taxes increase by 6%, and business subsidies are reduced permitting welfare transfers to households to remain high.

Limitations of the simulation
using this simple model

There are several limitations of this model. First it shows only flows, not balance sheets items; secondly, it omits banks and the monetary system, third it is highly aggregated, with only two sectors, and fourth, it lacks an underlying physical dimension. It would for example be useful to show workers, man- hours worked, and wage rates. Perhaps use of a more complex model that included these elements would depict the situation considerably more accurately. Nonetheless I believe that what the simple model has shown is useful, and makes a nonsense of the assertion that we cannot banish the continuing long recession and address the important tasks facing our society.

One thing has puzzled me with this simple simulation is that despite 3 percent supposedly real growth in year 5 – it nonetheless shows real or physical output not increasing at all. Consumption, investment, and the real part of government services (that is the part devoted to reducing the deficit) do not increase – of the apparent 15% growth in government services, all the increase, $31.3 billion, is simply deficit reduction – the deficit falls from 105.4 to 74.1 billion dollars – I do not clearly see what is 'real' – in the physical sense – about that. Perhaps use of the far more complex model mentioned above would elucidate the matter.

History of the Hypothesis of Underlying Societal Malfunction

About fifty years ago I formulated what I called a 'hypothesis of underlying society malfunction', and over the years since then I have clung to this same view of a seriously ailing society. It is surely interesting that a person should have so long adhered to the same unchanged view, despite enormous changes in our society – who would have thought fifty years ago that humans all over the planet would be connected directly with each other through small hand held gadgets, and that we could access nearly everything that has ever been published or reported on any subject without budging from our seats, or ask a SatNav to tell us how to get anywhere in a giant sprawling metropolis?

Yet despite these rapid changes I continue to believe in the same 'underlying societal malfunction', a misgoverned, unhealthy, society, poorly serving the people. And I have held to this view although no one else, as far as I know, has seen our society's ills in the same way. I have often circulated papers I have written but with only very few exceptions, have received no positive response. So the question arises, either my views were mistaken, or for some reason, though they were right, something was preventing many, many, brilliant and learned minds from seeing the truth. The latter would seem to be highly improbable, and so it is not surprising that already, forty years ago, ten years after I originally formulated the hypothesis, I asked: whether this hypothesis of mine was simply a delusion, what the cybermeticist Stafford Beer, called an *idée fixe*.

And now forty years later the same question can be asked. But now our society, in North America, is in great travail. Western economies for the last four years have been gripped in a Great Recession, still there is little sign of recovery, and there is huge contention over what must be done. And many writers and commentators believe the West, and especially its American half, is in a sorry, perhaps decadent state and in decline. New ideas are needed on how to mend the West, and perhaps 'the hypothesis of underlying societal malfunction' will be seen less as a deluded *idée fixe*.

In Chapter 4 I quoted the earliest statement of the hypothesis I have in my records, written forty-three years ago. Soon after that first formulation, I started to develop a 'society system model', and I reported on this in 1972, in 'The Society System Project: A Progress Report' – it is from that report that I quote in Chapter 4 Staffford Beer on the *idée fixe*. Preparing that paper was one of my most sustained efforts, I had no other job at the time, and I used it to apply for a research grant, but with no success – it was so much out of the realm of academic orthodoxy. As so much that appears in the present work was developed, or foreshadowed, in that document, I here quote from it at some length.

'Many of our cleverest people now believe that some present trends, unless checked, will lead ultimately to the loss of all that makes life worth living .... The juggernaut cannot be stopped, each day another green field is paved over, there is as little more stench and congestion, and another missile is placed in its underground silo. . . Society seems to be a many-headed hydra: do battle against one supposed evil, a proposed superhighway, say, or a supersonic transport, and ten more spring up in its place . . . . Governments pretend to have answers, but often simply get us more into a pickle . . .

Yet there *are* people who believe they see practical ways to reverse the ugly process. One approach is through long-term, in-depth, research into specific problems, often using the "systems approach" and multi–disciplinary teams . . . I am involved in this type of approach, but at a broader level, that of the societal system as a whole, the "body social-political-economic", which is the complete environment within which

each of our little "selves" attempts to make itself comfortable.' . . . .
'This paper is a progress report on my project germinated about ten
years ago' – that is, in about 1962, or fifty years ago.

[I have just this moment recalled, I had recently resigned from
the huge electric utility, Ontario Hydro, in order to find work that
interested me more. At Hydro I had first worked as a soil mechanics
engineer responsible for checking the stability of the many miles
long earth dykes containing the reservoirs at both the St Lawrence
Seaway project and the Niagara Falls pumped storage project. I had
then transferred to the Management Services Division as a systems
analyst, eventually becoming responsible for long-term information
systems planning. It was in fact there that I developed the systems
language that I later used in the 'society system model', here under
discussion].

- These were the main tasks of the Society System Project:

- 'Construction of a total Society System Model. The measure of
  the success in carrying out this task will be the extent to which it
  offers a plausible explanation of the most important phenomena .
  . . that our society exhibits'.

- Consideration of my particular hypothesis of underlying
  societymalfunction.

- Consideration of the possibility of "an integrated social science
  organised in a systems-economic framework", the economics
  component conceptually accommodating the so-called
  "intangibles" and "non-economic considerations" now largely
  excluded from orthodox economics.

Here is the hypothesis of underlying society malfunction as I framed
it in that report (as will be seen it is an elaboration of what I had
sketched out three years earlier and quoted in Chapter 4 of this book).

1. 'We must focus on the most important question: What makes the
   human animal really comfortable? Then we must reorganize the
   means at our disposal accordingly. The tail has been wagging
   the dog . . . Common sense suggests that a society should aim

explicitly at producing fulfilling "work", and the sense of self-realization, for everyone, and an easily available environment, both natural and man-made, not only the "consumer goods", and inavoidable government services, that doctrine states are the raison d'être of the "economic system".

2. 'There is a more serious danger from internal degeneration from underlying present trends in our society than from any external threats. . . . .

3. 'Another strand is enormous wealth misused, an extraordinarily innovative, and growingly productive, free enterprise system frantically producing many of the wrong things.

4. 'Related to this is the cancer of sales promotion and public relations run wild. Not only are the phenomena unappealing in themselves (my 'feeling' rather than 'scientific' self refers to them as this 'nauseating effluent', more significant, they represent an adjustment mechanism that has grown up through default, in the absence of a conscious effort by society to create machinery to make rational use of our accelerating industrial productivity and keep its people employed. Associated with this compensating mechanism is a value system increasingly permeating society, and beginning to exceed the bounds of viable society ethical structures.

5. 'The belief in the necessity for continual population growth to facilitate "economic growth" is another element of the madness that has gripped society.

6. 'It is not true that to point out these difficulties is to be a secret socialist . . . . Free enterprise could most effectively carry out the task at hand, if we provide it with a more intelligent framework of national policy making /. . . . In fact, we might end up with a leaner, less bloated, less bureaucratic government . . . .

7. 'It would not really be difficult to solve the problem of public funding of private enterprise to do public tasks. There are probably more effective ways than the progressive income tax for providing these funds, and for distributing income equitably.

8. 'We have a vicious circle in the weakness of our mechanism of governance. The government is an integral part of the existing total society system and shares all its myths. . . . The mechanism brings to the top few people who understand the long term predicament of our society, and encourages demagoguery and pandering to the immediate self-interest of particular groups . . .

9. 'While diagnosing the flaws in our societal system, we must recognise the priceless benefits it provides us, after centuries of painful evolution. We must cure these flaws, not throw out the system'.

The first item above is what in the present work I call ensuring our governance is in accord with the Social Contract. As for considering 'an integrated social science organised in a systems-economic framework', that is no other than what I have laid out in Chapter 12, 'The New Science of Economics'. When I wrote Chapter 12, I had not read what I had written on that subject so many years earlier, and was very surprised – indeed, an *idée fixe* – but I insist not a deluded one! I quote here what I wrote in 1972:

A Redefinition of the Social Sciences

'One inevitable result of attempting to define society as a system, and studying how changes come about in this system, is to ask oneself what the relationship is between this exercise, and the activities of the many academic disciplines referred to as the "social sciences".

'Certain tentative, and not yet very precise, ideas on this matter are beginning to emerge at this stage of the study. Can one begin to see a single "Social Science", whose field is the diagnosis of, and prescription for, the ills of the body-politic-social-economic, the system we call society? Would this parent discipline of social science then have its various branches concerned with the subsystems or "organs" of the total system? Continuing our analogy with medical science, we would then have our social science generalists, and our social science specialists. The society system model attached as

Exhibit 3 has three complementary parts, physical, monetary (Figure 4.3 of the present work), and informational, that seem to bear some relationship to the present major division of the social sciences into sociology, economics, and political science.

'Another matter for speculation is whether the new unified social science would consist of a sociological content accommodated within a "systems-economics" framework.

'The result might then be a new economics from which the present bugbear of "intangibles" and "non-economic considerations" is banished. These so-called intangibles, which in fact refer to some very tangible evils and benefits for the human race, need no longer be dealt with outside the conceptual framework of economics.

'Finally, it is speculated whether the new economics, or "systems-economics" might simply amount to the theory underlying the Grand Project, the Society programme to establish a beneficial control over human destiny, which is the subject of this particular study. The results that have already been achieved. . . . seem to provide a close integration of several branches of economics, and economics-related, disciplines, such as macroeconomics, input-output economics, monetary economics, growth economics, microeconomics, benefit-cost analysis, planning-programming-budgeting, and accounting.'

In all the years since I first formulated the hypothesis of underlying society malfunction I have never written a book – this is the first. The question arises, why have I been so tardy? The reason I gave in a 2004 paper[140] was that it would be 'fatal to be labelled a Cassandra with a boring hobby-horse, better to hold one's fire . . . My thinking has gone through three phases. First I was concerned with our economic system's perpetually expanding output capacity arising out of technological progress. Lacking a mechanism for its rational use, we continue to rely largely on the producers to induce people to absorb this output. The consequent degrading of values, I argued, was likely to lead to our society's decline'.

In the second phase 'my attention switched to one vital aspect of this inducement process, the hijacking of broadcasting – in its increasingly dominant form – as an advertising vehicle for corporations.

It is bad enough that this advertising - broadcasting system yields poor programmes, interrupted at frequent intervals by irrelevant, often offensive, breaks to tout tampax or toilet paper, worse is the damaging effect on society of this misappropriation of the main mass public communications system to serve not the public's, nor society's ends, but the sales and profit goals of business corporations. But I've found a reluctance to see broadcasting in this light. . . And this despite the fact that no valid argument has ever been made in favour of our present irrational way of organizing one of society's most important services. And the consequences of this reluctance to perceive this evil are becoming increasingly dire, at a time of innumerable societal, geopolitical, and environmental problems.

'Nonetheless I continued to restrain myself until now, at last, in the third phase, I have decided to risk the Cassandra curse, so acute are our problems becoming'. Now there was a 'growing perception, books are being written, on our societal degradation and societal rot . . . . Adding urgency has been an additional factor, the extension of misappropriation beyond broadcasting'. A similar misappropriation is spreading to other services, and to the support of 'worthy causes' – that is, so-called 'corporate social responsibility', for example. 'While symphony concerts are not interrupted once underway by the equivalent of television commercials, a corporation representative at the commencement may deliver a eulogy on his company's contribution. Another such misappropriation has been so-called 'sports marketing' which recently produced the absurd Tiger Bubble, and the sudden undoing of Tiger Woods.

Further I wrote in the 2004 paper, 'The West occupies what was the position of Rome in the ancient world[14], the centre of power, technology, and wealth, and of international standards of what is progressive. But the reference since September 11 to the "clash of civilizations" has ignored the rest of Huntington's title, " . . . *and the remaking of world order*" arising out of the West's internal rot. But, Huntington tells us, societies have sometimes reversed their decline and recovered. Most probably, though, this was through some fortuitous circumstances rather than from any deliberate programme of societal recovery. 'The issue now is whether now, in our time, we can mend our rot and correct what ails'. Even so, I did not rally myself to write a synthesis of my diverse ideas in a coherent work. Apart from a few papers circulated among a handful of people, I still failed to make any effort to publish. Instead I became immersed in what to do about global warming, and a paper I wrote on it in 2005[142] says substantially the same as what appears in the present work, for the simple reason that what must be done is quite obvious, at least to any physicist or engineer who puts his mind to it. The only reason, I argued, that society, especially North American society, hadn't acted has been its severe faults of governance. In particular, in this 2005 paper, I wrote of the perverted broadcasting system that addles peoples' minds.

There is no shortage of current works bewailing our society's dire state, indeed they are building up to a crescendo. A recent cover of Time Magazine shows George Washington with a black eye, and in giant letters 'THE GREAT AMERICAN DOWNGRADE', and a week later Time's cover picture was of a hooded London looter, with the caption 'THE DECLINE AND FALL OF EUROPE'. We are told that the economic union is unravelling. London is ablaze, and... the U.S. is too feeble to save the day or the euro. Say goodbye to the old order' Warnings, warnings, but little is offered by way of remedy, how to pull ourselves out of our nosedive. But in all my 'gestation' period I have remained constant not only on the nature of our sickness, but also on what we must do to extract ourselves from our mess. Right from the start, fifty years ago, I've had a number of recurring notions, in particular our society's gross contravention of the Social Contract, according to which human society has only one justification, the service of the people, otherwise why not return to a state of nature where life is nasty, brutish and short? Many of our ills will be seen to stem from institutional faults which allow this contravention. Our misappropriated broadcasting system, corporate social responsibility, and sports marketing, are all contraventions of the Contract, treating these vital activities, broadcasting, sport, and worthy cause support as sales promotion and public relations services for business corporations. Likewise, as a consequence of our inattention to the Social Contract, our society grossly misuses its magnificent production system, its business corporations, which could be better deployed. And all along I have thought that our so-called progressive income tax has been a poor way of raising public funds.

Also I have long been convinced that our so-called discipline of 'economics' is not a genuine science of the economy, in the sense that physics is the science of the physical universe, and medicine the science of the human body – but that economics could be vastly improved to become the genuine science of the complex system social-political-economic–environmental. Would any genuine science of the economy have two such diametrically opposed theories as market fundamentalism and Keynesian macroeconomics? Since the Great Depression of the 1930s, its orthodoxy has oscillated: / free market / Keynesian / free-market (of the most fundamental which pitched the world economy into its present Great Recession / Keynesian stimuli, / now to be countered by an anti-Keynesian dread of budget deficits.

Can one imagine the science of physics oscillating thus, between geocentric Ptolemaic and heliocentric Copernican? No, the Copernican far from being up-ended was progressively improved on through the Newtonian to the Einsteinian. Physics and engineering are grounded in the reality of the world around us, and a new economics too must be anchored to this real world. One might even say that the Ptolemaic formulation differed less from the Newtonian than does market fundamentalism from Keynesianism, in that the Ptolemaic could at least predict the positions of the planets through its ingenious 56 concentric spheres. At the time of Ptolemy perhaps physics was already more scientific than present day economics.

The failure of economics can also in part be linked to its lack of attention to the Social Contract. In fact the national accounts, from which GDP is estimated, in their structure imply the Contract – the distinction between the economy's 'final goods' which serve the people, and its 'intermediate goods' which are inter-company trade. But this fact is totally ignored by the economists – I have never heard the word 'social contract' emerge from an economist's lips. Had economists reflected at all on the Social Contract, they would long ago have shouted outrage at the perverted broadcasting system, hi-jacked by the business corporations, whose output, ostensibly serving the people, in reality is an intermediate good, an advertising service, bought by business corporations from other business corporations.

Also popping up continually in my mind has been the small boy who said 'but the king isn't wearing any clothes'!. I assume that the boy's mother simply said 'Shush Johnny, behave yourself'. I have never been able to understand why what I believed I could see wasn't evident to others. Here I'll make one more attempt to convince.

Throughout I have been partisan, I am pro-ourselves, our Western civilization. Though it is now sick, nonetheless, our society can correct its present failings, it can continue to represent the good society, the result of progress along the long trail from Greece, through Rome, and, after the Middle Ages decline, the Renaissance, the Reformation, the Enlightenment, and ultimately to the full establishment of what I call the 'western attributes', democracy, the rule of law, individual liberty, and human rights, that this long trail led to what *should* be the best, but of course vigilance is always required in human institutions. We have lacked vigilance, we have neglected the Social Contract, with tragic results.

I have talked of the *West's* sickness, but in fact the heartland of this sickness lies in the United States, whence in varying degrees it has spread to other nations. The United States in recent years, despite many shining qualities, and its magnificent means of production, the business corporations, has relinquished control of its destiny to serve the business corporations' goals, not because of any particular evil of the latter, the business corporations are amazingly innovative and efficient production machines, but they have been left to run amok because of severe failings of American governance, degrading the quality of their democracy. In contrast, some smaller West European nations, especially the Scandinavians, Switzerland and the Netherlands, are freer of this American governance malady.

My views, perhaps, have been moulded by the accident of a somewhat unusual life experience, graduating first as an engineer, and then in philosophy, politics and economics, then working successively as a civil engineer, management systems analyst, information systems planner, energy policy analyst, and economic statistician. This has perhaps made me less than enthusiastic about particular orthodoxies, with a tendency to meld bits of them together into my own conceptual framework. In this, flow diagrams and input-output models have been prominent to depict the national accounts and the structure of the economy, and of society. And perhaps I'm a lateral thinker. I see links, I slide off sideways in conversations and irritate profoundly individuals who argue in a syllogistic progression, this ergo that, stick to the point!

Finally there is the question of what this work should be named, it is a synthesis of diverse parts. Consistently I have talked of societal rot and recovery therefrom, of our breach of the Social Contract, of the failings of our economists. And I have expended much energy on the Great Battle of the Climate. And my writings on the latter were accompanied by a brief companion paper, 'Auxiliary Measures for the Battle of the Climate', the improvements of our societal governance if we were to engage successfully in the Battle. Most of our terrible woes are related: Had our governance, and our so-called 'economics', been grounded on the Social Contract, we would not have emitted huge amounts of carbon, nor would we now be in degradation and decline. I have chosen to name this work 'Launching the New Enlightenment', but with little reorganization it could equally have been called 'The Great Battle of the Climate', or 'The Great War of Civilization, or 'The League of the Social Contract', or the New Science of Economics. Indeed several years ago I started writing a book of the latter name, but abandoned it when I found that another book (the present) that I was writing was saying much the same thing.

Above I wrote that until now I have made no attempt to publish my work, and that is true apart from the several occasions a newspaper rejected a paper I had submitted. But I did pester many individuals with papers on, in particular, averting global warming, and reforming broadcasting. These attempts were without avail, except in the case of three individuals whom I mention in my Acknowledgements, whose encouragement proved crucial, and led eventually to this work. One consequence was that I expended much effort and time trying to communicate with Canada's political leaders –no doubt naively. In 2007 I sent to every member of the Canadian parliament a programme for curbing carbon emissions.

The following is my covering letter:

1 August 2007

To the Prime Minister of Canada,
The Members of the Cabinet,
The Party Leaders,
Members of the House of Commons

Honourable Ladies and Gentlemen,

Some weeks ago you received

MANIFESTO. THE GREAT BATTLE OF THE CLIMATE

(by both the House of Commons post office, and e-mail).

Attached is a very brief version, stating the set of particular actions that are necessary if Canada is to play its part in the great battle ahead.

With respect,
yours sincerely,
Michael Jaffey,
Ottawa

Then, ever naively optimistic, from November 2009 to May 2010 I made strenuous efforts to propose to the Liberal Party a radically different sort of party platform on action not only on cutting emissions, but also to bring about some of institutional reforms that are the subject of this work. Eventually, I tried to arrange a meeting with the new Party leader, Michael Ignatieff, by going through the party bureaucracy – it was naive of me to think one could get through to meet him this way – I should have tried to approach him outside government.

It was only when these efforts failed that I concentrated on writing a book. However in mid 2010 instead of resuming work on the New Enlightenment, I started another, 'The New Economics', which as I discussed in Chapter 12 embraces much of the same subject matter. But then in December I decided to return to the Launching the New Renaissance (as I called it until in April 2012 renaming it 'Launching the New Enlightenment' – it dawned on me that the Renaissance was essentially a cultural rebirth, and what we should now be aiming at was a re- Enlightenment in the spirit of Locke, Newton, Voltaire, Rousseau and their ilk. The following lists some of my earlier papers of which this work is a synthesis.

List of Selected Past Articles

The 'New Renaissance' is a synthesis of the ideas I have expressed over the years on various aspects of our society's difficulties. The papers appear together in the document entitled 'Collected Papers on Societal Dysfunction'.

1. Some Remarks on Wages, Productivity, Inflation and the 'Revised Sequence', (June 1969).

2. The Hypothesis of Underlying Social Malfunction (From 'The Society System Project', 25 March 1972).

3. The Conceptual Underpinnings of Public Broadcasting, (25 June 1996, paper presented at the seminar: Public Television at the Crossroads: Refinancing the CBC.
   McGill Institute for the Study of Canada).

4. The Battle for Civilization –The Broadcasting Front (30 Jan 2004).

5. Underlying Societal Problems (10 Apr 2004).

6. 21st Century Manifesto (22 Dec 2006).

7. The Great Battle of the Climate (31 Aug 08).

8. Auxiliary Measures for the Great Battle of the Climate (04 Aug 2007). (These were the correction of two major governance flaws which were impeding our efforts to engage in the Battle of the Climate, the perversion of broadcasting, and the faulty taxation system).

Acknowledgements

Particular events can exercise a strong influence on one's actions, and there is one that added to my confidence in writing this work. I mention it here because many of my ideas I have already put forward in earlier papers which were ignored, or even pooh-poohed. But one particular response gave me confidence. My ideas on mitigating global warming appeared in a paper I wrote five years ago, which was highly commended by Martin Rees, the Astronomer Royal, and until lately, the Master of Trinity College, Cambridge, and President of the Royal Society. This confirmed for me that I had not been talking nonsense, at least on climate change. I am deeply indebted to Martin Rees.

For the structure of this work I am indebted to Desmond Morton, the Canadian historian who wrote to me thus: 'When my students are at a loss for how to organise their essays, I return to my boyhood military learning . . . Orders followed the routine of SMEAC: Situation, Mission, Execution, Administration, Command and Signals'. I have adapted this thus: Symptoms, Diagnosis, Strategy, Action Plan (SDSA!).

Over the years I have talked much about our society's degraded state with my friend Anne Glyn-Jones. In her book 'Holding up a Mirror: How Civilizations Decline' she applies the Sorokin view of three competing mind-sets that societies exhibit, the ideational, the idealist, and the sensate. Much of Western Society is now in an advanced sensate, materialism-driven condition, with characteristics not unlike the 'Symptoms of Decline', discussed in my book's Part One. I am most grateful for Anne's critique of the book, and have moderated my excessive ranting on my *bêtes noires,* especially, the 'broadcasting perversion'.

I am also indebted to my brother, Anthony Jaffey for his careful reading. He has a huge capacity for detecting ambiguities and lack of clarity – so much so that I made several changes.

One person who has been important in reassuring me that I'm asking the right questions is Gavyn Davies, former BBC Chairman, and among his many activities, writer on macroeconomics for the Financial Times.

Most helpful in commenting on my global warming chapter has been Jeffrey Roberts, Dean of Science at Purdue University. Also of great help to me was Jason Smyth, who is an information technology expert.

I am an alumnus of St. Edmund Hall, Oxford, and I would like to thank Martin Slater, Emeritus Fellow, and until recently economics tutor. Over the years he has most generously given me of his time, to discuss economic questions, and my somewhat odd ideas.

A number of friends have kindly read my book and offered their suggestions, most notably Larry Heath with his nonsense-detecting Queen's Council mind, and Annie Horton, who travels much and has 'many goodly states and kingdoms seen' and so can compare them with her own. And there are others who have helped me by their comments, including Terry Winhold, David Barker, Deborah Jaffey, and Jon Tang.

And I am greatly indebted to Micheline Gauthier, who is a wizard at making my recalcitrant computer behave and organizing my chaotic files. This book is self-published, but the 'self' involved was not myself, but Bruce Broadfoot, who is himself a printer, and played a large part in the book's design and format, and also dealt with CreateSpace, the publishing subsidiary of Amazon.com. I am enormously indebted to Bruce.

Select Bibliography

Bennett, Oliver	Cultural Pessimism. 2001
Bronowski, J.	The Ascent of Man. 1973
Brown, Gordon	Beyond The Crash. 2010
Edsall, Thomas B.	The Age of Austerity: How Scarcity Will Remake
	American Politics. 2012
Ferguson, Niall	The War of the World: Twentieth-Century Conflict and the Descent of the West. 2006
————-	The Ascent of Money: A financial history of The world. 2008
————-	Civilization: The West and the Rest. 2011
————-	The Great Degeneration: How Institutions Decay and Economies Die. 2012
Freeland, Chrystia	Plutocrats: The Rise of the New Global Super-Rich and the Fall of Everyone Else. 2012
Fukuyama, Francis	The Origins of Political Order. 2011
Hedges, Chris	Death of The Liberal Class. 2011
————	Empire of Illusion. 2008
Huxley, Aldons	Brave New World. 1932
Jacques, Martin	When China Rules The World: The rise of the Middle Kingdom and the End of the Western World. 2011
Keynes, J, M.	The General Theory of Employment, Interest, and Money. 1936
————	Economic Possibilities for our Grandchildren. (in Essay in Persuasion, 1930)

Kotlikoff, J. &
Burns, S.   The Clash of Generations.

Krugman, Paul   The Return of Depression Economics and
                                       The Crisis of 2008. 2009
————————   End this Depression Now! 2012
Lovelock, James   The Vanishing Face of Gaia: A Final
                                       Warning. 2009
Lynas, Mark   Six Degrees: Our Future on a Hotter Planet.
                                   2008
Orwell, Georg   Nineteen Eighty-Four. 1949
Rees, Martin   Our Final Hour: A Scientist's Warning 2003
————————   From Here To Infinity. 2011
Roubini, Nouriel &   Crisis Economics. 2011
Mihm, Stephen
Russell, Bertrand   A History of Western Philosophy. 1946
Skidelski, Robert   Keynes: The Return of the Master. 2009
Stiglitz, Joseph   Freefall. 2010
Wapshott, Nicholas   Keynes Hayek: The Clash that Defined
                                       Modern Economics. 2011

Notes

1. The Society System Project: A Progress Report, 25 March 1972 (unpublished paper).

2. The Economist. 9th of December 2011.

3. From 'Our Final Hour: A scientist's warning: How terror, error, and environmental disaster threatens humankind's future'. Martin Rees is Master of Trinity College, Cambridge (this single college alone has had 32 Nobel Prizes), Astronomer-Royal, and former President of the Royal Society.

4. From an article published by The American Institute of Physics: 'In the 1960s and 1970s observations showed that . . . . the greenhouse effect had made Venus a furnace, while lack of atmosphere had locked Mars in a deep freeze. This was evidence that a planet's atmosphere could flip from a liveable state to a deadly one' (look for article)

5. Find reference in my papers.

6. Howard Covington and Chris Rapley: 'The Risks of climate disaster demand straight talking', in the Financial Times of August 5th, 2012. The authors are respectively chairman of the UK's national mathematics research institute, and a professor of climate science at University College London.

7. For the structure of this work I am indebted to Desmond Morton, the historian who wrote to me thus: 'When my students are a a a loss for how to organise their essays, I return to my boyhood military learning . . . Orders followed the routine of SMEAC: Situation, Mission. Execution, administration, Command

and Signals. I have adapted this thus: Symptoms, Diagnosis, Strategy, Action Plan (SDSA!).

8. Source: www.huntonprivacyblog.com

9. Reported in the Christian Science Monitor weekly edition of 19 July 2009.

10. BBC World News, 21 December 2011.

11. From articles in the G&M and NYT.

12. New York Times, 15 October 2011.

13. That was written of the previous State of the Union speech. In the latest though he stuck to 'green jobs' he slipped in the climate once.

14. 9th May 2011 – find reference.

15. Financial Times, 11 August 2011.

16. 'Worrying signs of 'Japanisation', Richard Milne.

17. Globe and Mail, April 2009.

18. The Economist. 10 March 2012.

19. Wikipedia.

20. Wikipedia.

21. Richard Tomkins in the London Financial Times (find date).

22. Shakespeare, Richard II, Act 2, Scene 1.

23. From 'Some Remarks on Wages, Productivity, Inflation and the "Revised Sequence", Michael Jaffey, June 1969, unpublished.

24. 'The Society System Project – A Progress Report'. Michael Jaffey 25 March 1973.

25. 'An idea that dominates the mind; an obsession (Oxford Dictionary).

26. In the Broadway musical 'My Fair Lady'.

27. Quoted from an abridged version of 'The Affluent Society', second edition 1969 (http:/abridge.me.uk/). The original edition was published in 1958. Keynes was successful in shifting the economics paradigm, but Galbraith, a quarter of a century later failed in this, much to society's misfortune.

28. Thomas Kuhn's highly influential 'The Structure of Scientific Revolutions' was published in 1962. 'Normal science' is the occupation of scientific orthodoxy, refining the current paradigm, until one day, when its shortcomings become increasingly evident, a new paradigm is put forward. Copernicus proposed a universe that no longer goes round the earth, Newton the laws of motion, house arrest (T).

29. A spending review for a diminished country. Financial Times 20 October 2010.

30. Bertrand Russell, 'The History of Western Philosophy', 1945.

31. 'China in the 21ˢᵗ Century'. Jeffrey N. Wasserstrom.

32. Ibid.

33. Martin Jacques, 'When China rules the World: The Rise of the Middle Kingdom and the End of the Western World'.

34. As quoted by Chris Hedges in 'The Empire of Illusion', 2009.

35. Freefall: America, Free Markets, and the Sinking of the World Economy. Joseph Stiglitz, 2010.

36. Chris Hedges, op. cit.

37. NY Times 13 November 2010.

38. Globe and Mail, 29 October 2011.

39. 'Why the world needs virtuous autocrats'. Robert Kaplan. Financial Times, 2 March 2011.

40. 'The Origins of Political Order' Francis Fukuyama 2011.

41. 'Can America be put back together? Timothy Garten Ash in the Globe and Mail, 4th August 2011.

42. David Brooks. 'Yanks in Crisis'. New York Times, 23 April 2009.

43. It is a hotly debated question in the United States how the Second Amendment is to be interpreted, whether it prohibits the gun control legislation that most other advanced nations have enacted. Did the framers of the Second Amendment allow the bearing of arms to be used solely in government regulated militias that might be formed to suppress insurrections against the state?

44. New York Times.

45. 'Off-road living: Curbing our cars' Globe and Mail, 22 August 2011.

46. The Economist, 27 November 2010.

47. Its actual current market value is different – the balance sheet values are the total of what was paid for each vintage at the lower prices of past years.

48. Agent France-Press, 5th August 2011 (check source).

49. Gillian Tett, Financial Times, 20th September 2012. 'Beware the costs and psychology of QE3'. This is a most illuminating article, on the hazy reasons behind quantitative easing, or at least QE3. Tett refers to a just-held survey of the chief financial officers of 887 large companies. 91 % said that a one percent interest rate reduction would not affect their business plans, and 84% said not even a two percent reduction would do so.

50. 'The IMF game changer'. Izabella Kaminska, Financial Times. 11 October 2012.

51. The Browser website, 'thebrowser.com', has a wealth of valuable information, including its FiveBooks series of interviews with

many prominent figures and experts, on the books that have most influenced their thinking.

52. OECD Factbook for 2009.

53. 'The Chancellor George Osborne is losing the argument on growth'. Philip Aldrick in the Telegraph, 16 August 2012.

54. 'Business leaders attack Osborne'. Tony Helm and Heather Stewart. The Guardian, 22 July 2012.

55. Moody's have just (February 2012) issued a warning that Britain has a 30% chance of being downgraded in the next eighteen months as a result of the eurozone crisis.

56. From the IMF fiscal Monitor of September 2011 (check this).

57. Shakespeare, Richard II.

58. In Canada, 20 percent of television air time is allowed for advertising interruptions which means 12 minutes per hour. If we allow that one minute of the twelve is used by broadcasters to advertise their own coming attractions, then eleven minutes each hour is given over to the advertisers who buy time. Television viewing statistics indicate that average daily viewing time is four hours, and that gives us our figure of forty-four minutes daily of commercial breaks.

59. A work on broadcasting by Andrew Graham, former Master of Balliol College, Oxford, has suggested that broadcasting standards are maintained provided the share of adverting-free broadcasting exceed about 35%.

60. Advertising in Canada: Its Theory and Practice. Zarry and Wilson (ed). McGraw-Hill Ryerson, Copyright, Association of Canadian Advertisers, 1981.

61. Stalking the Elephant: My Discovery of America. James Laxer, 2000.

62. 'The future of the CBC' in 1996 (check title and date).

63. Social Communication in Advertising. Leiss, Kline, and Jhally. Second Edition, 1990, Nelson, Canada. Page 107.

64. Address by Newton Minow, Chairman of the Federal Communications Commission, 1961.

65. For simplicity I omitted net exports, that is, exports less imports, which may be positive or negative. If positive it increases C, G, and I, and if negative it reduces them (if negative, if a nation is spending beyond its means as has the U.S., the nation's external debt is increase.

66. Total world advertising is $500 billion, and American advertising is $300 billion.

67. There is also an increasing amount of 'infomercials', very long commercials without accompanying programmes. So there are people willing to endure a smarmy-voiced salesperson droning on even without program consumer-bait.

68. The Oxford Dictionary, 2011.

69. Chris Hedges. Empire of Illusion. 2009. Hedges, a former New York Times writer, is a journalist, author, and war correspondent, and worked for the New York Times as a foreign correspondent for fifteen years. He has written several books on what he believes is a dying culture. Hedges' background is interesting: he graduated first in English literature, and then as a Master of Divinity from Harvard Divinity School. Recently he was arrested in New York in connection with the Occupy Wall Street movement. One might say that it says much for the underlying strength of American democracy that the likes of Hedges are unmuzzled – it was doubtful that one could have said that in Senator McCarthy heyday. Similarly in, for example, Britain and France, such robust political opposition remains possible, and that gives hope for the possibility of igniting a New Enlightenment.

70. It is not only in the United States that excessive power has flowed to business corporations. The late Anthony Sampson

wrote 'The Anatomy of Britain' in 1962, and updated it over the years. His last edition written in 2004 he names 'Who Runs this Place? The Anatomy of Britain in the 21st Century' There had been a huge transformation, the power of business corporations and financial institutions was greatly magnified, that of Parliament shrunk.

71. I am here discounting what some may believe casts doubt on my proposal, that we have the present system because that is what people like, they prefer it to pure programme without programme.

    I suggest instead that they are merely inured to what is now broadcast, they believe that's just the way the world must, It's always been. Further I believe they would eventually very much like the future form of broadcasting here advocated.

72. From "The conceptual underpinnings of public broadcasting", J.M. Jaffey, 1996.

73 . 'Twitter's Changing Revenue Model Signals No More Free Rides'. Barry Silverstein. Aug 1, 2011, www.revenews.com/affiliate-marketing.

74. Most of the numbers appearing in the two diagrams are those in the published statistics, but assumed values were used where the required categories were not readily available, for example personal savings, the amount of personal dividend income, the split of the capital consumption allowance (CCA) between business and government activity, and the change in the public debt during the year. These assumptions were far from arbitrary, having to be in balance with other values: For every component element of each diagram, the sum of its inputs must equal the sum of its outputs (each of the two flow diagrams could have been presented in the form of a Leontief input-output table of the economy).

75. Margaret Wente. Globe and Mail. 4th December 2010.

76. Per James Lovelock, the eminent scientist who is also an environmentalist explains this question of instability in his recent 'Farewell to Gaia'.

77. James Lovelock, ibid.

78. Our Final Hour: A Scientist's Warning. Martin Rees. 2003.

79. Andrew C. Revkin, 'Industry Ignored Its Scientists on Climate'. New York Times, 23 April 2009.

80. One reason is that the share of services in the economy is increasing, and most services, whether professionals or clerks use little energy. Not only that, their methods don't change much, whether lawyers, artist, or clerks. Perhaps in the future energy will grow by more than 1% more slowly than GDP, even in the absence of public policy to curb emissions, as so many of the consumer products now being produced, electronic gadgets and the like, do not need much energy.

81. It would surely be unwise from a safety and environmental viewpoint to rely on nuclear propulsion of the world's entire fleet of ships. We'd need only a few ship captains like the hapless man of the recent Italian cruise ship disaster which filled the world's television screens.

82. The amount of emissions of the fossil fuel supply industry has been assumed to be a constant proportion of the total emissions of the three other sectors that use its output – very crude, but accurate enough for present 'ball park' purposes.

83. The Sir Adam Beck Pumped Storage Reservoir at Niagara Falls.

84. Wikipedia, 22 April 2009.

85. Hitler's demented refusal to capitulate right to his bitter end in the bunker is the subject of Ian Kershaw's book, 'The End'.

86. A Farewell to Fossil Fuels: Amory Lovins, in the March/April issue of the journal 'Foreign Affairs'.

87. World Nuclear Association. 'Plans for new reactors worldwide (updated Feb 2012)'.

88. Le Figaro, 9th March 2012. 'The Nuclear Station should never have been flooded'.

89. From website of EDF, the French publicly-owned electricity supply company.

90. 'The risks of climate disaster demand straight talking'. Howard Covington and Chris Raply. Financial Times. 5 August 2012.

91. John Kay. Visiting professor at the London School of Economics and fellow of St. John's College, Oxford, in the Financial Times. 25 August 2011. This article discusses the scientific method now being used by economists in government agencies as well as universities.

92. Paul Krugman in the New York Review of Books.

93. In fact this is not precisely true, the weighted average value is slightly different from the total economy value for reasons not clear to me – but the near-equality is surely sufficient to make my point.

94. In fact it is a little more sophisticated than that. Each category of stock is not assumed to have the life L, but some sort of distribution, for example a normal distribution about L, that distribution also being assumed with little evidence. It is doubtful whether this added sophistication adds much to estimates' accuracy.

95. The Netherlands is an exception. There the statistical agency actually visits corporations every few years and learns from their accounts how much equipment they have of each vintage. This gives them the 'gross' stock, regardless of age. They then use assumed lives to estimate not only the in-between year gross stocks, but also the amount of capital consumption and the net stock – the stock value allowing for each stock vintage's age. With FAASM all these different values can be determined

accurately and cheaply without any need for life assumptions. In 1995 (check) I visited the Netherlands to discuss their method. Subsequently, I designed a version of FAASM which tied the system to the kind of periodic benchmark gross stocks for even greater accuracy.

96. While the wealthy would certainly save part of their income, this might be offset by others spending more than they earn through massive credit card purchasing.

97. 'The Society System Project: A Progress Report. 25 March 1972.

98. Development of a Comprehensive, Dynamic Economic System Model. 23 Nov.1982.

99. Guardian 25 March 2010.

100. Francis Fukuyama. The Origins of Political Decay 2011.

101. Chrystia Freeland, Editor, Thomson Reuters Digital. In the Globe and Mail, 1st June 2012.

102. Wikipedia.

103. 'The election is set to break all records, with a group of 30 or so billionaires spending more on the polls than the rest of America combined'. Edward Luce in the Financial Times, 3rd June 2012).

104. Report in the Financial Times, 25 March 2012.

105. Wikipedia.

106. Timothy Egan in the New York Times of the 2nd August 2012.

107. To be more complete we should add a fourth category of current spending, foreign aid, help to 'third world' countries.

108. Capital consumption, or depreciation, is the money set aside out of operating costs to cover the replacement of worn out facilities.

109. Wikipedia, which refers to a criticism by The Economist.

110. In fact this is not strictly accurate: Canadian government statistics treat grants tp Crown corporations, for example, the Canadian Broadcasting Corporation as a transfer payment. But in fact such transfers are very different in kind from what might be called the 'social safety net'.

111. 'The Vocabulary of Fiscal Balance' Michael Jaffey, 1997.

112. From 'Project Syndicate', 11 November 2011. (Project Syndicate describes itself as providing 'the world's foremost newspapers with exclusive commentaries by prominent leaders and opinion makers', for example Martin Feldstein, Mohamed el Arean, Lord Skidelski, Christine Largarde (who heads the IMF), and Joseph Stiglitz, the Nobel prize winner.

113. Martin Wolf in the Financial Times of the 21st May 2011.

114. This account is from Martin Jacques' compendious and fascinating work, 'When China rules the World: The Rise of the Middle Kingdom and the End of the Western World'. Martin Jaques, Allen Lane, 2009.

115. Interview of the reporter Mark Mackinnon in Beijing with Chan Koonchung, a writer of a recent Orwellian novel with a large underground readership.

116. From brief description of Niall Ferguson's book, 'The Great Degeneration: How Institutions Decay and Economies Die'. This is the description given by the publisher, Penguin UK. An article by Ferguson in Newsweek (30 October 2011) says much the same thing.

117. 'Our Final Hour: A Scientist's Warning'. Martin Rees. 2003. Martin Rees, the Astronomer Royal, and until lately, the Master of Trinity College, Cambridge, and President of the Royal Society.

118. Ibid.

119. Ibid.

120. To be exact, not 3%, but 3.02%: The product of 1.01 and 1.02 is 1.0302.

121. 'Troublesome Young Men', Lynne Olson, 2009.

122. GDP at purchasing power parity.

123. The 2010 edition has been used, but later editions are little different.

124. For each of the three indexes I've converted the particular units used by the index makers so that a rating of 0% is the worst score possible and 100% in the best possible.

125. Compiled every two years by the Intelligence Unit of The Economist magazine.

126. Published annually by the US organization, the Fund for Peace, in conjunction with the magazine 'Foreign Policy'. It has twelve factors: demographic pressures. Massive movement of refugees and internally displaced peoples, legacy of vengeance-seeking group grievance, chronic and sustained human flight, uneven economic development along group lines, sharp and/or severe economic decline, criminalization and/or deligitimisation of the state, progressive deterioration of public services, widespread violation of human rights, security apparatus as a 'state within a state', rise of factionalised elites, and intervention of other states or other factors.

127. Published annually by Transparency International (check).

128. Wasserstrom.

129. Ayaan Hirsi Ali, the remarkable young Somali woman who escaped to Holland to avoid a forced marriage, learnt Dutch, and became a member of parliament, writes[3] that young Muslims continually have to bottle up any contrary ideas they have and defer to authority figures, father, teachers, and imams, and so are liable eventually to explode in rage and violence.

130. Find references, eg NYT articles or editorials.

131. Wikipedia article on advertising (check).

132. Oliver Bennett. Cultural Pessimism. 2001. Bennett defines cultural pessimism as 'the conviction that the culture of s nation, a civilisation . . is in an irreversible process of decline'. In 'the last few decades of the twentieth century narratives of decline emerged throughout the West in widely disparate fields' that were deeply pessimistic'.

133. Martin Jacques, ibid.

134. Martin Jacques, ibid.

135. Daily Telegraph, London, 14th March 2011.

136. Globe and Mail. 3rd May 2012. James Hansen has been one of the scientists at the forefront of the climate issue.

137. Throughout this work I have talked of five estates, each with its own proper function. If I had had time for a more precise analysis, I would have used six estates, separating the financial system from the business estate. But I believe the use of six estates would make very little difference to the diagnosis I have offered of our society's problems.

138. 'Speech, Apathy, Lies'. Jason Stanley. New York Times 30 August 2012.

139. 'Life Span Shrinks for Least Educated Whites in the US'. New York Times, 20 September 2012.

140. The Battle for Civilization: Societal Problems underlying the Perversion of Broadcasting. June 2004.

141. Not strictly accurate. The East had great civilizations of a different sort. Little was known of China in the West before Marco Polo's great journey. And of course, there were India and Persia.

142. Meeting the Kyoto Goals, 04 October 2005.